**Living Political
Biography**
Narrating 20th Century
European Lives

Ann-Christina L. Knudsen · Karen Gram-Skjoldager (eds.)

Living Political Biography

Narrating 20th Century European Lives

AARHUS UNIVERSITY PRESS · 2012

Living Political Biography:
Narrating 20th Century European Lives

© The authors and Aarhus University Press
Tilrettelagt af Carl-H.K. Zakrisson & Tod Alan Spoerl
Cover design by Camilla Jørgensen, Trefold
Printed by Zeuner Grafisk, Denmark
Printed in Denmark 2012
ISBN 978 87 7124 057 3

AARHUS UNIVERSITY PRESS

Aarhus   *Copenhagen*
Langelandsgade 177   Tuborgvej 164
DK – 8200 Aarhus N   DK – 2400 Copenhagen NV

www.unipress.dk

Published with the financial support of
Aarhus Universitets Forskningsfond
Forskningsrådet for Kultur og Kommunikation
Oslo Contemporary International History Network
Lademanns Fond

INTERNATIONAL DISTRIBUTORS
White Cross Mills
Hightown, Lancaster, LA1 4 XS
United Kingdom
www.gazellebookservices.co.uk

ISD
70 Enterprise Drive
Bristol, CT 06010
USA
www.isdistribution.com

Preface

International historical research and writing, as most who have engaged in this exercise will probably agree, is rewarding yet cumbersome. The original ideas for this book were conceived in connection with a conference held at Aarhus University called "Locating Europe. Ideas and Individuals in Contemporary History" in June 2008. In the period since the conference, while we have been developing the contributions in dialogue with the authors, we have been pleased to note that historical biographical research has become a focus of attention in leading academic journals, as we also discuss in the introduction.

A volume like this is the product of numerous collective and individual efforts. Our first acknowledgement and debt is to the contributors to this volume. Some contributors delivered their articles shortly after the conference, while others took a little longer. Unfortunate family circumstances and omnipresent university responsibilities and duties kept the editors from bringing the work into print with the dispatch that its contributors deserved. We hope that their extraordinary patience eventually receives its just reward with the publication of the book. Besides paying tribute to the patience of the contributors, we also wish to acknowledge their responsiveness to our suggestions for revisions and clarifications. Further acknowledgements go to the anonymous peer reviewers who provided encouragement and constructive comment on the manuscript. Finally, the book would not have been possible without generous financial support from Aarhus Universitets Forskningsfond, Forskningsrådet for Kultur og Kommunikation, the Oslo Contemporary International History Network and Lademann's Fond.

Abbreviations in the text

ADK	Arbeitskreis demokratischer Kreise
BN	Bekende Nederlander
BTO	Brussels Treaty Organisation
CDU	Christian Democratic Union in the Federal Republic of Germany
CHR	UN Commission on Human Rights
CIE	Confederation international des étudiants
DWNC	Danish Women's National Council
EC	European Communities
ECHR	European Convention of Human Rights
ECSC	European Coal and Steel Community
EDC	European Defence Community
EFTA	European Free Trade Association
EP	European Parliament
EPA	European Planning Authority
ERC	European Reconstruction Corporations
EU	European Union
EUI	European University Institute
Euratom	European Atomic Energy Community
HR	Human Rights
ICW	International Council of Women
ILO	International Labour Organisation
IWA	Icelandic Women's Association
LGA	League General Assembly
MEP	Member of the European Parliament
NAA	North Atlantic Assembly
NATO	North Atlantic Treaty Organisation
NS	National Socialist
NSDAP	National Socialist Party
OEEC	Organisation for European Economic Cooperation
PACE	Council of Europe's Parliamentary Assembly
PR	Public Relations
SAC	Second Action Committee
SDP	Social Democratic Party in the Federal Republic of Germany
SPD	Sozialdemokratische Partei Deutschlands
UDHR	Universal Declaration of Human Rights

UK	United Kingdom
UN	United Nations
UNGA	UN General Assembly
US	United States

Archival collections and their abbreviations

ABA	Library and Archive of the Labour Movement (Arbejderbevægelsens Bibliotek og Arkiv, ABA), Copenhagen.
ACDP	Archiv für Christlich-Demokratische Politik, Sankt Augustin.
BB	Bodil Begtrup's private papers, DKNA.
BL	Bodleian Library, Oxford.
CAB	Records of the Cabinet Office. UKNA.
CARDOC	Archive and Documentation Centre of the European Parliament, Luxembourg.
DKFA	Archive of the Danish Ministry of Foreign Affairs, DKNA.
DKNA	Denmark's National Archive, Copenhagen.
DKUN	Archive of the Danish Mission to the UN, DKNA.
DWNC	Danish Women's National Council, DKNA.
FO	Foreign Office, UKNA.
GdF	Geoffrey de Freitas Papers, BL.
HEJ	Nachlaß Hans-Edgar Jahn, ACDP.
HF	Hartvig Frisch papers, ABA.
HH	Hans Hedtoft papers, ABA.
JOK	Jens Otto Krag papers, ABA.
LAB	Ministry of Labour and National Service, UKNA.
MC	Ministry of Commerce, DKNA.
PREM	Records of the Prime Minister's Office, UKNA.
SD	State Department, USNARA.
UKNA	United Kingdom National Archives, Kew, London.
USNARA	US National Archives and Record Administration, Washington D.C.
VN	Vincent Næser's private papers, DKNA.

Introduction

Living Political Biography
An Introduction

Ann-Christina L. Knudsen and Karen Gram-Skjoldager
Aarhus University

Shortly after Sir Geoffrey de Freitas (1913–1982) had passed away his wife Helen wanted to publish his sketch for an autobiography. Sir Geoffrey had had a long and solid political career since he joined the House of Commons with Labour's sweeping victory in 1945 until he retired from politics in 1979. Britain's first prime minister after the Second World War, Clement Atlee, had appointed the young Geoffrey as Parliamentary Private Secretary and as junior minister, and they became so close that the Atlee family invited him to spend Christmas with them at Chequers. Early in his career, Geoffrey had been a delegate to one of the very first General Assemblies of the United Nations. When Labour was pushed into opposition in 1951 he began to engage himself more systematically in the transnational political work related to international organisations, first as representative to the Council of Europe's Parliamentary Assembly (PACE), and in 1955, he became one of the founders of the North Atlantic Assembly (NAA), that is, the parliamentary arm of the North Atlantic Treaty Organisation (NATO). Returning to Britain after having served as Britain's High Commissioner in Ghana between 1961 and 1964, Sir Geoffrey re-entered political life and soon won a new Labour seat. There was no front bench positions available, and he opted for a specialisation as Labour's representative in PACE and the NAA, and, from 1975, also in the European Parliament (EP). When in 1974 Sir Geoffrey was asked by a local British newspaper what he considered to be the "high points" of his political career, his answer was: "My election as President of the Assembly of the Council of Europe in 1966, and my re-election in 1967 and 1968."[1] This sense of pride and triumph was, no doubt, equally great when he became President of the NAA (1977–1978). In his personal archive, Sir Geoffrey kept the notes of congratulation sent to him from statesmen and senior political figures from many different countries as well as press cuts from his meeting with US-President Jimmy Carter at the White House. The pinnacle of Sir Geoffrey's political career was clearly abroad.

The de Freitas-couple seemed well aware of the privileges that such a political career and life had brought them, and in the last years of Sir Geoffrey's life, Helen assisted him in writing up his memoirs. Admittedly, the draft manuscript was incomplete, anecdotal, and it was not presented as a linear, chronological story. When Helen in 1983 took it to Penguin Books, it was rejected. The same happened with several other publishing houses before she finally accepted to pay most of the publication costs herself with a minor publisher.[2] The replies that she received suggested that the life of Sir Geoffrey – a globetrotter throughout his life, a democratically elected representative for more than three decades, and a founder and president of multiple international parliamentary assemblies – was not considered to be interesting enough for the political biography market.[3]

The life and biographical endavours of Sir Geoffrey illustrate several problematiques related to the biographical genre in political history. On the one hand, (auto-)biography is generally a best-selling category in bookstores, but it is also a genre that relies on certain conventions. This was also revealed in the reactions and rejections to the de Freitas-manuscript from the publishers: namely the need

1. Bodleian Library [henceforth BL], Oxford, Geoffrey de Freitas papers [henceforth GdF], box 43, Answers by the Right Hon. Sir Geoffrey de Freitas KCMG MP to the Northamptonshire Evening Telegraph Questionnaire, 23 March 1974.
2. BL, GdF, box 44, folder of GdeF's book and papers, in particular, letter from Constable Publishers, 1 March 1982.

3. After she had engaged with the manuscript herself, and solicited assistance from various friends and family members, the memoirs were published as Geoffrey and Helen de Freitas, *The Slighter Side of a Long Public Life*, 1985. The name of the publisher does not appear on the book. While it is catalogued in major bibliographical databases such as www.worldcat.org, it does not have an ISBN.

for a narrative that draws in faces and places that are familiar to the readership. The national political and cultural settings are considered important in framing such biographies. By contrast, Sir Geoffrey had used the world stage as the foil for his life and his biography. Apart from certain scenes – as when in his capacity as President of the NAA he had met President of the United States Jimmy Carter at the White House – the manuscript was full of the names of French, African and other politicians and civil servants that only few English-language readers would have known. Besides, the parliamentary organisations he served in had no formal powers. The concerns of the publishers were clearly that his life did not comply with the conventions relating to nation and narration to which importance is attached at the commercial market for political biographies.

On the other hand, the meeting with historical characters like Sir Geoffrey presents us with challenges of an academic nature in relation to historical political and biographical research. Sir Geoffrey was exemplary of a growing number of political representatives who gave life to the new international organisations that were created in the twentieth century or who tried to grasp and conceptualise regional and international phenomena. Their conceptions of the boundaries between the national and the abroad tended to become blurry, and the relationship between the two was not necessarily perceived as one of conflict. In this book, we take up some of the key challenges of narration, framing and methodologies in relation to this type of historical research. This chapter offers an introduction to the aims of the book, and the following section outlines key developments in literatures that have been relevant in developing the book and in facing these academic challenges.

The politics of undertaking historical political biographical research, and of portraying and narrating the lives and activities of those involved in the changing political scenario in 20th-century Europe, are key themes in this book. The contributions come together around the overarching aim of exploring and explicating the analytical potentials and shortcomings of political biography research in view of the recent transnational and sociological 'turns' in international and European political history. In doing so, the book attempts to facilitate exchange between scholars of biographical and of 20th-century European political historical research. In the following sections we outline recent twists, turns and crossroads that inform and frame this book in the fields of international and European political history as well as in biographical historical research.

International history has traditionally aimed at analysing and explaining interstate bargaining and policy outcomes.[4] This has resulted in biographical narratives in which statesmen and diplomats have been attributed importance – often implicitly – according to their formal functions in the political processes and the negotiations under scrutiny, and sometimes possibly also according to the personal favouritism of the author. This approach to international history has however been challenged from several angles in recent years.[5] In particular, historians of transnational history have pointed to the need to relax the stronghold of the national in 20th-century international and European history.[6] While historians of the trans-

4. P. Finney, "Introduction: What is international history?", in: Patrick Finney (ed.), *Palgrave Advances in International History*, London 2005, pp. 1–35; W. Loth and J. Osterhammel (eds.), *Internationale Geschichte: Themen, Ergebnisse, Aussichten*, Oldenbourg 2000; C.S. Maier, "Marking Time: The Historiography of International Relations", in: Michael Kammen (ed.), *The Past Before Us: Contemporary Historical Writing in the United States*, Ithaca 1980, pp. 355–87; M. Trachtenberg, *The Craft of International History. A Guide to Method*, Princeton 2006.

5. A theoretically informed study that in many ways stay at the territory of traditional international history and biography is: D.L. Byman and K. M. Pollack, "Let Us Now Praise the Great Men. Bringing the Statesman Back In", *International Security*, vol. 25, 2001, no. 4, pp. 107–146.

6. C.A. Bayly, S. Beckert, M. Connelly, I. Hofmeyr, W. Kozol, and P. Seed, "AHR Conversation: On Transnational History", *American Historical Review*, vol. 111, 2006, pp. 1440–64; Patricia Clavin, "Defining Transnationalism", *Contemporary European History*, vol. 14, no. 4, 2005, pp. 421–439; A. Iriye and P.-Y. Saunier (eds.), *Palgrave Dictionary of Transnational History: From the mid-19th century to the present day*, London 2008; K.K. Patel, "Transatlantische Perspektiven transnationaler Geschichte", *Geschichte und Gesellschaft*, vol. 29, 2003, pp. 625–647.

national are often reluctant to give clear definitions of what the transnational really is, one conceptualisation of transnational spaces involves "keying into historical realities and perceptions of space that, in geographical terms, did not necessarily coincide with the territorial demarcations of given political entities".[7] The relevance of this has been shown, for instance, in studies on the advent of international and non-governmental organisations, as well as transnational political networks that cut across national boundaries.[8] These developments have been particularly relevant in research on 20th-century European history due to the intensive political and institutional integration beyond the nation-states and by the many headquarters of international organisations on the continent. These international organisations range from the League of Nations in Geneva, through NATO in Brussels, to regional cooperative initiatives such as the Council of Europe and the European Communities (EC) and present day European Union (EU).

In recent years historians have begun to find inspiration in socio-cultural approaches to the study of international, transnational and European political developments. This has, on the one hand, moved attention away from political events, meetings and agreements to the making and shaping of the ideas and norms that inform the 'rules of the game' in the social world of politics across national boundaries. In this research, the strict divisions between formal and informal politics typically found in traditional international history are removed, and the narrative strategies employed by researchers are different. Scholars examine the emerging transnational political spaces through the groups of agents who inhabit them, the recruitment, careers and social properties of these agents, and the

7. M.G. Müller and C. Torp, "Conceptualising transnational spaces in history", *European Review of History – Revue européenne d'histoire*, vol. 16, no. 5, 2009, pp. 609–617, here p. 613.

8. Akira Iriye, *Global Community. The Role of International Organizations in the Making of the Contemporary World*, Berkeley 2004; W. Kaiser, B. Leucht and M. Gehler (eds.), *Transnational Networks in Regional Integration. Governing Europe 1945–83*, London 2010.

networks they form across and within national boundaries.[9] Readers will encounter these approaches in this book; Kristine Midtgaard's chapter on Bodil Begtrup, a Danish human rights activist and diplomat, and Jan-Henrik Meyer's chapter on Hans-Edgar Jahn, who was a German war-time Nazi turned pro-European politician and environmentalist activist, specifically take the transnational and networking approaches on board. The chapters by Anne Deighton, on the British trade union leader and politician Ernest Bevin, and by Jan van der Harst, on Max Kohnstamm, a Dutchman who had a career as a top-level civil servant in the context of European-level organisations, address in different ways the informality of politics in the lives of those who had a part in creating European political organisations and institutions in the 20th century.

On the other hand, this new socio-cultural inspiration in historical biographical research has opened up perspectives in relation to the notion and role of gender. It seems clear that the lack of female statesmen, politicians, diplomats and civil servants has long ensured that political biographical research remained relatively oblivious to what role, if any, gender might play in political life. Biographers of prominent female agents, by contrast, have tended to attribute crucial importance to gender in their narrations and interpretations

9. W. Kaiser, *Christian Democracy and the Origins of European Union*, Cambridge 2007; A.-C. L. Knudsen and Karen Gram-Skjoldager, "Hvor gik statens repræsentanter hen, da de gik ud? Nye rolleforståelser hos diplomater og parlamentarkere efter 1945", *Temp – Tidsskrift for Historie*, vol. 1, 2010, no. 1, pp. 82–113; M. Rasmussen, "Constructing and Deconstructing 'constitutional' European Law: Some Reflections on how to study the history of European Law", in: H. Rasmussen and H. Koch et al. (eds.), *Europe:* *The New Legalism: Essays in Honor of Hjalte Rasmussen*, Copenhagen 2010, pp. 639–660; P.-Y. Saunier, "Circulations, connexions et espaces transnationaux", *Genèses*, vol. 57, 2004, pp. 110–126; K. Seidel, *The Process of Politics in Europe. The Rise of European Elites and Supranational Institutions*, London/ New York 2010. See also for instance J. M. Brown, "'Life Histories' and the History of Modern South Asia", *American Historical Review*, vol. 114, 2009, pp. 587–595, here p. 590.

of the life of the biographee.[10] In this book, the politics of gender is thematised in three chapters. In her contribution, Birgitte Possing delivers a sharp critique of the classical biographical rendering of prominent male characters while Midtgaard demonstrates empirically how a pioneering woman navigated the overtly masculine world of diplomacy and (trans)national politics. The question is, of course, whether the historical political biography is ready to go beyond the classical gender "essentialism"?[11] A different way in which gender can play a role in biographical politics is shown in the chapter by Christoffer Kølvraa, which takes an innovative approach to examining how the biographies of people like Jean Monnet have been used in the construction of Europe's "founding fathers".

A further recent development in international history has been a growing interest in the ideational and intellectual aspects of politics. To historians of international history, it was interesting to observe that political scientists in the closely related field of International Relations rediscovered ideas as relevant analytical categories in the early 1990s,[12] and began conducting historically sensitive and contextualised analyses of various political intellectuals and activists.[13] For historians, researching ideas in international history never really went out of fashion. What has changed in this histori-

---

10. For an excellent example of the thematisation of masculinity, see for instance Andreas Marklund, *Stenbock. Ära och ensamhet i Karl XII's tid*, Lund 2008. For a relatively classical discussion among Danish historians of the relevance of gender and political power in biographical research, see N. Thomsen, "Biografiens nye bølge – en skæv sø?", Sidsel Eriksen, "Niels Thomsens relevans" and Birgitte Possing, "Biografien – en frisk eller en skæv bølge", all in *Historisk Tidsskrift* (Copenhagen) 1997, no. 2, pp. 414–429, 432–438 and 439–450.

11. L.W. Banner, "Biography as History", *American Historical Review*, 2009, pp. 579–586, here p. 581.
12. J. Goldstein and R.O. Keohane (eds.), *Ideas & Foreign Policy. Beliefs, Institutions and Political Change*, London 1993; M. Finnemore, *National Interests in International Society*, Ithaca 1996; C. Parsons, *A Certain Idea of Europe*, Ithaca 2003.
13. H. Suganami, *The Domestic Analogy and World Order Proposals*, Cambridge 1989; D. Long and P. Wilson (eds.), *Thinkers of the Twenty Years' Crisis. Inter-War Idealism Reassessed*, Oxford 1995; Parsons, *A Certain Idea of Europe*.

cal research, however, is that scholars have taken a more explicit and theoretically informed interest in the varied and changing normative and ideational contexts of the international and European political, legal and social orders that emerged during the 20th century.[14] This is also highly relevant to the work on historical political biography, as several chapters in this book demonstrate. The contributions by Mark Gilbert on the British historian, diplomat and journalist E. H. Carr, and by Karl-Christian Lammers on Herman Heller, a legal scholar in Weimar Germany, show how intellectuals were related in different ways to the changing political forces and ideological developments in inter-war Europe. The chapters by Karen Gram-Skjoldager and Thorsten B. Olesen, and by Niels Wium Olesen and Johnny Laursen, show a particular sensitivity to the overlap between the writings and intellectual aspirations of two Danish politicians who engaged with the idea of Europe in the abstract and in practice, namely Hartvig Frisch and Jens Otto Krag.

At its best, historical biographical research is capable of reaching a wide public audience. However, to what extent a serious academic career is compatible with the popularising of historical research remains a controversial topic, and there are certainly different positions to be found among historians and different academic traditions. In the United States, for instance, young academics have often simply been advised to refrain from writing biographical works.[15] Yet in recent years, historical political biography has risen to new academic prominence, including in the United States. This

14. See for instance: J.C.E. Gienow-Hecht, "On the Diversity of Knowledge and the Community of Thought: Culture and International History", in: J. Gienow-Hecht and F. Schumacher (eds.), *Culture and International History*, Oxford/New York 2003, pp. 3–26; D. Laqua (ed.), *Internationalism Reconfigured: Transnational Ideas and Movements between the World Wars*, London 2011; A.-C. L. Knudsen, *Farmers on Welfare. The Making of Europe's Common Agricultural Policy*, Ithaca 2009.

15. D. Nasaw, "AHR Roundtable. Historians and Biography. Introduction", *American Historical Review*, vol. 114, 2009, pp. 573–78, here p. 573.

became clear in 2009 when the leading journal, the *American Historical Review*, ran a discussion of biography as a genre.[16] Interestingly, however, the emphasis on the articles in the *American Historical Review* was on national narrative traditions for historical biographical research, and the special volume did not raise the inherent problems of methodological nationalism that are also embedded in the genre. A key feature of the historical political biographical genre has been that presentations are usually framed by the national context of the person portrayed, and so both the chronological life story of the political actor and the self-understanding of author and readers are implicitly or explicitly defined in relation to the national.

Meanwhile, several changes can be identified that challenge the national framing of biographies, which in fact resemble the reorientation in international and European historiography outlined above, although they come from a very different starting point.[17] On the one hand, recent works of biography on prominent political actors in 20th-century international and European history, such as Gustav Stresemann, Aristide Briand, Konrad Adenauer and Jean Monnet, have been based on archival research in a variety of countries. This has resulted in narratives that to some extent relax the traditional tensions between the national and the international.[18] On the other hand, a recent collection of historical writings on *Transnational Lives – Biographies of Global Modernity* specifically rebelled against the tradition whereby "biographies have often been pressed

16. *American Historical Review*, vol. 114, 2009. See for instance also the focus on new biographical research in *Geschichte im Wissenschaft und Unterricht*, 10/09, and *Mitteilungsblatt des Instituts für soziale Bewegungen*, 45, 2011.17. See also the broader theoretical outline in T. Wengraf, P. Chamberlayne and J. Bornat, "A Biographical Turn in the Social Sciences? A British-European View", *Cultural Studies – Critical Methodologies*, no. 2, 2002, pp. 245–269.
18. S. Pedersen, "Back to the League of Nations", *American Historical Review* vol. 112, 2007, no. 4, pp. 1091–1117, here p. 1093–4; W. Kaiser, "From state to society? The historiography of European Integration", in: M. Cini and A. K. Bourne (eds.), *Palgrave Advances in European Union Studies*, London, pp. 190–208, here p. 198.

into the service of the nation".[19] While all the contributions in this book sympathise with this approach, the book's first section on "Biographical Politics" also addresses two further themes that have rarely been problematised in historical biographical research. Firstly, biographies often follow the convention of telling the life story as a linear chronology. This narrative strategy has been criticised by, among others, the sociologist Pierre Bourdieu, who in a classic essay pointed out that lives are not lived and understood from the cradle to the grave, but are rather experienced in fragments that are not necessarily coherent or well-connected.[20] A consistent cradle-to-grave biographical portrait is therefore, according to Bourdieu, an illusion.[21] This critical argument is taken seriously and pushed further in Possing's chapter on deconstruction and reconstruction techniques in biographical research. Secondly, biographical research has served many different political purposes; for instance, it has been used and abused in the construction of political and territorial identities. What lies behind such biographical politics is taken up in the chapter by Kølvraa, which applies a highly original psychoanalytical perspective to the realm of European and transnational politics. Kølvraa takes a meta-biographical approach to examining the way that the life and biography of Jean Monnet – often seen as the founding father of the European Community – has been used in attempts to construct a European identity.

19. D. Deacon, P. Russell and A. Woollacott, "Introduction", in: Deacon, Russell and Woollacott, *Transnational Lives*, pp. 1–11, here p. 2. See also V. Berghahn and S. Lässing (ed.), *Biography between Structure and Agency. Central European Lives in International Historiography*, New York 2008.
20. P. Bourdieu, "L'illusion biographique", *Actes de la recherche en sciences sociales*, no. 62/63, June 1986.

21. While Bourdieu was skeptical of the biographical genre, he actually, albeit reluctantly, made an autobiographical portrait in P. Bourdieu, *Sketch for a Self-Analysis*, Chicago 2008. Importantly, other sociologists have in fact brought new inspiration to the biographical genre such as B. Latour, *The Pasteurization of France*, Cambridge MA 1993 and N. Elias, *Mozart: Portrait of a Genius*, Berkeley 1993.

The contributions in this book draw in various ways on the perspectives opened up by the transnational and sociological approaches outlined above, exploring the range of insights that may be gained by adopting a biographical approach. Rather than focusing on the leading statesmen that are most typically portrayed, their subjects also include intellectuals, diplomats, bureaucrats and parliamentarians – sometimes several of these roles are embodied in one person at different times – who have come to inhabit and/or intellectualise the transnational political realm. The points made in this introduction should not necessarily be read as an encouragement to write biographies about each and every historical actor who used the new windows of opportunity to interact with international organisations, but as a call for a theoretically and methodologically more reflective use of biographical research in 20th-century European and international history.

The contributions are written by an international group of historians who are experts in the fields of biographical research and 20th-century European history. Moreover, the contributors have all carried out extensive multiarchival research, and through their work they have tried to place this historical research in relation to theoretical and methodological and inter-disciplinary academic debates. Their chapters are all products of original research, and many of them are based on source materials and literatures in languages other than the English presented here to an international audience for the first time. By virtue of the biographical focus, all this work shares two features that are different from the representation of history found in traditional international and European integration historical research. For one, it challenges the way in which the great wars of the 20th-century are often seen as decisive breaks with the past; from the perspective of biography, the wars do not necessarily provide the 'natural' or most significant dividing lines. A second difference is that political history often divides the world up according to formal organisational structures – for instance the European Community and European Union – yet the contributors in this volume demonstrate how many political and diplomatic actors moved around between various national, international and transnational institutions during their educations, careers and lives. The chapters in this book also share an active engagement not only with the prospects, but also with the constraints, of the use of biographical research in historical research.

The book is divided into three sections. The first section on "Biographical Politics" brings out some key questions of theory and methodology relating to political biography by presenting and juxtaposing two innovative and provocative contributions from the fields of biographical research and European history. In her opening chapter, "Portraiture and Re-portraiture of the Political Individual in Europe: Biography as a Genre and as a Deconstructive Technique", Birgitte Possing, as mentioned earlier, offers a series of theoretical and methodological reflections on narrativity in political biography. An accomplished and innovative biographer herself, Possing draws on her own extensive research experience, and presents some of the postmodern criticisms that have been levelled against the coherent cradle-to-grave narrative in classical political biography. At the same time, she also thematises the gender perspective in political biography.

Beyond problematising the questions of narrativity and gender, Christoffer Kølvraa's chapter "Who's your Daddy? The Construction of Jean Monnet as a Father Figure for the EC in the 1980s" takes an original approach to biographical politics and the construction of the EU/EC.[22] He considers the criticism made by the prominent historian of European integration processes, Alan Milward, of the tendency among some of his colleagues to establish a hagiography of a select number of "European Saints", that is, a small group of men who were repeatedly characterised as "founding fathers" of the EC/EU. Kølvraa points out that these men have been accorded the status of ideological father figures whose "vision" for Europe is referred to not as one political position among others, but as

22. A different discussion of psychohistorical interpretations in historical biographical research in Banner, "Biography as History", p. 580.

something of a secular gospel for the community of Europe. Instead of investigating Jean Monnet's political life, Kølvraa adopts a psycho-analytical perspective to explore the biographical politics relating to Monnet after his death. Kølvraa shows that it was in Monnet's afterlife that his real legacy as a founding father was created, which then became a core element in the discourses on European identity in the 1980s. Kølvraa takes the metaphor of "founding father" literally and uses psychoanalytical theory to further our understanding of how father-figures function as a mode of symbolic power in political communities – and not least in the context of a more diffuse political entity such as the EC/EU.

The four contributions in the second part of the book, "Politics of European Lives", are united by their aim to explore different analytical potentials of the biographical approach in relation to the tracing and making of international and transnational political organisations and institutions. A further commonality of the contributions is the identification of phases and continuities in lives that challenge the widespread assumption that the Second World War was a decisive break with the past. Each chapter in its own way underlines that in order to grasp the significance of the political agents inhabiting the post-war European diplomatic and political realm, it is necessary to include their inter-war ideas and experiences. Moreover, they highlight the need to take a perspective that crosses formal political boundaries, since the narratives themselves are not contained within organisational boundaries.

In the first chapter in this section, Anne Deighton scrutinises one of the key political figures in Britain to have entered the scene of European politics after 1945, namely Ernest Bevin. Bevin held multiple public positions during his political career, notably as a trade union activist and leader, as well as minister of foreign affairs (1945–1951). Deighton approaches Bevin's biography in relation to his views on the emerging European human rights regime in the context of the Council of Europe. It is an area of Bevin's life that has been largely overlooked, perhaps because he did not succeed in getting what he wanted. Deighton demonstrates how Bevin's ideas about human rights, when translated into political practice, were mediated and adapted by chance and by domestic and international political forces. In doing so, Deighton points out how political biography reveals the limits of the political impact of individuals and their ideas, and how biographies also become narratives about what was possible – and impossible – in practice, with all the compromises, sub-optimal decisions and failures that are an inevitable part of the political process.

Further new approaches are taken by Kristine Midtgaard and Jan-Henrik Meyer in the two ensuing chapters. As pointed out earlier, both are interested in individuals who would typically not be placed on the political map if considered in classical terms of political offices or impact, but who merit attention here because their lives and career trajectories can in different ways shed light on the changing rules of national and transnational political games during the 20th century. In her chapter "Bodil Begtrup: Career, Network and Individual Agency in International Organizations and National Embassies, 1926–1973", Midtgaard demonstrates how Begtrup, a Danish human rights activist and diplomat, was a "multipositioned" agent who moved between various international and transnational networks and organisations that emerged and increasingly overlapped during the 20th century. While explaining that Begtrup was struggling to convert the political capital she had built up as a womens' rights activist when entering the Danish diplomatic service, Midtgaard also shows how Begtrup continuously managed to take advantage of her formal representations as platforms for her work on her main interest in women's rights.

In his chapter "Hans Edgar Jahn – Anti-Bolshevist, Cold Warrior, Environmentalist", Jan-Henrik Meyer also looks into the ideas and life of an individual who moved between and inhabited various political and institutional worlds. Tracing Jahn's movements from a position as a stern Anti-Bolshevist and Nazi propagandist in the Third Reich, through his involvement in the German Christian Democratic Party, to his position as a strong proponent of European environmental cooperation in the European Parliament, Meyer shows how these worlds eventually conflicted and collided. Rather than achieving a legacy as a "good" European, Jahn's career ended in public disgrace once his Nazi past was made public towards the end of the 1970s. However, as Meyer points out, unravelling Jahn's political career also alerts us to questions of continuity and change in interpretations of and advocacy for Europe. As Meyer demonstrates, the key idea of a united Europe that Jahn cherished and promoted throughout his post-1945 career was shaped by the anti-Bolshevist worldview he acquired as a National Socialist before 1945.

Based on extensive experience with biographical research and European integration history, Jan van der Harst's chapter focuses on the mix of methods that can be employed when the subject of a biography is still alive, and he reflects on some of the limits that exist in terms of ethics and (self-)censorship. Van der Harst's subject is Max Kohnstamm, a Dutch-born civil servant from a bourgeois family who was closely involved with the establishment of European organisations such as the High Authority of the European Coal and Steel Community. Max Kohnstamm worked closely with well-known personalities such as Jean Monnet, but he also stayed out of the limelight as much as possible. Van der Harst and his collaborator set themselves the task of writing a biography that would avoid the hagiographic traits that biographies of the European 'founding fathers' traditionally had. In doing so they moved from writing macro-level to micro-level history and adopted a set of new research methods such as oral history interviews and observations, along with consideration of the large amounts of written materials available about Kohnstamm and his contemporaries.

The theme of "Biography and Intellectual Politics" is taken up in the book's third part, in which the contributors demonstrate how a biographical approach can serve as an analytical entry point into the diverse spectrum of ideas of Europe. In the chapter by Karl Christian Lammers, the constitutional struggle in the Weimar Republic is viewed in a broader European perspective. This chapter is concerned with the German social democratic constitutional thinker Hermann Heller and his attempts to defend the European constitutional state against surging fascism. Lammers shows how, shaped in part by first hand experiences of Italian fascism, Heller became a harsh critic of fascist ideology and developed the concept of "Sozialer Rechtsstaat" (the social constitutional state), a political regime in which state and government are bound by the rule of law and legitimised by the political subjects through a community of values and social compromise. Lammers follows the development of Heller's writings at the intersection of his own political development and experiences amongst the changing winds of politics in Europe in the 1920s and 1930s, and inside the Weimar Republic where one of Heller's competitors in constitutional theory at the time, Carl Schmidt, was also active. In exploring this theme, Lammers introduces interesting reflections on the contributions from, and limits to, a pro-democratic thinker in inter-war Germany who is often overlooked in writings on German and European history.

Other authors demonstrate that the Second World War or particular organisations cannot provide the right demarcation lines for individual stories. In their chapter "Promise or Plague", Karen Gram-Skjoldager and Thorsten Borring Olesen examine the intellectual roots of Danish foreign policy between 1920 and 1950 as seen through the writings of Hartvig Frisch, a Social Democratic politician and prominent university academic. The authors position Frisch as a transformative figure at the nexus of political and intellectual circles. The biographical perspective opens up new understandings both of how Frisch's intellectual and ideational development unfolded during this period of tremendous international political change, and of changes within Danish political culture. The chapter looks at how Frisch's ideas on Norden, Europe and wider international forms of interactions and cooperation were related to each other and developed over time. It points out how, during the 1930s, the fascist and radical communist tendencies displayed on the continent gradually alienated Frisch from Europe and prompted him to take a strong pro-democratic stance based on a juxtaposition of violent and radicalised Europe with peaceful, social democratic Norden. This conceptual collocation, as well as Frisch's burgeoning interest in the idea of peaceful international development in the world through the League of Nations and the United Nations, became a key element in Danish national and international self-understanding in the following years. However, the two authors also show how Frisch gradually became marginalised as he transmuted some of his ideas into a neutralist conception of foreign policy which included a fierce defence of Danish cooperation with the Nazi-regime during the war, and a hesitance towards membership of NATO cooperation. His personal ideas of Europe therefore also came to position him outside of the Danish foreign policy mainstream.

A very different view of intellectual politics and ideas of Europe is presented in the chapter by Niels Wium Olesen and Johnny Laursen. Through a portrait, or rather several portraits, of the former Danish social democratic Prime Minister Jens Otto Krag, they alert us to some of the problems involved in doing biographical research on a political figure who has gained almost legendary status in the general historical outlines of post-war Denmark, as well as in several biographical studies. The two authors argue that Krag himself has managed to influence and shape much of the biographical research that has been done about him through a conscious and systematic effort to create a political legacy for himself. The dominant biographical narratives about Krag are, according to Olesen and Laursen, too well-ordered and coherent, and attempt to give a purpose, order and direction to his political life that it did not in fact have. They challenge this narration of Krag's life through a discussion of three core episodes in Krag's political career, and re-evaluate the assumed coherence in and importance of Krag's political ideas. Contrary to conventional wisdom, they point to the relatively limited impact of Krag's plan for post-war reconstruction in 1945. They describe the development of Krag's ideas about and support for European integration and EC membership as a gradual and dynamic process, and they argue that his internationalist, Atlantist visions were not as strong and unambiguous as has often been claimed. In this way their chapter takes on board Possing's suggestions for a deconstructive technique, and underlines Deighton's argument that the ideas of an individual, even one who had a central political role, are analytical entities and causal factors are to be treated with the utmost caution.

The chapter by Mark Gilbert centres on one of the most prominent political and historical thinkers of the 20th century, namely
Edward Hallett (E. H.) Carr, and it moves the focus towards the
question of how the political ideas of intellectuals contribute to
the framing and shaping of politics. Carr was a historian; during the
inter-war years he had a diplomatic career, and later he moved into
a journalistic career working as an editor for *The Times* in London
during the Second World War. These different worlds shaped Carr's
worldviews, yet Gilbert argues that Carr's influence was not on
immediate events, but in the way that intellectuals usually have
most impact: through the contributions he made to eroding established mental structures and through his dissemination of new
concepts which would become part of the patrimony of political
discourse over the next thirty years. More specifically, the chapter
argues that Carr was one of the thinkers in wartime Europe
who contributed most to the creation of the historical rationale for
European integration as it took shape after the war. One rationale of
Gilbert's chapter – and of his other writings – is therefore that
the "idea of Europe", which so often is equated with the European
integration process in the context of the EC/EU, should not be
understood in a teleological fashion, but as a dynamic, plural and
multidirectional process.

These chapters demonstrate diversified and innovative approaches to historical political biographical research. The promise of this
type of research and perspective, which we hope historians of
European, transnational and international history will appreciate,
lies not in its ability to retell the life stories of historically powerful
political characters (usually male actors), but in its ability to prob-
lematise and go beyond conventions of chronological narration
and national framing.

Part I
Biographical Politics

Portraiture and Re-portraiture of the Political Individual in Europe:
Biography as a Genre and as a Deconstructive Technique

Birgitte Possing
The Danish National Archives

Biographical fascination and illusion

There are biographies here, there and everywhere, and the list is growing. In spite of this cornucopia of biographies we see the academia, especially in the Scandinavian countries hesitate accepting or dealing with the biography as a genre. So, let us try to define: what is a biography? The short answer is that it is a description of a life, *bios graphein*, written by someone other than the person who lived the life. A biography is a telling of a life. In contradistinction to an autobiography. And in contradistinction to a lived life.

Given the validity of this definition the long answer is that the genre has a lengthy history, going right back to Antiquity;[1] that the genre during the centuries has served many purposes vis-à-vis its readers; that the genre is like a bar of soap slipping from our grasp when we pick it up; that the genre shares borders with many a branch of learning and cuts across specialisation; that the biographical genre has a robust tradition of gender imbalance, which was

1. B. Possing, *Viljens Styrke. Natalie Zahle – en biografi om køn, dannelse og magtfuldkommenhed*, vol. 1–2, Copenhagen 1992 and 1997; P. France and W. St Clair (eds.), *Mapping Lives. The Uses of Biography*, Oxford 2002; H. E. Bödecker (ed.), *Biographie schreiben*, Göttinger Gespräche zur Geschichtswissenschaft, vol. 18, Göttingen 2003.

first broached in the twentieth century; and last, but not least that the genre has a tradition of presenting a cohesive picture of life, but is today open, polyphonic and speaks with many voices. Biography deals with lives lived by individuals, and therefore exercises a strong fascination. But can we allow this fascination to be unreflective when it has long since been recognised that the linear life story is a construction in need of epistemological analysis, as demonstrated by Pierre Bourdieu in his 1986 landmark article *L'Illusion bio-graphique?*[2] Bourdieu maintained that the biographical construction of separate events in a chronological sequence bears an inescapable similarity to the *bildungsroman* of the literary agenda, in which the lived life is rendered on a model of linear, subjectivised – and objec-tivised – coherence. Bourdieu rightly disputes that this construction might well be worthy of preservation in terms of aesthetics, but that it is not worthy in terms of theory or scholarship.[3]

Does this mean that, in a scholarly context, biography should thus be passed over? Is a biography only a biography if its intention is to follow the progression of a life? Can an individual's under-takings, thoughts and feelings be reconstructed from one end to the other in a biography substantiated by simple reference to the begin-ning of life at birth and the end at death? Can a life be reconstruct-ed without deconstructing the supposition that this life has an underlying coherence? Does time, in itself, create narrative? Do bio-graphers employ a chronological narrative technique – from one end to the other? The answers are just as complex as the process of writ-ing a biography. The biographer does not have to spend much time with her or his material before it becomes apparent that the idea of using the sequence of the life story as the basis for a biographical interpretation is not workable. This is nothing new. In the 16th century, Michel de Montaigne pointed out the inconsistencies in

2. P. Bourdieu, "L'Illusion biogra-fique", in *Actes de la recherche en sciences sociales,* no. 62/63, June 1986, Editions de Minuit, Paris 1986. Danish translation by Eva Bertram in *Kontext* 2, pp. 39–45, Politisk Revy, Copenhagen 1988.

3. P. Bourdieu, "L'Illusion biogra-fique". Om biografi som dekonstru-erende metode", in: J. Kofod and D. Staunæs (eds.), *Magtballader. 14 fortællinger om magt, modstand og menneskers tilblivelse,* Copenhagen 2007.

every individual's life,[4] just as Chateaubriand in the 19th century stated that the individual did not have just one, but many lives.[5]

It is precisely this inconsistency, paradox and ambivalence which, to my mind, makes for the fascination of the genre and for the history of the Individual. Writing of this fascination 250 years ago, Samuel Johnson, the biographer who also had a biography written about him, claimed: 'No species of writing seems more worthy of cultivation than biography, since none can be more delightful or more useful, none can more certainly enchain the heart by irresistible interest, or more widely diffuse instruction to every diversity of condition.'[6] Despite Johnson's claim, the biography enthrals in its compelling tales of life, but provides only diffuse guidance as to how life should be tackled, given that circumstances differ and can change radically over the course of a lifetime.[7] Biographers have been aware of this ever since the Renaissance saw the stirrings of a biographical form endeavouring to encompass a rounded character. This type of biography evolved from the Enlightenment by way of the 18th-century preoccupation with the bourgeois individual's development seen in a Romantic-evolutionary light. At the beginning of the 20th century, the modern, 'revelatory' or demythologising life story was introduced by the Bloomsbury group, starting with Lytton Strachey's *Eminent Victorians*.[8]

4. M. de Montaigne, *Essays*, vol. 3 [1580], translated by C. Cotton, revised by W.C. Hazlett and E.C. Hill, New York 1910, p. 9.

5. Chateaubriand, cited in P. Auster, *The Book of Illusions*, London/New York 2002.

6. Samuel Johnson in *The Rambler no. 60*, 1750, cited in: P. France and W. St Clair (eds.), *Mapping Lives*, New York 2002, p. 3. James Boswell wrote *The Life of Samuel Johnson* in 1791; this biography is still considered to be the pioneering work of study into the process of intellectual and character development and in the identification of threads between a life's work in the public arena and its anchorage in a private life, based as it was on a huge amount of empirical material comprising letters, interviews, literary and private documents.

7. This is a somewhat contrary discussion about life coherence than presented in L. W. Banner, "Biography as History", *American Historical Review*, vol. 3, 2009, pp. 579–586.

8. L. Strachey, *Eminent Victorians*, London 1918.

The new aspect of biography today, however, is neither its diversity nor its cornucopia of publications. Innovation comes by way of the complex choreography, reflection and research applied to the biographical genre. This development was brought about by the gradual post-war paradigm shift from modernism to post-modernism. In this transformation, autobiography and biography were key battlefields on which the struggle between old and new was fought out. Inspiration was gleaned from complex literature such as Proust's *À la recherche du temps perdu*. History is made by individuals, famous and anonymous alike. In advanced biographical research, the question today is not how the individual life is read in or behind the work. Modernistic concepts such as identity, truth and development have been challenged and set in motion; where answers were previously sought to the question of the person behind the myth, or endeavours were made to reconstruct an individual's life and work in a search for 'the truth' about this individual's 'identity', the issue now is how the individual constructs personal experience or is constructed via others' stories and via other tracks than their own. Where, for example, the new criticism employed in comparative literature considered interest to be centred on the work rather than the life that had created it, the focus is now on uncovering, not the person, but 'the textural structures which construct – or fail to construct – the I that belongs to the narrator', as expressed by the Swedish professor of literature Lisbeth Larsson in her study of biography and autobiography, *Sanning och Konsekvens* [Truth and Consequence], 2001.[9] With the research-based biography's vigorous experimentation and expansion in the historical, literary, aesthetic, theological and sociological disciplines, we find a valid wish not just to incorporate passions, irrationalities and human idiosyncrasies in the decoding of a life's work, but also to see truth, identity and memory as historically-determined constructions rather than as concepts with a fundamental nucleus.

9. L. Larsson, *Sanning och konsekvens: Marika Stiernstedt, Ludvig Nordström och de biografiska berättelserna,* Stockholm 2001.

Thus, today biography is more than ever both a narrative and an analytical genre. It is not a case of either-or:

> In recent decades, biographical research, as well as research into autobiographies, has been part of the extensive critique of the so-called Grand Theories[10] about Humankind, History, the Individual and the Truth. The joint critique of these concepts, their dissolution and their new definition as epistemologically historically-determined constructions has, however, served two in principle completely contradictory purposes. On the one hand, deconstructive, given that the concept of truth is drained and dissolved. On the other hand, one that could be described as *re*constructive, given that the concept's diverse implications are demonstrated in relation to the formerly alleged homogeneity, and given that the biographical texts were used to show that there are other stories, other individuals and other truths than those which were formerly sanctioned.[11]

There continues to be an expressed intellectual need for open reflection on pictures of living individuals' search for a point of orientation in life – a need to read another person's life as a form of '*Owner's Manual*'.[12] But interest now moves on to a need to see the long and complex biographical process as being authorisation of the legitimacy of the stories told about the individual in question. Not as a writer's quest to legitimise the actions or works of the central character, but as a biographer's orientation instrument in complex interpretations of time: 'The object of study for the new biographers is not just the construction of identities but also and inevitably, the contested nature of inventing selves.'[13]

10. Grand Theories mean in this connection the ideologies of the 20th century such as liberalism, communism and socialism.
11. Larsson, *Sanning och konsekvens*, pp. 13–14.

12. M. Thing, *Portrætter af ti kommunister*, Copenhagen 1996, p. 272.
13. J.B. Margadent (ed.), *The New Biography. Performing Femininity in 19th Century France*, Berkeley 2000, p. 9.

Fiction writers can create coherence and identities; they can also construct various identities for the same central character. The Norwegian writer Jan Kjærstad did just this in his celebrated trilogy about Jonas Wergeland, using three different versions of the same man. He created a fictional *coherence* in an individual's *life* (*Forføreren* 1993, *Erobreren* 1996, *Oppdageren* 1999; in English: *The Seducer* 2003, *The Conqueror* 2007, *The Discoverer*, 2008).

Can a scholarly historian, littérateur, anthropologist or scholar in the humanities do the same thing, based on sources from documented reality, on empirical studies of historical figures who have actually lived! As far as I have been informed by the editors, this is one of the purposes of this anthology, namely to show how lives can be deconstructed, and how biographical research can be used to tell new versions of mainstream history. Another question is about historical biographies' possibility of having scholarly legitimacy and at the same time having a narrative function? In academic circles, some will claim that this is so while others will chime the death knell – over and over, according to my own survey over the literature and the research debate in the Scandinavian countries. But the urge to prove oneself in the genre is strong, in academia too, and it is not unusual to see *several biographers* applying themselves to the same principal character; prominent national and major international figures often inspire the attention of a number of biographers. We frequently hear that now the 'definitive' biography of Churchill, Hitler or Queen Victoria has been written. In Denmark, three biographies of Churchill were published within the space of three years: *Statsmand og myte* [Statesman and Myth],[14] and translations of *Churchill: A Life*[15] and *Churchill: A Biography*.[16] But which is the *most* ultimate? None of them – because biographies are always a mirror of their times, their biographer and their readers.

14. J. Sevaldsen, *Statsmand og myte*, Copenhagen 2004.
15. M. Gilbert, *Winston Churchill. A Life*, London 1992.

16. R. Jenkins, *Churchill. A Biography*, London 2001.

Biographical narrativity:
reconstruction or deconstruction?

Is it good or bad that biography is everywhere said to be a story that starts in the cradle and ends on the brink of the grave? The Danish historian Jens Christian Manniche has suggested: "[...] actually, the biggest problem of the biography is perhaps the perceived biographical convention that an individual's life has to have coherence."[17] His book on Anna Hude, the first female historian and D.Phil. (*doctor philosophiae*) in Denmark, was at first turned down by a commercial publishing house for being too fragmentary and ambiguous. The editorial consultant had asked for a picture showing the coherence of Hude's life, but biographer Manniche could not *see* any coherent whole. In rejecting the manuscript, the consultant wrote that the contemporary reader *insisted* on coherence in a life story, and went on:

> That is [...] why biographies, fictional biographies and historical novels are so popular. Every individual interprets his or her own life, more or less consciously, and makes for a coherence which is perhaps present, perhaps not. And we read these books for the sake of recognition, to find structures that can explain, create purpose and meaning in what appears to be random.[18]

A desire to create something that does not exist. Eventually, however, Manniche's book was published – by Gad publishing house – and it was praised to the skies!

Nevertheless, biographers persist in constructing a thread which runs through a postulated cradle-to-grave coherence. We create a construction – not because of, but in spite of the life story it is telling. But who is to say that in the life as lived there was one destiny that created purpose, meaning, coherence? One destiny that can be

17. J.C. Manniche, "Om biografi", in: *Jens Christian Manniche 1942–2003. Biograf, historiograf, koloni-* *historiker,* Den jyske Historiker, Aarhus 2003.
18. Manniche, "Om biografi".

read biographically in retrospect and explain the life? Well, ye-e-s … Kirkegaard summed it up: 'life is lived forwards and understood backwards.' And we are all on Freud's tail – brought up believing it. But what if we anchor biography in a life-story context that is not one of continuity, but of rupture and complexity? Should we then keep up the biographical convention – or should we make room for other perceptions? Can the biography's scholarly legitimacy in the 21st century be found in interpretations that are open, documenting ambiguity in text and sources, constructing a narrative without an unequivocal linearity? In other words: putting the reader to work?

It is, of course, a postmodernist question. And yet …! Ambiguity has been an element of human interpretation for longer than we would like to think. Five hundred years ago, an elderly Montaigne wrote in his essay 'Of the Inconsistency of our Actions':

> Such as make it their business to oversee human actions,
> do not find themselves in anything so much perplexed as
> to reconcile them and bring them into the world's eye with
> the same lustre and reputation; for they commonly so
> strangely contradict one another that it seems impossible
> they should proceed from one and the same person.[19]

Chateaubriand – the Romantic ego above all Romantic egos – wrote in the 19th century: "Man has not one and the same life. He has many lives, placed end to end, and that is the cause of his misery."[20] Nonetheless, countless biographies tell the story of a life going forwards, without explaining it going backwards – or from the side. This is not hard to understand: narrative theorists tell us that stories might well be read sequentially, but they are interpreted and comprehended retrospectively. It is the end that makes sense of the beginning and the story as such; i.e. in a good story, it is not until the end that the story reveals its overall significance. The ending, the main idea, the plot – all in all, are prerequisites for the creation

19. Montaigne, *Essays*, p. 9
20. Chateaubriand (1768–1848) was the exponent par excellence of self-awareness in French Romanticism. The citation is taken from Auster *The Book of Illusions*.

of a story. But when the historical biography is told step by step as a chronological story, then it is, so to speak, an unfinished narrative – and, as such, meaningless. Unless it has a contention – an interpretation.

And if it has a meaning – an interpretation – then it also has a thread running through it; most historians have learnt this technique from the littérateurs. The biography stage manages the past and commits itself to an explanation along the lines of: it happened like it happened because it happened like it happened – because the story, the narrative exposition, has direction and coherence vis-à-vis where it ends. The Danish politician and former prime minister Jens Otto Krag (1914–1978) did *not* succeed as an artist, the painter or writer he aspired to be, because he was a politician. Because he made the wrong choice when his days as an active politician came to an end. Then he *had* to succumb to drink, which eventually killed him. And here I am not only alluding to the interpretation made by his celebrated biographer, Bo Lidegaard,[21] but to the construal of most biographers. The story is predetermined because the ending is known in advance; see also the chapter by Laursen and Wium Olesen for a case discussion of this. This kind of predetermination will be at stake, too, even if the biographer has gone behind the myth of 'great lives' and has demythologised the individual life, as I myself did 19 years ago in relation to the pioneering Danish educationalist Natalie Zahle (1827–1913).[22] The objective and function of the Natalie Zahle biography was *partly* to open up a life and times universe across a whole century, to be the catalyst for a story that had not been written, and *partly* to reveal the person behind the myth. The myth of an individual who embarked upon an enterprise rooted in divine inspiration, and who started from scratch. And, instead, to understand her as a bearer and breaker of cultural rules, as a woman who suffered misgivings and sorrows along the route of her journey. As the pioneer who, on a private basis, founded a

21. B. Lidegaard, *Jens Otto Krag,* vol. 1–2, Copenhagen 2001–2003.

22. Possing, *Viljens Styrke.*

school empire, who designed educational models and the prototype of a state school system destined to operate far into the future. It was a unique achievement for a woman working within a Victorian environment. She created an organisation that required her to exercise power and authority over her surroundings. This needed to be explained: she was *both* hero and villain. Just that single demythologisation was new in itself, but it also generated a new – feminist – myth, because we knew the ending of her being as an outstanding pioneer having founded her own female family with herself in the lead. During her lifetime the ending was, of course, unknown. She had had the option of marriage – and seeing her creation fall to pieces. She could have gone to live in Russia – and written herself out of the history. But that about which we have no knowledge cannot amount to anything other than speculation in a historical biography. So how can we postulate linearity if it was not to be found in the lived, empirical life? If life and work was too complex, contradictory and catch napping (= surprising) to foresee?

Quite another question which is not to be developed here is the question about ethics. The act of writing a biography, an intellectual juggling act with destinies, involves not only documentary and narrative challenges. Furthermore, it involves ethical challenges – if, that is, the biography is to be faction rather than fiction. The challenges of an ethical and methodological nature arise from the role of the biographer as arbiter of the life of an individual who is defenceless. If biographers wish to uphold the humanist project, respect for the dignity of others, how far is it then possible to go[23] – as regards crossing boundaries set by individuals to their private lives, for example. In the scholarly genre we learn to reveal hidden truths. But what should we do with evidence of private and ethical issues which the individual in question has chosen to erase and thus delete from any potential future reference? Should this wish be respected or not in a time and period of world history where the boundary

23. Professor Eva Østerberg, oral critique, contribution at the publication of H. Rosengren and J.   Östling (eds.), *Med livet som insats. Biografin som humanistisk genre*, Lund 2007.

between private and public has shifted so radically as is the case with those spheres during the last 50 years? I just have to be content with the statement that the biographer's ethical respect towards the protagonist is an issue that has to be seriously considered over and over again when facing the actual protagonist of the biography. But the question of biographical ethics is a subject upon which one should develop a series of arguments which I am doing in another work to be published in a near future. Here, I will just underline that this is an important issue that any scholarly biographer needs to consider. Also the question of the selection of sources and the documentary fundament of the biographical reconstruction and narrative is a classical ethical one within the biographical genre. Virginia Woolf's comments on biography have been quoted countless times; when writing a biography of her late friend Roger Fry, she wondered: 'How can one make a life out of six cardboard boxes full of tailors' bills, lovers' letters and old picture postcards?' And she asked: 'What are you really like?'[24] Put a little crudely: if she told a good story, she was interpreting a possibly non-existent direction followed by a life; if there was no direction, it was a bad biography. The answer to that question is not simple – and it is not just necessarily one of coherence.

The renewed interest in biography has been seen by many over the last decade as something of a humanistic reaction against the postmodern, fragmented subject. But more and more biographers are abandoning the endeavour to identify coherence. Instead, the approach is given a different slant, as described by the American historian Jo Burr Margadent: 'The subject of biography is no longer the coherent self but rather a self that is performed to create an impression of coherence or an individual with multiple selves.'[25] The convention of coherence is questioned. The reconstruction of a coherent life story is deconstructed.

24. Cited in: L. Edel, *Literary Biography*, London 1957, and L. Edel, *Writing Lives. Principia Biographia*, New York 1984.

25. Margadent (ed.): *The New Biography*, 2000.

Biographical polyphony

Thus, biography has acquired new significance. Denmark in the early 1990s witnessed a robust public debate about the relevance and role of the personality in history, inspired by my biography of Natalie Zahle. The public debate blew up again in the early years of the new century following the publication of the theologian Joakim Garff's biography of Søren Kirkegaard.[26] In both cases, the arguments of the debate were focused on the interpretation of the protagonist and her/his impact and influence on the national Danish identity. Or in general, on the role of the individual personality in history compared to structures and ideologies. In the 1990s we saw a huge public enthusiasm as a welcoming reaction on the re-writing of Natalie Zahle into Scandinavian history. In 2003–04 the opposite issue was at stake, when a critic of the Kierkegaard biography claimed the (copy)right of 'the truth' and 'the true' interpretation of the protagonists' actions and thoughts as a national figure. Why was the tone so vehement? I believe that it was not only due to the status of Zahle and Kierkegaard as Danish national icons. The discussions were robust because the biography is 'historiography's humanistic primary genre', as the Swedish professor Gøran B. Nilsson has called it.[27]

In other European countries it is the pioneering nature of biographical research which wins particular recognition. A central aspect to the discussion was inspired by David Macey, author of biographies of Lacan and Foucault, who invented the concept of *compartmentalisation*.[28] In this view, 20th-century cultural liberation of the modern individual is seen to have liberated identity. One individual's many identities provide the potential for changing track in the course of a lifetime. In his biography of Michel Foucault

26. J. Garff, *Søren Kierkegaard. A Biography*, translated from Danish by B. H. Kirmmse, New Jersey 2005.
27. G.B. Nilsson, "Biografi som spjutspetsforskning", in: R. Ambjörnsson, P. Ringby and S. Åkermann (eds.), *Att skriva Människan. Essäer om biografin som livshistoria och vetenskaplig genre,* Stockholm 1997.
28. D. Macey, *The Lives of Michel Foucault,* London 1993.

(1993), Macey showed that Foucault lived many lives – an academic, a political activist, a child and a homosexual. Biographer David Macey is challenged by the multiplicity in Foucault's life, because the range of elements made it difficult to reach any satisfactory periodisation of his work. The concept of compartmentalisation reflected the fact that modernity gave humankind the opportunity to have one identity at the workplace, another in a minority culture, a third in the family, a fourth in a sports setting or political context etc. Each identity could have its specific signals and attire, and no single culture was overarching for the individual's inclusive identity. Consequently, a biography can be seen in contexts other than the chronological. Foucault himself was amused to note that he was perceived as anarchist, Marxist and anti-Marxist, ultra- and neo-liberal and Gaullist technocrat etc.: 'It's true that I prefer not to identify myself and that I'm amused by the diversity of the ways I've been judged and classified.'[29]

A number of biographers have abandoned the cradle-to-grave convention and taken a particularised approach in order to confront the complexity: for example, Stephen Walton on Ivar Aasen, Yvonne Hirdman on Alva Myrdal, Toril Moi on Simone de Beauvoir, Seyla Benhabib on Hannah Arendt, and myself on Bodil Koch.[30] With this individualisation, the biographical genre has acquired a new productive layer – it has become a prism for a multitude of specialities; it has been post-modernised. Today, the theoretical bearings of a scholarly biography within the humanities have to be interdisciplinary, navigating through literature, history, anthropology, sociology, psychology, philosophy, and possibly theology and art history. Also needed is an empirical corpus comprising analysis of texts, pictures and sources. There are thus considerations of both theoretical and methodological nature that are bound to

29. Macey, *Lives of Michel Foucault.*
30. S.J. Walton, *Ivar Aasens kropp,* Oslo 1996; S.J. Walton, *Skaff deg eit liv! Om biografi,* Oslo 1998; Y. Hirdman, *Det tänkende Hjärtat. Bokan om Alva Myrdal,* Stockholm 2006, Larsson, *Sanning och konsekvens*; T. Moi, *Simone de Beauvoir : the Making of an Intellectual Woman,* Oxford 1994; B. Possing, *Uden omsvøb. Et portræt af Bodil Koch,* Copenhagen 2007.

apply regardless of whether the biographer is a literary or a political historian, and whether the biographer is an author or a politician.

And what do I mean by that? The protagonist of our biographies is and has been a fully nuanced human personality in real life – and thus cannot be phrased in a one-dimensional literary, anthropological, psychological or another disciplinary frame without losing some dimensions of his or her life. So, the best biographies are the ones that open up the biographical analysis understanding the individual from different disciplinary angles. When I wrote my first Natalie Zahle biography, for instance, I was aware of painting her into a social, private, cultural, educational and even political context, but on the other hand I had to be painfully aware that I did *not* approach her as a theologian researcher. I had to realize the limits of my theologian skills.

Later, when I published the biography on the internationally well known Danish Minister of Cultural and Ecclesiastical Affairs Bodil Koch (1903–72), the situation was different. In this case, I had to include the theologian approach, because Bodil Koch's religious feelings and understandings were extremely important in order to understand her national visions of international relations and foreign politics. In my biography on her, it was not an imperative to include an interpretation of her private life as it was in the understanding of the pedagogic pioneer Natalie Zahle, because Zahle had been unable to succeed in building her educational school empire, had it not been for the special construction of her social families.[31] As for Bodil Koch, though, the understanding of her private life was less important to the understanding of her public career than her religious beliefs. So, as a biographer I had to educate myself within theology in order to understand and analyse the theologian issues. Working with disciplines that are new for the biographer and in which the biographer is not educated or skilled, it is necessary to read a lot, but also to test the approach among more skilled colleagues. Being a more experienced historical biographer it is easier to deal with a broad series of disciplines within the humanities and

31. B. Possing, *Awakening the Promise of the Soul,* Copenhagen 2001.

social sciences that should be needed for a well situated biography. The important point is that the protagonist of a biography is not to become a victim of a pedagogic game that the biographer plays, framing him or her in a narrow one-dimensional disciplinary thinking. After all, the scholarly educated biographer should be able to develop a cross disciplinary methodological approach in order to understand the personality and the protagonist of the biography.

Most biographers operate with at least three basic ingredients: an individual, the (life's) work and the times – attributing them widely different prominence. The biography as a genre gives the biographer scope to feel privileged and to crisscross; and to develop the intellectual scope to surmount narrow specialisms. This liberates the biographical research, enabling it to pursue many directions, albeit the chronological convention is tenacious. Innovation is on its way – and often it comes from the feminist approach. Rising numbers of scholarly biographies are being written by women, which will perhaps change some perspectives in the gender imbalance. The historical biography as genre was previously dominated by men writing about statesmen, financiers or male scientists. Ten years ago, only 8% of biographies had female protagonists and only 4% were written by female biographers, if the review sections in European and US historical journals are to be believed.[32] Changes have been afoot during the last 20–30 years, and that is not to be sneered at, because we have to go all the way back to 79 BC to find the single swallow, Chinese Liu Xiang, who in *Biographies des femmes illustres*[33] showed that female personalities could also be worthy of biography. The interesting renewals and new perspectives in the historical biographical genre have come from feminist biographies because biographers have to include new views and new understandings to recognise, visualize and reconstruct female lives in history because of the simple fact that women have been differently situated in history than men.

32. B. Possing, "The Historical Biography", in: N. J. Smelser and P.B. Baltes, *Encyclopedia of Social and Behavioral Sciences,* vol. 2, Amsterdam 2001.

33. Lui Xiang, *Lienü zhuan*, BC 79–78. Translated into French by M. Kaltenmark, *Biographies des femmes illustrés,* Peking 1953.

Biographical deconstruction and alternative stories

A biography might have many functions. The biography can function as catalyst for something else, something that could be difficult
to extrapolate: an alternative story. A biography is constituted by
the coherences of the biographer's choice: the theologian and mu-
sic expert Jørgen I. Jensen wrote a biography of Carl Nielsen[34] which
would be over in the first two lines of page 1, with Carl Nielsen's
birth on June 9 1865 and death on October 3 1931, if it had been
a cradle-to-grave life story. Nevertheless, Jensen wrote a – learned –
biography, more than 500 pages, about religious yearnings, audience attitudes, crises and conflicts both private and international, in
the social order of which he was a part. When biography is viewed
from this vantage point, it becomes a polyphonic genre with end-
less potential to understand life, work and times: a genre going
beyond traditional academic disciplines; a genre that is thematic, analytical and narrative. Modernistic concepts such as truth, identity
and development are thus irrelevant in relation to the protagonist.
It is a case of deconstruction – and reconstruction. 'By means of
biographical texts, it can be shown that there are other accounts,
other individuals and other truths than those which were formerly
attributed credence.'[35]

My last book about Bodil Koch, the former Danish Minister
of Ecclasiastical Affairs and Minister of Cultural Affairs, titled *Uden
omsvøb* [*To the Point. An Incisive Portrait*],[36] endeavours to de-
construct the stories told about her in Danish and international history – and to reconstruct alternative stories dealing with religion,
feminism, culture, foreign and domestic policy. The stories are documented in an abundance of sources, but told in my interpretation.
The biography does not start in the cradle and does not postulate

34. J.I. Jensen, *Carl Nielsen –
danskeren: musikbiografi*, Copenhagen 1991.
35. L. Larsson, "Biografins återkomster", in: Rosengren and Östling
(eds.), *Med livet som insats.*

36. Possing, *Uden omsvøb.*

linearity of direction in her life. It seeks answers to the conundrum as to the efficacy of her voice and her efforts – for her personally, for her contemporaries, and for the generations to come. It seeks clarification as to why she was perceived as provocative, impulsive, gifted and naïve – at one and the same time. And it seeks an explanation as to why she has been so ineptly represented in Danish and international historiography alike when she was actually well-known around the world for her robust and intellectual critique of the Cold War division of nations into two blocs, East and West. She was an internationalist, travelled the globe and would rather 'thaw out than freeze'. A photograph of Bodil Koch – wearing evening gown, string of pearls, brandishing cigar, finger raised – remonstrating vehemently with the US Secretary of State John Foster Dulles, during the NATO conference hosted by the Danish government in Copenhagen in 1958, was circulated throughout the world's media. His expression was one of surprise and consternation: was this a woman or a man with cigar and pearl necklace? Was this Danish minister, who criticised the US and his foreign policy, a friend or foe of NATO?

The book places this construal of Bodil Koch within the analytic framework of two paintings of her made in the same year. They were titled, respectively, *Vision i rødt* [Vision in Red] and *De lukkede øjne* [The Closed Eyes], and both were painted by the Danish painter Kirsten Kjær – but they show completely different interpretations of the sitter. First Kirsten Kjær painted *De lukkede øjne*, which is a portrait of a despairing woman, in pastel shades, with an anaemic, introverted expression. Her eyes are actively closed, but the portrait expresses yearning and inward-looking despair. Bodil Koch hated this portrait, which the artist, on the other hand, saw as *her* truth about the sitter. Madam Minister of Church Affairs demanded re-painting. A re-portrayal. For the first and only time in her career, Kirsten Kjær conceded and painted another portrait. This one was *Vision i rødt*, which showed the sitter in an eruption of colour, red, yellow and green – a woman poised for action and on the alert, with a focussed gaze, but nonetheless with a body that exploded and scattered and was full of holes.

Uden omsvøb deals with re-portrayal. Re-portrayal means questioning the former portraits and narratives of the protagonist looking for new empirically situated contexts, new and non-chronological angles in describing, reading and understanding the individual, acting protagonist from concrete situations, thus shedding new light on a well-known personality. I find the concept of re-portrayal extremely relevant in the making of new political biographies of nationally situated, but internationally oriented protagonists as Bodil Koch. Because she, being an outspoken Protestant and a Danish national, democratic representative, insisted on questioning the given order of international politics. Thus, she was an unusual political figure: She was a modernist that claimed that the given political order had to be questioned again and again. She did not want to be categorized only as a Danish Minister of Ecclesiastical Affairs, because she involved foreign politics, art and cultural politics, democracy and technology in the global society. She claimed that international affairs were and should be the fundament of all politics. So, to understand her as a political individual, as a biographer I realized that I had to do the thinking and analysis of intersectionality, of transnational understanding and on the personal scale – of a certain degree of compartmentalisation. I had to focus on the crossing of borders, be it within politics, nations, ideologies, life spheres or sections. This is what the methods of re-portrayal are about. It would certainly not have been possible to explain the life-long advanced and Socratic effort of Bodil Koch in neither national nor international politics if you had not integrated the understanding of her un-pragmatic combination of a social liberal, democratic humanistic, protestantic, feminist and politically naïve personality.

So, my biography on her seeks out the stories between the two portraits of my protagonist, between Bodil Koch and the extreme stances of the Cold War and the battle to win over hearts and minds. It searches for what Bodil Koch saw as "rupture of form" in art, in modernity – and in humankind. Via forensic investigation of manifold source material and, not least, the holes in this material, the book centres on the picture between the two portraits and during the Cold War's extreme debates on modernity and power over mindset. The re-portrayal deals with why Bodil Koch became a controversial critic of her own government's foreign policy, and of the Church for which she was the government minister, and of the women for whom she was the feminist, and of the democracy she loved, and of the Cold War spirit which travelled with her, and of the family in which she was mother and wife. I approach Bodil Koch from the outside – devise a strategy – and examine her objective. On the intellectual and political level, her ambition would seem to be a vision of humanistic democracy which was not only in permanent motion, but which developed by means of paradoxical thinking and confrontation. And on the human, personal level, it would seem she aspired to that which in her own life she endeavoured to cover up, hide and remove from the public arena. This had a democratic function publicly, but came at a high price privately.

With this approach to a biographical portrait of a complex personality, my intention is to show that political biography can still retain its power to fascinate even when life and work are analysed thematically by means of a number of stories crisscrossing the chronological sequence of a life as lived. The objective has been to show that this construction can come close to a complex and stratified response to a series of precisely posed questions – possibly to an even greater degree than a chronologically structured biography can, given that the portrait here focuses on ruptures and dramatic confrontations as well as a smooth sequential narrative of single events. It can, however, be difficult to trace and describe the coherence of a life story which might indeed exist even though it cannot be seen in the conventional positivist sense. But why not take up this challenge?

Doing so as a biographer, you might present a 'ruptured' biography of a life that contained several directions, but in certain historical cases, this might be the most appropriate response to the challenge.

Conclusions

In this article I have argued that the biographical genre is a genre of its own right, and that it should be treated and looked upon as a genre. I have argued that scholarly educated biographers to a still greater degree realize that the genre in modern and postmodern times is characterized by complexity in form, structure and aims. The living political biography of today is both a narrative and an analytic genre where the conventional coherence of biographical, chronological life-linearity of the individual protagonist is questioned. The cradle-to-grave perspective of a biography still being a living convention within the genre, the experiments of understanding a life story and its context as one of rupture and complexity began to be practised to a great degree through the twentieth century, and now at the beginning of the twenty-first century. Furthermore, during the époque we see that changes are afoot in the male-dominated biographical genre; we now see more biographies with female protagonists – and more biographies written by female biographers. Last, but not least the concepts of intersectionality and social constructivist re-portrayal have been introduced in the historical biographical genre taking its first tender steps, and this – the making of a biography, the telling of a life – might lead to an even more fascinating and complex challenge than ever before. But, I suppose, this is a consequential reflection of the complexities for the living individual personalities in real life.

Who's your Daddy?
The Construction of Jean Monnet as a Father Figure for the EC in the 1980s

Christoffer Kølvraa
Aarhus University

Jean Monnet, European Identity and the making of a father figure in the EU

In recent years European identity has been studied extensively both in anthropology, political science, history and sociology[1]. Much work has already been done in analysing the manufacturing of symbols, the ideological foundation of co-operation and the emerging networks of interdependence which might all be said to be dimensions of a wider construction of a common European identity.

In the literature on the different political attempts at constructing a European identity, much attention has been paid to the European Community's' policies of overt symbol creation in the 1980's. It was in this decade that the institutions of the EC, first and arguably most forcefully tried to cultivate a common feeling of 'being European' in the populations of the continent. European integration was no longer to be a closed and technocratic process seemingly

1. C. Shore, *Building Europe – The Cultural Politics of European Integration*, Houndsmill 2000; K. Wilson and J. van der Dussen, *The History of the Idea of Europe*, Houndsmill 1993; U. Beck and E. Grande, *Cosmopolitan Europe*, Cambridge 2007; O. Wæver, "Insecurity, Security and Asecurity in the West European Non-War Community", in: E. Adler and M. Barnett (eds.), *Security Communities*, Cambridge 1998, pp. 69–118; Z. Baumann, *Europe – An unfinished Adventure*, Cambridge 2004.

spawning ever more bureaucratic confusion as it lumbered forward
on neo-functionalist autopilot. Instead Europe should be presented
to the public as a great historical endeavour in which the peoples
of Europe could invest both their pride and their identity. This
required that the origins, ambitions and achievements of European
integration be communicated to the public in ways which did not
require a law degree to understand. Material symbols and common
rituals are forms of communicating and reinforcing community belonging which were used extensively and successfully in the construction of the modern nation-state[2], so it is perhaps not surprising that the EC in its endeavour to construct a European identity in
the 1980's saw fit to invent among other things a common flag, a
community hymn and a 'Europe day'.

The most ferocious critics of the EC's new symbolic politics
reject the entire notion of a common European identity as 'artifi-
cially constructed' and therefore any attempt to symbolise it as ideologically loaded[3]. Indeed the very ambition of forging a common
European identity could be seen as the last trick of those who from
the beginning had secretly harboured federal ambitions for European integration. When Jean Monnet is (mis-)quoted for having
said 'If we were to do it all again we would start with culture' it often serves – for good or for bad – to implicate him in the 'cultural'
or symbolic policies of the 1980's, even if he had died in 1979[4].

However to think of Jean Monnet as the hidden architect behind
the attempts to construct a European identity from the late 1970's
onwards, overlook the true nature and form of the power that Jean
Monnet exerted posthumously in the construction of European

2. E. Hobsbawm and T. Ranger, *The
Invention of Tradition*, Cambridge
1983; E. Hobsbawm, *Nations and
Nationalism since 1780 – Programme,
Myth, Reality,* Cambridge 1991.
3. This kind of critique of course
only makes sense, if one explicitly
(cf. A.D. Smith, "National Identity
and European Unity", in: P. Gowan

and P. Anderson (eds.), *The Question
of Europe,* London 1997 or implicitly
(cf. Shore, *Building Europe*) operates
with a contrast to communities
(most often the nation) which are
somehow less constructed and
more authentic.
4. Shore, *Building Europe,* p. 44.

identity. It was as a symbol himself rather than as an actor that Jean Monnet came to play a prominent role in the construction of European identity.

In fact this was implicitly acknowledged already by Alan Milward who in his 'The European Rescue of the Nation-State' pointed out that EC supporters as well as most historians tended to write the history of European integration as a hagiography of a select number of 'European Saints';

> Monnet, Schuman and Spaak are honoured above others in the calendar, although Adenauer and de Gasperi stand in almost equal rank. Their photographic icons decorate the walls of the Berlaymont building, while cheap coloured reproductions of the arch-saint Monnet adorn the desks of their faithful servants on earth.[5]

Milward's agenda was to launch an alternative thesis about the hidden logic of European integration, and as such he was not particularly interested in how, when or why these men had become 'canonised'. It is however exactly these questions which I will attempt to treat in the following. It must be pointed out however that the religious metaphor which Mil-ward employs is entirely of his own making. Among their 'faith-ful servants' the preferred imagery around these men was always that of paternity. Monnet, Schuman, Spaak, Adenauer and de Gasperi are those select few who are most often designated as the 'Founding Fathers' of Europe. They are part of a small group of historical actors who have ceased to be simply 'eminent predecessors' of contemporary bureaucrats and have become by now ideological father figures whose 'vision' is referred to not as one political position among other, but as something of a secular gospel for the community of Europe.

5. A.S. Milward, *The European Rescue of the Nation-State*, London 1992, p. 281.

What I shall argue here is that it was in the 1980's, and as part of the political push from the European institutions for engendering a popular European identity, that these men were elevated and presented to the public as common European 'Founding Fathers'.

Since it would seem impossible to cover even this restricted group of 'fathers' in the present frame, I will focus primarily on Jean Monnet[6]. It is around his person that I will attempt to track the transformation from political individual to pure symbolic reference that is proper for a community's central father figure. This is justified by the fact that he today enjoys a position as the primary paternal figure in the rhetoric of the EU – rivalled only at times by Schuman. And indeed as it was around the figure of Monnet that the most forceful and varied activities of constructing a common father-figure in the 1980's took place.

When attempting to analyse the construction of a community's father-figure, the questions which arise are not biographical – my primary concern is not the life, historical context, actions and actual opinions or strategies of the man later singled out as father-figure. Instead I am interested in how the references to him and to his vision carry ideological power in the discourses about European integration, and how this symbolic power came to be constituted. In short our interest is not the actual political biography of Jean Monnet, but instead the 'biographical politics' which after his death made the reference to him as the founding father, a core element in the discourses on European identity.

Furthermore I intend to take the metaphor of 'founding father' seriously to the extent that in order to investigate a concrete instance of a community father-figure being constructed, it is necessary to develop a theoretical understanding of the function of father-figures in relation to community belonging and identity. Here psychoanalysis both in its original Freudian and its later Lacanian form entails a determination to understand the position of the father-figure both

6. In any case this seems something of a plastic category. Although it would seem fair to claim that Jean Monnet and Robert Schuman reside at its very centre, an actually rather long list of 'lesser fathers' can also be included and often is if the needs of political rhetoric requires it.

in the family and in other kinds of community. Initially therefore I will use psychoanalytic theory to generate a general understanding of how father-figures function as a mode of symbolic power, also in wider political communities such as the EC.

Psychoanalysing the Father Figure: Law, Absence and Guilt

It might initially seem counterintuitive to draw inspiration from a theory originally conceived to describe dynamics of the individual psyche, in order to theorise what is clearly a collective and ideological phenomenon. But the psychoanalytic understanding of the role of the father in the child's development was already by contemporaries – and by Freud himself – thought to be applicable also to the symbolic constitution of authority in communities wider that the bourgeois family[7]. The French psychoanalyst Jacques Lacan's post-structuralist reading of Freud, fully released the theory of paternal authority from the restraints of the individual psyche and from the immediate context of the family. Here the understanding of the symbolic function of the 'paternal metaphor' is instead connected to a wider theory of language and identity equally applicable to political communities, and to the modes of legitimacy and authority which constitutes them[8]. For a fundamental understanding of the idea of 'the Father' in psychoanalysis it is necessary to start with its original formulation as tied to the (in)famous Oedipus complex.

The relationship to the father, as it is formed through the Oedipal complex is an inherently ambiguous one. It is characterised equally by fearful submission and loving admiration, as well as by an ever looming presence and a necessary absence. In short Freud theorised that the Oedipal complex is initiated as the (boy)child becomes aware that he is not the sole focus of his mother's attentions

7. Cf. S. Freud, *Group Psychology and the Analysis of the Ego*, New York 1922, Rev. ed.1959.

8. B. Fink, *The Lacanian Subject*, Princeton 1995.

and love, but that his father is also the object of her desires. The child will therefore engage in fantasies of killing his father and possessing his mother for himself. Eventually however the little boy realises that such a confrontation with the father would inevitable end with his defeat and instead starts to identify with the father, emulating him and completely submitting to his authority[9]. In this first (lost) confrontation, the foundational law of the incest-taboo is laid down by the father, and on it is built the whole matrix of moral codes which the child will gradually internalise. It is by this first prohibition that the human subject is made to understand that certain objects of desire (the mother) are appropriate from certain positions in the symbolic code (that of the father) and not from others (the son). As Jean-Michell Rabaté points out "A father is not simply an 'individual', but mainly a function; paternity is that place from which someone lays down a law, be it the law of sexual difference, the law of the prohibition of incest, or the laws of language"[10].

The point is that the child learns that he cannot posses 'a mother' unless he himself becomes a father. In other words this is not simply a case of bending to overwhelming force, but of transforming the former antagonist into an ideal for ones own identity. The father therefore emerges not just as the centre of the moral universe – as the authority whose power ultimately enforces its dictums – but as an ideal whose approval the subject will continuously seek. Indeed so complete is the child's capitulation that the voice of the father is internalised and becomes the foundation of what Freud termed the SuperEgo; that voice of our 'bad conscience' through which we judge ourselves and in relation to which we feel guilty when falling short of internalised ideals. The father is an awesome creature in

9. Freudian theory in fact speculates more specifically that because the boy also at this time becomes aware that little girls and the mother lack something he and the father has (the penis), he actually develops a fear that the father will punish him by castration, which is what he assumes happened to his sisters and mother.

10. J.-M. Rabaté, "A Clown's Inquiry into Paternity: Fathers, Dead or Alive, in Ulysses and Finnegans Wake", in: R. Con Davis (ed.), *The Fictional Father – Lacanian Readings of the Text*, Amherst 1981, pp. 73–114.

Cf. S. Homer, *Jacques Lacan*, London 2005.

Freudian theory; at once the authority which anchors the moral rules by which we live, the (impossible) ideal that we strive to imitate, and the punishing power in whose voice our guilty conscience speaks when we fail[11].

It is of course not all real fathers who are worthy of the symbolic role of 'the Father'. There is in other words an inherent tension between the symbolic position of 'the Father' and the actual man attempting to fill it. Ordinary men are not awesome creatures; they have their own failures, repressions, perversions, limitations, doubts and insecurities[12]. The irony therefore is that 'the Father' is never more forcefully present, than when the inherently limited man filling this position is actually absent[13]. The absence of the real father in a sense secures that his limitations do not disturb the image of him as 'the Father'. The power of the father, and his internalisation as the SuperEgo is facilitated, not by his own physical implementation of his authority, but by the way in which others in the child's surroundings mobilise the reference to him as a 'borrowed power'. The classical example would be the mother's warning; 'Just you wait till your father gets home', or better, catering directly to the emerging SuperEgo; 'What if your father could see you now!'[14]. It is these 'third party references' to the paternal figure which entrench his status in the psyche of the child, a status which

11. For a more detailed discussion of the Oedipal complex, also in its later Lacanian elaboration see L. Chiesa, *Subjectivity and Otherness – A philosophical Reading of Lacan*, Cambrdige MA 2007 or Homer, *Jacques Lacan*. Freud's idea of the Oedipal complex can be found in S. Freud, *The Ego and the Id*, London 1927).

12. P. Verhaeghe, "The collapse of the function of the father and its effect on gender roles", *Journal for the Psychoanalysis of Culture and Society*, vol. 4, no. 1, 1999, pp. 18–30.

13. Indeed Freud argued in Totem and Taboo that the first human communities were established around the figure of a dead Father (S. Freud, *Totem and Taboo*, New York 1918). For a discussion about the 'absent Father' in literature see R. Durand, "The Captive King: The Absent Father in Melville's Text", in: Con Davis, *Fictional Father*.

14. L. Munk Rösing, *Autoritetens Genkomst*, Copenhagen 2007.

ironically can be undermined by the actual presence of the real father because such presence will tend to reveal him as what he really is behind the idealisation; just an ordinary man. Many of Freud's hysterical patients indeed suffered from the symptomatic repercussions of too devastating or too sudden a fall of their father figure.

But in fact it is the eventual disillusion with the godlike idealisation of the real father which was theorised to open up for the shift of the paternal dynamics' to the wider societal or political sphere. As the Italian psychoanalyst Sandor Ferenczi and contemporary of Freud pointed out "The feeling of awe for the parents, and the tendency to obey them, normally disappear as the child grows up, but the need to be subject to someone remains; only the part of the father is transferred to teachers, superiors, impressive personalities; the submissive loyalty to rulers that is so widespread is also a transference of this sort"[15]. We desperately need and search for father figures also beyond the confines of the family. Jacques Lacan thus observed that references to an absent idealised authority also structured wider communities. All communities in Lacan's view were structures by what he termed a Symbolic Law, a web of explicit and implicit rules and codes for behaviour and dispositions; a regulating matrix for appropriate and inappropriate desires and (subject-)positions[16]. The central point of this web – its lynchpin or anchoring point – was constituted by references to what Lacan termed 'the-Name-of-the-Father'[17]. This functioned as the basic and fundamental level of a community's symbolic construction of the world; something which could not be questioned or debated but had to be accepted as a pure metaphor for the ultimate authority and ordering principle of the whole world view. Historical examples of 'Names-of-the-Father' for wider communities could thus be 'God'

15. S. Ferenczi, *First Contributions to Psychoanalysis*, London 1952, p. 80.
16. Lacan's idea of the symbolic Law is, admittedly, somewhat more complicated that this (cf. J. Lacan,

"The function and field of speech and language in psychoanalysis", in: J. Lacan, Écrits, London 1977, pp. 30–113.
17. Lacan, Écrits, p. 67.

or indeed 'the Economy', or perhaps most obviously references to 'founding fathers' or national heroes[18].

The essential point here is that the existence of such paternal 'disembodied' or purely symbolic authorities do not eliminate the possibility of debate or internal disagreement. Exactly because the father is an *absent* authority, debate unfolds between different interpretations of his will (or Law). Founding fathers are mobilised to lend pathos and support to various different positions and arguments, which are by no means necessarily congruent. Therefore the father's absence is not a limitation to be handled, but a necessary condition for him to become the father in the first place; it is his absence which allows him to become a unifying paternal symbol existing and functioning beyond the immediate 'cut and thrust' of everyday politics in communities. If the 'Name-of-the-Father' is thought of as the supreme symbol around which communities and their unifying moral code are formed then D. I. Kertzer's point that it is the binding force of symbols that makes political solidarity (and as such the continued existence of community) possible even without political consensus, is all the more true when it come to this paternal 'master-symbol'[19].

This of course does not mean that all interpretations of the father's will is accepted as equally valid, or that all members of the community has equal right to offer authoritative interpretations. All communities have their 'clergy'; an elite with special interpretative rights and privileges. The battle for political hegemony from this view is the battle to close the gap between the father's will and its mere interpretation; to establish one interpretation as singularly true; to convince the people that one does indeed speak with the father's voice.

18. B. Benvenuto and R. Kennedy, *The Works of Jacques Lacan*, London 1986, pp. 126–141, and Chiesa, *Subjectivity*, pp. 60–103.

19. D.I. Kertzer, *Ritual, Politics and Power*, New Haven 1988, p. 14.

If successful this is indeed a formidable victory, because political opponents cannot challenge the father figure, without seeming to opt out of the very foundations of community. If one political party successful positions itself as representing 'the Nation' as such, then its opponents are by definition national traitors. Of course the actual achievement of such total hegemony is rare in democratic systems[20]. But as a rhetorical strategy the attempt to depict the opposing view as one in conflict with common fundamental values (associated with the father) is not. In such strategies the father's will be mobilised as an admonishing 'collective SuperEgo', as a voice which demands that we feel guilty for our failures, or more specifically that certain political opponents feel ashamed of their 'treacherous views'. It is the political version of the maternally delivered guilt-trip; 'What would the founding fathers not think if they could see you now ....'[21]

This then sets the parameters for the analysis below. In analysing the construction of Jean Monnet as 'The Father of Europe' attention must be paid to the extent to which he became a central figure in the community's wider symbolic matrix, or more specifically how his memory became intertwined with the construction of a European communal identity. But it is also necessary to look at how the references to him functioned in the rhetoric of political struggles and by who and for what purposes his name and voice was called on. First however it is worth taking the centrality of the father's absence seriously. If indeed the elevation of a certain person to the symbolic privilege of a father-figure, to some extent requires

20. The political philosopher Claude Lefort has in this vein argued that what distinguishes democracy is that the 'place of power' is kept empty. Unlike in totalitarian systems no one party or individual is allowed to embody power fully – to become we might say a present God-like father. Cf. C. Lefort, *The Political Forms of Modern Society*, Cambridge 1986.

21. An example of this might the Irish anti-EU organisation Coir, which during the debate on the Lisbon Treaty in Ireland printed posters depicting the heroes of Irish independence with the text "They won you Freedom – don't throw it away".

his physical absence, then it should be possible to detect a difference between the kind of centrality that Monnet enjoyed while he was very much present and active in community politics, and the kind that he came to enjoy after he had departed from the political stage.

All too present: Jean Monnet as 'Father of Europe' before the 1980's

It is of course true that Jean Monnet, along with his close collaborator Robert Schuman, can be thought of as 'Fathers of Europe' in the very real sense that it was their co-authored declaration, which in 1950 set in motion the process of European integration. However here I am interested in the symbolic function of father-figures for political communities and as such I will seek instead to ascertain whether Jean Monnet already from the beginning enjoyed such symbolic privilege.

Academic literature and journalistic discourse quickly seized on the catch-phrase of designating Monnet – and for that sake also Schuman – as the founding fathers[22]. However this did not immediately spill-over into political discourse. From a more official

22. In the academic literature we find at the earliest use of a paternal metaphor already in 1958 with E. Strauss referring to Monnet as *"The true founding father of the community"* (E. Strauss, *Common Sense about the Common Market*, Crows Nest, NSW 1958, p. 71). When Schuman the same year visited Los Angeles, the Los Angeles Times introduced him to its readers as a man *"who has often been called the 'father of Europe'"*(*Los Angeles Times*, 23 March 1958). When the 1968 the book series *Persönlichkeiten der Europäischen Integration* devoted a volume to Monnet , it stated in its introduction that; *"Man hat Jean Monnet mit Recht den 'Vater Europas' genannt"*(L. Hermann, *Jean Monnet*, Freudenstadt 1968, p. 7). Also beyond these few examples we find that already from the late 1950's designators indicating the primary role of Monnet and Schuman abound in academic and journalistic discourse; they are entitled as 'architects', 'Baumeistern', 'founders', 'originators', 'initiators' and indeed as 'fathers'– a trend which gathers speed in the 1960's and is apparently somewhat of a journalistic and academic convention by the 1970's.

position there does indeed seem to be a correlation between the use of the paternal metaphor and the either actual or expected absence of the man himself. It is true that something of an internal ritual praxis of celebrating the anniversaries of Schuman Declaration developed in the Parliamentary Assembly from the 1950's onwards, and that these micro-ceremonies always involved speeches praising Schuman's role as the originator of European integration. But in fact the term founding father was not used. In 1960 as he retired Schuman was honoured by the assembly electing him 'Honorary President', and in this connection the Head of the High Authority Piero Malvestiti did indeed describe him as the father of the European enterprise. The fact that it has since then often been claimed by voices sympathetic to Schuman and his legacy that he was thus officially 'declared' the father of Europe, illustrates that the paternal metaphor has a power and authority which not even the actually afforded title of 'Honorary President' can compete with[23]. It is a curious fact therefore that when the paternal metaphor is used in Schuman's obituary – at a point were his absence had become a physical fact – it refers to a seemingly official precedence which does not actually exist. Printed in the Bulletin of the European Economic Community the obituary states that "The three European Communities owe their existence to him. (...) He therefore well deserved his title of the 'Father of Europe'"[24]. This in fact was the first time the 'title' 'Father of Europe' was conferred on Schuman.

Monnet is mentioned in the obituary when it speaks of 'The famous declaration of 9 May 1950 – embodying an idea of Jean Monnet – in which Robert Schuman put forward on behalf of the French Government the Plan which bears his name'[25], but not as a 'father', only his deceased friend was given that honour.

23. C. Constantin, 'Le future passé' de l'intégration européenne. Discours et pratiques mémoriels des élites européennes (1950–2007). Congrès AFSP 2009. Available from epi.univ-paris1.fr/ [Accessed 28 January 2011].

24. Bulletin of the EEC, September/October 1963, 9/10, p. 5.

25. Bulletin of the EEC, September/October 1963, 9/10, p. 5.

And indeed Monnet could in no way in these years be regarded as absent. After he stepped down as president of the High Authority in 1955 to form his 'Action Committee for the United states of Europe' he emerged as the voice of a specific vision for European integration and this was not by any means a vision that everybody agreed with. Such a controversial and opinionated actor could not be elevated to the symbolic position of a father-figure, without risking to elevate his specific political views beyond reproach[26]. Indeed in some circles Monnet and his ideas about European integration were despised rather than revered. Particularly De Gaulle labouring for a *Europe des Patries* had little regard for Monnet, and sought to marginalise him whenever the opportunity arose. One such opportunity, although of a more petty kind, presented itself at Schuman's funeral where De Gaulle's representative invited the distinguished French ex-premiers present for a luncheon afterwards, but expressly left out Monnet. Such an insult would hardly have been possible had Monnet already enjoyed the position of a Father-figure.

It was not until 1975 that Monnet – now aged 86 – finally withdrew from the frontline of integration politics. On the 25th anniversary of the Schuman Declaration he dissolved the Action Committee and finally retired to his small country estate in Houjarray to work on his memoirs.[27]

It seems almost as though the institutions of the EC had been waiting for him to step back just enough to give them a 'safe' opportunity to honour him. Already in April of the following year the European Council voted him the first 'Honorary European Citizen'[28]. Still however the paternal metaphor was not used; the resolution which conferred on him the title of Honorary European carefully steered clear of pronouncing him 'father of Europe' or 'founding

26. *Time magazine*, 13 September, 1963.
27. For a detailed biographical treatment of Monnet's life, work, and to some extent 'afterlife' as a uniting symbol for the EC, see

F. Duchêne, *Jean Monnet. The First Statesman of Interdependence*, New York 1994.
28. F.J. Fransen, *The Supranational Politics of Jean Monnet*. Westport, 2001, p. 134.

father'[29]. Another late honour conferred on Monnet was the institution of the Jean Monnet Lecture series at the European University Institute in Florence, itself an institution founded by the by the six original EC members in 1972. In the first of these lectures on the 27th of October 1977 Max Kohnstamm, Principal of the European University Institute, explained: "why we have given this annual lecture the name of Jean Monnet (...) There are very few men of whom you can say, 'without him the European Community would not have existed'. It can be said of Jean Monnet – and that is why we are so pleased that he has agreed to the lectures being given his name"[30]. Arguably Kohnstamm here moves rhetorically very close to the paternal metaphor but still it is not used.

For this honour Monnet had to be truly absent, not just from active politics, but from life itself. In perfect parallel with the fate of his friend Schuman it was also for Monnet only at the event of his death that he was pronounced 'founding father' from within the European institutions.

Jean Monnet died on 16 March 1979. And in the memorial addresses for him there is no longer any hesitation about affording him a paternal status. In the European Parliament the president told the members that it was with great sadness that he had to inform them about the death of the "creator of the first European Community; the Father of Europe" and added that "the European Parliament acknowledges the greatness of this man and the significance of his accomplishment, and it will preserve his memory in grateful recollection"[31]. Likewise the Council now saw fit to designate Monnet 'one of the community's founding fathers'[32].

29. For the exact wording see P. Fontaine, *Jean Monnet – A Grand Design for Europe*, Luxembourg 1988, p. 47.
30. Kohnstamm, *First Jean Monnet Lecture*, 27 October 1977. Source: http://www.eui.eu/Research/ EUIPublications/Lectures/Jean-MonnetLectures.aspx.

31. *EP debates*, C241, 16 March 1979, p. 233–234.
32. 569th *Council meeting Press release*, 19 March 1979, 5632/e79 (Presse 25), p. 3a. Archive and Documentation Centre of the European Parliament, Luxembourg (CARDOC).

It was not until his death that the European institutions and the actors in and around them, started to wholeheartedly elevate Monnet to the semi-sacred status of founding father. It was only when his personal absence could be trusted to be permanent, that a symbolic presence could be constructed around his name and memory. During the 1980's he would be crafted into the core symbolic figure of the European Communities; his name would emerge as something of a rhetorical trump card with which politicians could berate each other for falling short of the father's vision, and his memory would be sacralised and memorialised as the lynchpin around which the symbols and narratives of a European identity might be constructed. Both the former tendency – Monnet's function as a political SuperEgo for the Communities – and the latter one – his function as a metaphor for a common fundamental Symbolic Law – are already indicated in the memorial speeches after his death. For instance the President of the European Parliament exclaimed that; "To everybody who is gathered here today, and whose task it is to work for the ideals, which was his [Monnet], his message is directed: 'I have never had any doubt about which road should be chosen, but how far this road is uncertain. The Construction of Europe takes time, as do all peaceful revolutions'"[33]. Monnet's ideas and opinions about the method, speed and direction of European Integration were here already being lifted out of the political realm were they could be doubted, disagreed with or even refused, and installed at the level of fundamental ideals under which all served, and thus in relation to which their shortcomings could be judged and berated.

Almost immediately as soon as Monnet was no longer there to argue for his ideas, they had become indisputable. But the elevation of Monnet as a father figure was only just getting started – his presence would be felt both in the community's political rhetoric leading up to the SEA and Maastricht, and in the construction of a symbolic universe around the notion of European identity, which the communities wholeheartedly engaged in especially from the beginning of the 1980's.

33. *EP debates*, C242, 23 April 1979, p. 2.

The Father's Law: European identity and the making of a father-figure in the 1980's

It is therefore of course not irrelevant that Jean Monnet died at a time when questions of a common European identity and the need for unifying symbols were making their way up the European agenda. Already in 1973 a 'Document on European identity' had been issued by the Council[34]. And it was soon followed by the Tindemans report (1975)[35] containing a number of suggestions as to how the EC might win the favour of the by now seemingly disenchanted populations, thus reinforcing its somewhat waning legitimacy. The 1985 Adonnino report engaged fully with the idea that what was needed was unifying symbols around which a sense of common 'Europeaness' might emerge[36]. As part of the so-called 'A People's Europe' project, the Community had by the mid 1980's acquired both a common flag, a European hymn and a joint day of celebration on the 9 May[37]. This European 'manufacturing of symbols' is well known. Especially Cris Shore has covered and criticised what he seems to consider an attempt at illegitimate ideological indoctrination from the European institutions. And Jean Monnet is certainly not exempted here. But Shore is content to criticize Monnet in the context of what he calls the EU's 'rewriting of history' in the 1990's. Here he claims that the EU now began to disseminate a idea that "The true saviours of Europe from the horror of Nazism, Fascism and military aggression during the Second World War are thus not the leaders of the Resistance or the wartime Allies, but Monnet, Spaak, Schuman, De Gasperi and Adenauer (...)"[38]. I am not

34. *Bulletin of the European Communities* 12, 1973, pp. 118–127.
35. "European Union", Report by Mr. Leo Tindemans, Prime Minister of Belgium, to the European Council, printed in *Bulletin of the European Communities*, Supplement 1/76, 1976, pp. 11–36.
36 P. Adonnino, "A People's Europe: Reports from the Ad Hoc Committee", printed in *Bulletin of the Euro-pean Communities*, Supplement 7/85, 1985.
37. P. Odermatt, "The use of Symbols in the Drive for European Integration", in: J.Th. Leerssen and M. Spiering (eds.), *National Identity – Symbol and Representation, Yearbook of European Studies*, vol. 4, 1991, pp. 217–238.
38. Shore, *Building Europe*, p. 58.

disputing that the EU indeed cultivated such a 'myth' of itself as a grand peace project and that this narrative was tied to the 'heroic' deed of the founding fathers[39], but Shore's critique remains at the level of 'myth-busting' – he is interested in revealing the 'myths' distance from historical fact. Therefore his analysis does not in any depth explain the process through which Monnet became installed in the symbolic position of a founding father. As another scholar interested in European symbols, Peter Odermatt, at least acknowledges in passing, the elevation of Monnet was well established long before the EU started 're-writing history' in the 1990's [40]. In fact his name and memory was given a central place already as the EC from the early 1980's began to dabble in the symbolic construction of identity. Monnet was here positioned as the father-figure around which the community's symbolic law and thus collective identity would coalesce.

This is especially illustrated by the early decision and dogged determination – involving several of the European institutions – to purchase the house at Houjarray where Monnet lived, worked and finally died during the last thirty years of his life. This can be understood as an acquisition of what Pierre Nora has called a *Lieu de Mémoire*; a site which would serve to anchor and materialise Monnet's memory and his symbolic position[41]. In fact this central piece of symbolic construction predates most of the 'symbol-manufacturing' usually covered by scholars of European identity and indeed it seems to have been largely forgotten, since none of the scholars so avidly deconstructing the European symbols of the 1980's makes any mentioning of it. But as is clear from the sources around this purchase the actors were in no doubt as to what they were doing; they were acquiring a monument, a shrine even, around

39. Cf. C. Kølvraa, *Imagining Europe as a Global Player. The Ideological Construction of a New European Identity within the EU*, Bruxelles 2012.
40. Odermatt, *The Use of Symbols*, p. 228.

41. P. Nora, "From lieux de mémoire to realms of memory", in: P. Nora and L. D.Kritzman (eds.), *Realms of Memory: Rethinking the French Past*. vol. 1: *Conflicts and divisions*, New York/Chichester 1996, pp. XV–XXIV.

which and from which the vision of the father could be disseminated to the as yet ungrateful populations of Europe.

The idea to purchase Monnet's House in the small village of Houjarray emerged within the European Parliament but along the way came to involve several other institutions of the EC. What is striking when reading the correspondence and documents passing between the different actors is that they implicitly reveal that we are here at the very genesis of Monnet's construction as a father-figure, exactly because even if these actors are engaged in elevating Monnet to this position, they cannot as of yet take for granted that such an endeavour will be considered legitimate and worthwhile by other parties. Even if those involved are from the beginning well aware that this purchase is carried out for purely symbolic purposes, there is a constant worrying that such justifications might not be enough to secure its realisation. In fact, when the idea first emerged in the office of the President of the European Parliament in 1980, a first confidential note evaluating it for the director of the Presidents Cabinet, Francois Scheer, mercilessly pointed out that "Practically, one can say that the Parliament does not have any foreseeable use for this house. This situation makes it difficult to underpin an intention of acquisition, for which the Parliament obviously needs to provide precise justifications."[42] And indeed on 'practical' grounds the house in Houjarray left a lot to be desired. Situated forty kilometres from Paris, far from any main high ways, at the end of a country lane

42. CR. Legrand-Lane: *Note confidentielle á l'attention de Monsieur Scheer,* 13. October 1980, CARDOC. This note in fact echoes how an earlier idea came to an end, namely that idea that had emerged already in the late 1970's about acquiring the *birth* house of Monnet. This earlier idea was received positively in the Bureau of the European Parliament at a meeting almost immediately after Monnet's death, but send of to the College of Questors for a full evaluation. Here it was slapped down and advised against exactly on the grounds that this house (Monnet's birth house) had no practical use for the Parliament. See in particular *Minutes of the Bureau of the European Parliament,* Meeting Rome, 4/5 April 1979, p. 27, PE 58.009/Bur; *Minutes European Parliament College of Questors* Meeting Strasbourg, 15 October 1980, p. 5, PE 68.418/Quaest, all in CARDOC.

Quotes from documents and letters in the following section have been translated from french by the author.

which became all but impassable in the winter months, the house was small and generally in need of thorough restoration.

This did not however dissuade the forces behind the idea to purchase the house in Houjarray and at a meeting of the enlarged Bureau of European Parliament in December of 1981 it was decided to move ahead with the plans[43]. There was still however the matter of how one could go about such a requisition in legal and budgetary terms. This was the main issue discussed in a series of letters between the President of the European Parliament Pieter Dankert and the President of the Commission Gaston Thorn leading up to the actual purchase of the house in late 1982. These letters clearly reveal that neither men was going to let the practical deficiencies of the house deter them in what was now clearly articulated as part of a wider symbolic construction of Europe. Dankert writing to Thorn in the summer of 1982 thus informed him that with this purchase "The European Parliament thus intends to contribute to the safeguarding of the historical inheritance of the Community"[44] and asked that Thorn voiced any objections that the Commission might have to such an ambition. Thorn certainly had no objections but requested that the Council be let in on the initiative, which, in his words 'is undoubtedly of a nature which contributes to the joint efforts of our two institutions, aiming to raise public awareness of the "European idea"'[45]. Dankert could in turn thank him for the support in moving forward with what he now described as "a symbolic act which aims to honour the memory of the man which contributed so much to the European construction"[46]. Finally on 3 November 1982 Thorn could assure Dankert that the legal and budgetary matters had been taken care of and that the Parliament could "in the name

43. *Minutes of the Enlarged Bureau of the European Parliament*, PE 76.113/ BUR, Meeting 17/25 November 1981, p. 32, CARDOC.
44. *Letter from President of the European Parliament Pieter Dankert to the President of the Commission Gaston Thorn*, Strasbourg 17 June 1982, CARDOC.
45. *Letter from the President of the Commission Gaston Thorn to President of the European Parliament Pieter Dankert*, 23 July 1982, CARDOC.
46. *Letter from President of the European Parliament Pieter Dankert to the President of the Commission Gaston Thorn*, Brussels, 11 August 1982, CARDOC.

of the European Communities"[47] safely acquire the house. In late 1982 Monnet's final residence became the property of the European Parliament, but there still was no precise plan for what to actually do with the property. As a monument – which was what it was in symbolic terms – it was of course, as are all monuments, inherent useless for practical purposes. But as a building it seemed necessary that some sort of activity had to be attached to it and unfold within its walls for the acquisition to make any sense what so ever.

The task of coming up with a use for the house was given to the European Parliament's Committee of Youth, Culture, Education and Sports. In December of 1983 the Committee received a presentation from Francois Fontaine, the chairman of the Friends of Jean Monnet Association – an organization composed of 'former collaborators and close friends of Jean Monnet' – in which Fontaine argued that after a thorough restoration the house could be used as either accommodation for foreign researches and visitors, a centre for training courses for young Europeans or a specialised European cultural centre[48]. Even if the Committee commended Fontaine for his suggestions as to a possible use, they had however in no way lost sight of the symbolic value of the building. This was no mere office space – and it was made clear in the minutes of the meeting that the Committee had a "strong desire that, in view of the special associations of the Jean Monnet house, its structure should not be altered as a result of the use to which it is ultimately put"[49].

47. *Letter from the President of the Commission Gaston Thorn to President of the European Parliament Pieter Dankert*, 3 November 1982, CARDOC.
48. *Letter from Bouke Beumer, chairman of the European Parliament Committee for Youth, Culture, Education, Information and Sports, to President of the European Parliament Pieter Dankert*, Strasbourg 15 December 1983, (BUR/AX/2866/1) (PE 88.143/BUR). Annexed Note from Francois Fontaine to Bouke Beumer regarding the House of Jean Monnet (PE 88.143/BUR/Ann), CARDOC.
49. *Letter from Bouke Beumer, chairman of the European Parliament Committee for Youth, Culture, Education, Information and Sports, to President of the European Parliament Pieter Dankert*, Strasbourg 15 December 1983, (BUR/AX/2866/1) (PE 88.143/BUR). Annexed Note from Francois Fontaine to Bouke Beumer regarding the House of Jean Monnet (PE 88.143/BUR/Ann), CARDOC.

Finally it was decided that after the necessary restoration was carried out in the next couple of years, the house should be an 'Information centre on Jean Monnet and the European Construction'. The actual running of the House was given over to the newly established 'Association of the Friends of Jean Monnet's House', whose founding constitution clearly spelt out that the association would do much more than simply tend the grounds at Houjarray. Its main purpose was nothing less than to: "to make known the European thought and the action of Jean MONNET, as well as the great moments of European construction"[50]. In a letter to the chairwoman of the Committee of Youth, Culture, Education and Sports Winifred Ewing in the summer of 1986, the new President of the European Parliament Pierre Pflimlin could now suggest a display of "photographs of Jean Monnet surrounded by the personalities which played a part in determining European History (...). These photographs will be underlined by comments drawn from the Memoires of Jean Monnet (...)"[51]. At Houjarray then, the European public could flock to gaze at the father and be introduced to his wisdom – to the symbolic law which would underpin their new European identities. But would they come? With this move Monnet had been instituted as a central symbolic figure in the attempt to forge a European identity, but so far it had been an elevation effected only within the symbolic universe of the European institutions. As a father-figure Monnet would have to be brought to the people. And indeed as the restoration work on the house finally concluded in 1987, a new grand idea on how to bring the father to the people was already in the making.

The emergence of what was to become something of a celebratory climax, started rather inconspicuously. On 7 July 1987 Council President Martens spoke to the European Parliament on the implementation of The Single European Act and – almost in passing –

50. *Association des Amis de la Maison de Jean Monnet a Bazoches dans la Region de Rambouillet; Statuts*, Annexed to Letter from Jean-Maurice Duval to General secretary of the European Parliament Monsieur Vinci, 16 April 1986, CARDOC.

51. *Letter from President of the European Parliament Pierre Pflimlin to chairwoman of the Committee of Youth, Culture, Education and Sports Winifred Ewing*, 15 July 1986, CARDOC.

remarked that "at this new phase in the construction of a united Europe, it is appropriate that we are reminded of those who formed the foundation for this endeavour"[52]. He therefore went on to suggest 1988 – the centennial of Jean Monnet's birth – might be made 'the Jean Monnet Year'. Both Commission President Jacques Delors and a Parliamentary resolution backed the suggestion already that same day[53]. The actual planning of activities to be undertaken in connection with the Jean Monnet year, was soon delegated to the ever present 'Friends of Jean Monnet' association.[54]

1988 therefore represents something of a highpoint as regards Monnet's elevation to a father-figure. The Commission had convinced the Members states to issue a joint commemorative stamp featuring Monnet's friendly face and the Association of the Friends of Jean Monnet had lobbied more than 1500 cities to name public places after Monnet. Also in the European Parliament a mood of reverence and sacred awe found expression. On 25 February a motion for a resolution was presented to the parliament which suggested that the newly started Channel Tunnel between France and Britain should be named the 'Jean Monnet – Europe Tunnel'[55]. Presumably as a gesture towards the national sensibilities of one of the tunnel partners the motion was sent to the political committee and came back slightly altered; the tunnel was now to be named 'The Winston Churchill-Jean Monnet tunnel'[56]. In the debate which ensued in the parliament only a very few critical voices was heard. A majority instead dreamed that linking the name-of-the-Father to the great tunnel project would "give Europe soul", "enshrine the essential values", be "a symbolic contribution to the development of the European idea (...)" and indeed "all Europeans using the tunnel in the future would be reminded both of Europe's past and of

52. *Europa parlamentets forhandlinger*, 2–354, 7.7.1987, p. 30.
53. *De Europæiske fællesskabers
tidende*, C246, 14.9.1987. p. 40.
54. 250.000 ECU was budgeted
to support such activities, *De
Europæiske fællesskabers tidende*,
C160, 20.6.88 p. 23.

55. *European Parliament session
documents*, 25 February 1988, Series B,
Document B 2–1783/87.
56. *European Parliament session
documents*, 3 October 1988, Series A,
Document A 2–202/88.

the great idea of uniting our continent, which Jean Monnet saw as the driving force of European Integration(...)"[57]. The motion was passed, but the paternal euphoria that it expresses was apparently not shared in the national capitals of France and Britain[58].

None the less this seemed a fitting warm up for the ritual high-points to come. Already on 2 October the symbolic headquarters at Houjarray served as a fitting frame for a ceremony in which the president of the Parliament planted an oak tree in the garden to symbolise the memory of Jean Monnet[59]. But it is perhaps ironic that for the ceremonial climax which arrived on Monnet's birthday on 9 November one still reverted to the tried and tested ritual framework the nation state. Here an official ceremony was held in Paris and attended by a wide spectrum of European heads of states. It culminated with Monnet's ashes being interred in the Panthéon in Paris, the highest honour available to French citizens. Despite this seemingly national reclaiming of 'The Father of Europe', the French President Mitterrand professed to be speaking to all of Europe when he said, in his memorial speech for Monnet: 'We need to offer great examples to our youth, here is one'[60]. The father of Europe, here almost a decade after he had departed in a biological sense, seemed more symbolically present than ever.

But this of course was just the ritual dimension of the Jean Monnet year; the spectacles through which the people and their politicians would hopefully be struck with paternal awe and admiration. Along side this a steady stream of publications up to and during 1988 aimed to disseminate the biography and wisdom of Monnet to the public. There is no ambition or endeavour to remain neutral, distanced or remotely critical in this information campaign. Indeed its major message is clearly that Monnet should not be related to

57. Phrases used in the European Parliament debate, 13 October 1988, *Europa-parlementets Forhandlinger* 1988–1989, p. 236–239.
58. Neither the archives of the European Parliament nor those of the Commission contain any trace that the governments even bothered to answer the Parliament.
59. *Europa Parlamentets forhandlinger*, 2–371/31, 15 November 1988.
60. Quoted from F. Lewis, "Quiet Power endures", *New York Times*, 13 November 1988.

through a 'historical' frame of reference. The point is not to deliver
a portrait of Monnet's 'life and times' associating him with a specific *and past* set of historical issues and challenges. Rather his paternal authority clears him of any restraining connection to a particular context and allows him to be associated with issues and events
that he could not have foreseen.

For example in Pascal Fontaine's booklet 'Jean Monnet, A Grand
Design for Europe' Monnet's vision is connected to the 1992 dead-
line envisaged in the Single European Act; 'Working towards this
goal, which calls for a level of determination and commitment on
the part of our leaders and the European Institutions comparable to
that shown by the pioneers, is a concrete way of paying tribute to
Jean Monnet'[61]. And beyond this – in a section headed 'Monnet's
message today' – something of a political programme for the contemporary Community, including the completion of the single market, the prospect of a common currency, increased democracy and
the European pillar in the Western Alliance, is presented as apparently blessed by the fathers approval. This 'contextlessness' – or in
other words the universality of the father's symbolic law – is taken
to an extreme in another publication entitled 'Jean Monnet: A message for Europe'[62]. The booklet contains a short historical section in
which Monnet's personal biography and the Community's history
are weaved together. Besides this it presents a selection of quotes in
which the presumably reverent public can find appropriate paternal
wisdom – in the form of Monnet dictums & sayings – on such subjects as 'Why right must take precedence over might', 'How to unite
people', ' The force of simple ideas' or 'How to create trust'. There
is no elaboration necessary, certainly no critical reflection invited
and no reason to doubt the seemingly profound truths disclosed.
The quotes offered have no years, no indication of sources or any

61. Fontaine, *Jean Monnet*, p. 9.

62. Kontoret for de Europæiske
Fællesskabers Officielle Publikationer, *Jean Monnet – et Budskab
til Europa*, Luxembourg 1988.

hint of the concrete context in which they were uttered. This is 'the Law' in its most abstract, foundational, unmediated and untouchable form: one need know nothing of its particular emergence, its context or its alternatives; one need know only that this is the voice of the Father[63].

Even for the most Euro-sceptic of political leaders one could not at this point transgress against the father without good reason. As the political leaders gathered for the ceremony of interning Monnet's ashes in the Panthéon, there was one noticeable – but perhaps not surprising – absence; the British Prime Minister Margret Thatcher. However even in the most euro-sceptic of national parliaments she was during the next sitting required to give an explanation for her absence. Here perhaps one could expect to find a clear challenge to Monnet's paternal status. It was certainly at this point no secret that Thatcher had severe reservations about the direction of the European project, especially as it was advocated by Commission President Jacques Delors. And Delors had – as I will return to below – almost from the instance of his appointment made ample use of references to Monnet and the founding fathers in general. It says a lot, therefore, that Thatcher when answering a question in her own parliament did not choose to challenge Monnet's symbolic status. Neither did she point out, for example, that her own political views were so dissimilar to those of Monnet that it would have been hypocritical for her to honour him – and indeed she did not argue that she considered the EC a purely practical framework for cooperation, in which such pomp and circumstance had little place. She

63. This structure is also observable in the short film 'Jean Monnet; Father of Europe' released on the occasion of the Jean Monnet Year. The film crosscuts archive material and weaves Monnet's personal life story inseparably into that of Europe's 20th century. It concludes with shots of Monnet as an old man walking through his garden as his voice exclaims from elsewhere; "This is only the beginning of what needs to be done in Europe if we are to achieve lasting unity, prosperity and peace". Although his voice reveals that this statement is made by a much younger Monnet, its presence here transforms its object and instantiates the illusion that Monnet is speaking to us about our contemporary context.

chose instead to recognise Monnet's symbolic status and excused herself on purely practical grounds, stating simply; 'I gladly pay tribute to Jean Monnet. We were not able to go from here because we had a state visit in this country'[64]. Even if she had been unfortunately indisposed entertaining the President of Senegal while everybody else was in Paris, not even the Iron Lady could – at this zenith of his symbolic presence – avoid giving Monnet a minimum of paternal respect.

What this anecdote might also indicate is that Monnet was not only a core symbolic presence in the efforts to relate a European identity to the public. His name had also become part of political rhetoric in a more direct sense, namely as the signifier through which politicians could berate and attack each other for falling short of the fathers ideals and vision. Jacques Delors played a major part in establishing this discursive practice and at times seemed to employ it mercilessly – never more so than in arguing for the SEA and Maastricht treaties in 1986 and 1992.

The Paternal Guilt-trip: Monnet in the political rhetoric of the EC

What I have tentatively called Monnet's function as a collective SuperEgo in the rhetoric of the EC, points to the invocation of his name by political actors, in order to at the same time legitimate their own agenda *and* to suggest that their opponents should not only agree, but should indeed feel guilty for having opposed or disappointed the paternal ideal.

As demonstrated above this rhetoric of the paternal guilt-trip, was already used in the memorial speeches after Monnet's death, but it starts to surface more regularly in political arguments around the Single European Act of 1986. Even in more technical documents such the Commissions White Paper on the completion of the internal market submitted to the council 14 June 1985, one finds it clearly articulated;

64. *The Times*, 11 November 1988.

[T]he Community should now take a further step along
the road so clearly delineated in the Treaties. To do less
would be to fall short of the ambitions of the founders of
the Community, incorporated in the Treaties; it would be
to betray the trust invested in us; and it would be to offer
the peoples of Europe a narrower, less rewarding, less secure,
less prosperous future than they could otherwise enjoy.
That is the measure of the challenge which faces us. Let
it never be said that we were incapable of rising to it.[65]

Commission President from 1985 Jacques Delors who elsewhere
professed to the belief that 'We are still drawing on Jean Monnet's
legacy as a source of inspiration and ideas for our work in the service
of Europe'[66] used an almost identical rhetoric in his Jean Monnet
Lecture of November 1986. Here he portrayed the SEA as a 'moment
of truth' where the Europeans would either honour or disappoint
the 'calling' given to them by the founder of the community;

We have staked our honour on realizing Europe's potential,
and thus lending impetus to the political plans which reflect
our deepest conviction. In doing this we are paying a well-
deserved tribute to those eminent champions of a united
Europe who today are calling upon us to act with greater
determination. Those who created this vision of Europe
to which we aspire, ladies and gentlemen, are now urging
us to remain true to them by taking action where action
is possible.[67]

Monnet's voice could thus be called on to admonish those whose
ideas about the direction Europe were not in tune with the fathers
vision – as it was now being interpreted by Delors. And it does in-

65. European Commission,
Completing the Internal Market –
White Paper from the Commission
to the European Council, COM(85)
310 final, 14 June 1985, p. 57.
66. Quoted from Fontaine, *Jean
Monnet*, p. 10.

67. Jacques Delors, "The Single
Act and Europe, a moment of truth",
European University Institute,
Florence, 21 November 1986,
pp. 36–37.

deed seem that Delors and the Commission were in these years manoeuvring to become the primary authoritative interpreters of Monnet's vision[68]. This authoritative position meant that one was not bound to the issues and statement which Monnet actually dealt with and made during his life time. There is a wide margin in which authoritative interpreters are free to imagine 'what the father would have wanted'.

In the following years Monnet in this sense blessed the ambitions for a common foreign policy[69], a slow and cautious approach to the formerly communist bloc countries of Eastern Europe[70], the associations agreements later envisioned with the East and central European countries[71], and of course especially the aims, methods and ambitions of the Maastricht treaty[72]. As the Commissioner of Agriculture Ray Mac Sharry at one point ominously warned potential opponents: 'Do not underestimate (...) the Commission's ambition for Europe, it was given to us by Monnet (...)'[73].

When the European Heads of states finally gathered for a signing ceremony in Maastricht on 7 February 1992, it was – for some at least – apparently an achievement of which one could be proud. And perhaps more importantly it was an achievement of which the father would have been proud. Several of the speakers on the occasion make no secret of that fact that they considered this a founding moment comparable to that instantiated by the original 'founding fathers'.

68. It might not come as any surprise therefore that Delors eventually received two newly initiated awards bearing Monnet's name. Firstly the 'Jean Monnet Prize' of the Goethe Foundation on 3 November 1988 and secondly the Parker Jean Monnet Golden Pen Award on 21 April 1989.

69. Sir Leon Brittan, *The European Community : What Approach should it adopt towards the Rest of the World?*, SP/92/63, Faculte De Droit, Caen, 19 June 1992, CARDOC.

70. Jacques Delors, *Lors de la Seance Commemorative De la Decleraion Schuman* – Brussels, SP/90/39, 8 May 1990, CARDOC.

71. Frans Andriessen, *Der Weg Europas ins nächste Jahrtausand*, SP/90/38, Hannover, 9 May 1990, CARDOC.

72. Cf. MR Ray Mac Sharry, *Maastricht, Ambition and Reality*, SP/91/131, Dublin, 29 November 1991, CARDOC.

73. Ibid.

It is up to us to ensure that the European Union becomes
a true beacon that will lead Europe to a safe harbour and
to steer the European vessel towards a more cohesive, juster
and more progressive Europe. We must therefore continue
working so that new generations of Europeans may see themselves in our example, as we do in relation to the founders
of the Community. Without them and without their
generous dedication to the European ideal, this moment
today would not have been possible.[74]

Even if the president of the Council Cavaco Silva speaking at the
signing of the Maastricht Treaty, here drifts close to imagining himself in the fathers place, the last sentence prudently reinstall their
primacy. It is as always to the father that the primary honour goes,
leaving the diligent sons only to revel in his imagined approval. Delors and the Commission likewise allowed themselves the comfort
of such approval. In the Commission Communication issued immediately after the signing it was reassuringly stated that: "At Maastricht, meanwhile, the Community has set itself ambitious goals
commensurate with the hopes entertained by its founding fathers"[75].

They would need this reassurance because before long it would
become apparent that the attempt to deliver Monnet's vision to the
broader public left something to be desired. Already in June the
Danish electorate rejected the Treaty, but perhaps more alarming
was that fact that in Monnet's home country, in whose capital he lay
interned with its greatest heroes, the treaty slipped through on the
smallest of margins.

It could thus be argued that the anticlimax constituted by the
marginal approval of the Maastricht treaty ended the EC's first
attempts at underpinning the European project by grand symbols.

---

74. President of the European
Council Cavaco Silva, *Speech given
at the signing of the Treaty of European Union*, 7 February 1992, Communication a la Presse, 4504/92,
Presse 21, CARDOC.

75. European Commission, From the
Single Act to Maastricht and Beyond:
The Means to Match our Ambitions,
COM(92) 2000 final, 11 February
1992.

As the so-called De Clercq rapport advised soon after Maastricht one should now 'concentrate instead on presenting the European Union to the public as a 'good product' with an emphasis on the beneficial effects "for me"'[76]. Europe would be 'sold' to the individual citizen depending on the immediate benefits and practical improvements for him/her specifically. The grand narratives, imposing symbols and indeed revered father figures was replaced with a focus on how the new invention of a 'European citizenship' made life a little better and easier. Europe should be a convenient arrangement rather then an awe inspiring historical endeavour. Furthermore it sounded increasing hollow in the mid 1990's to keep narrating the father's great vision of peace in Europe, as Yugoslavia ripped itself apart next door, and the Union, despite premature triumphalism, seemingly could do nothing to stop the carnage.

As I have endeavoured to show elsewhere[77]– but which is beyond the scope of this article – one could argue that the grand symbolic rhetoric of the European Project was rediscovered only with the Prodi Commission and the new millennium. Several developments aided such a 'return of enthusiasm'. Firstly there was a general optimistic *fin de sicle* mood, an idea – as articulated in the Laeken Declaration of 2001 – that this would be Europe's century. There was the prospect of the Eastern Enlargement, and with it a vision of Europe 'whole and free', of Europe finally healed from the wounds of the 20th century. And there was, as a consequence of disagreements about the conduct of the war on terror, a rising awareness that Europe was no longer the lesser part of 'the West' but an actor on the global stage in its own right. The Iraq war, despite dividing the European governments, ironically only served to reinforce the image of a European public united across nationalities, around a grand peace project; now with ambitions both in Europe and beyond it. Even the ill-fated constitution does not seem to have dampened moods completely.

76. Shore, *Building Europe*, p. 55.
77. Kølvraa, *Imagining Europe,*
passim.

And as an air of grandeur, of mission and of pathos has returned to EU rhetoric so has the 'name-of-the-Father'. References to Monnet were prolific in the speeches of the Prodi Commission, a style which has been taken over by the Barroso Commission. As the EU celebrated the 50th anniversary of the Rome treaty, Monnet's name was again present in many of the speeches, here in the words of Vice president of the European Commission Margot Wallström;

> We should think of those who have built the European
> Communities. Jean Monnet, Robert Schuman, Paul-Henry
> Spaak, Alcide De Gasperi. How profound was their inspira-
> tion and how forward looking they were! How steadfast was
> their will and motivation when they launched and imple-
> mented the idea of uniting, after centuries of wars on Euro-
> pean soil, the nations that were used to fighting each other.
> Nobody should ever forget this starting point.[78]

Monnet is again being made the lynchpin of a European symbolic universe, and especially of a uniquely European narrative about overcoming war and division[79]. As I have attempted to show this is not a recent discursive innovation. The ground work for Monnet's presence as father figure for the European Community was laid already in the 1980's, initiated almost immediately after the man himself became permanently absent.

Conclusion

In the EU's rhetoric today Jean Monnet is first among those referred to as the 'founding fathers'. In order to understand how a man, who was hardly uncontroversial when he lived and worked for European Integration, have been elevated to the symbolic position of father-figure within the European institutions, one has to go back to the

78. Margot Wallström, *Europe of those who are constructing Europe*, SP/07/189, La Sapienza University, Rome, 24 March 2007, CARDOC.

79. Cf. Kølvraa, *Imagining Europe*.

years immediately following his death. In Freudian terms this makes perfect sense. The real father – that inherently flawed and limited actual person who originates something – must be absent for the idealised image of him as 'the Father' to emerge undisturbed.

Monnet was in the 1980's made object of diverse symbolic and ritual initiatives. His house was purchased and renovated to serve as a *Lieu de Mémoire*, a year (1988) was dedicated to his celebration and memory, his body was given the company of the greatest heroes of France in the Panthéon, and the channel tunnel was hoped to bear his name. He became in these years a centre piece of the EC's ambitions to forge something like a European identity, the central father-figure around which a communal symbolic law was constructed.

But Monnet also became a favourite rhetorical reference, repeatedly employed in the political arguments legitimating the SEA and eventually Maastricht. Here the function of Monnet's name was instead akin to that of a collective SuperEgo. It served as a way of undercutting opposing arguments by rendering them in contradiction to the father's vision.

Along with the symbolic and ritual endeavours, this rhetorical strategy of the 'paternal guilt-trip' elevated Monnet to a position were his vision could no longer be directly challenged, but where it was also de-contextualised so that his name could be mobilised in justification of issues that he could not have dreamed of.

That Jean Monnet has emerged as 'the Father of Europe', is therefore not simply because of what he did in his life, but also because of what was done to him after it had ended.

Part II

Politics of European Lives

Defensive Personal Leadership and its Unintended Consequences
Ernest Bevin and Human Rights in Europe, 1948–1950

Anne Deighton
Oxford University

Biography and the study of individuals should not blind us to the complexities of political decision-making. This chapter will show that the ideas of an individual, even one who had a central a role, were mediated and adapted by chance, by domestic, and by international forces. This truth presents particular challenges to biographers, especially biographers of twentieth century politicians in countries with strong institutional regimes in government, parties, business, and in society more widely. Further, for an international statesman, the existing realities of the international system – geographical, resource-based, political and strategic, cannot be ignored. For these reasons it is unrealistic to expect that the vision of one individual – however powerful the person may seem at the time – to be directly translated into practical policies. So political biography necessarily also becomes a narrative about what was possible in practice, with all the compromises, sub-optimal decisions and failures that inevitably accompany such analysis. In the case of Ernest Bevin, British foreign secretary, 1945–1951, the biographer's problems are compounded by the fact that Bevin wrote little down – we lack journals, letters, or a range of his own published material.

This chapter will first briefly outline the career of Bevin up to 1945, for his earlier experiences deeply influenced his ideas and priorities by 1945. It will then show how he influenced the development of the postwar human rights regime in Europe. Bevin was the

British foreign secretary during one of the most productive periods of British twentieth century history, the period in which Germany and Europe were divided, and when the United Nations, the Organisation for European Economic Cooperation (OEEC), the Council of Europe, NATO, the European Coal and Steel Community (that was to lead to the European Economic Community) were all invented. During these years, Britain also gave up its imperial role in India, Ceylon, Burma, and Malaya, as well as in Palestine; recognised the new communist China; and decided to build an atomic bomb. A Human Rights (HR) regime in Europe was thus but one part of a vast political agenda that confronted Bevin.

The chapter will then look at Bevin's role in the creation of this postwar international HR regime. Building it was but one of a multitude of often interlocking institutional and political developments over this period, but one which has continued to underpin the subsequent history of the continent. The history of the early Cold War years has generally been structured by the narratives of territory, strategy, nuclear questions, and relations between the US and Soviet Union, as well as more latterly, by studies on intelligence, decolonisation, and propaganda. However, the use of rhetoric was always a very powerful element of the Cold War which emphasized the ideological nature of the conflict. The 1947 Truman Doctrine claimed that the world faced a choice between alternative ways of life: one that advanced various freedoms and the other that relied on oppression, terror, and control.

Yet the formation of the UN charter with its commitments to HR, the agreement on the Universal Declaration of Human Rights (UDHR) in December 1948, and the European Convention of Human Rights (ECHR) in 1950 have not yet been fully woven into accounts of early Cold War European history, despite the fact that the idea of competing ideologies is one that has existed in accounts of the period from the very earliest days of scholarship on the Cold War. For example, the issue is barely mentioned in Alan Bullock's three volume biography of Bevin, which, in Britain, is still the core text of the period.[1] The questions that therefore drive this

1. A. Bullock, *Ernest Bevin: Foreign Secretary, 1945–1951*, London 1983.

investigation are whether Bevin thought that the international HR dimension was an aspect of identity politics that helped Western countries to explain to themselves who they were after experience of World War I and World War II, or whether he saw some form of Human Rights regime more instrumentally, in the context of his prosecution of the early Cold War.

Ernest Bevin

British Foreign Secretary between 1945 and 1951, Bevin had already had earlier careers. Although he had a humble and inauspicious background, and was largely uneducated, he rose to the top of the trade union movement in the interwar period. He founded and led the national Transport and General Workers Union for unskilled workers (1921–40), and was on the General Council of the Trades Union Congress (1925–40). He had shown an early interest in the international dimensions of politics, flirting with communist ideas early in his career and initially opposing the war in 1914, before he became disillusioned with communism and its potential to undermine the British and international trade union movements.

As a trade unionist, he was closely involved with the international trade unionists at International Labour Organisation (ILO) in Geneva, where he acquired a high reputation. Part of the rationale for the ILO had been to head off communism after World War I by delivering a fairer capitalist system to working people. He negotiated on behalf of the trade union section of the tripartite system in the ILO on the proposed changes to the rights of the employers of dockers and seamen – the latter whose working conditions obviously required an international approach. His early opposition to Hitler, and anti-appeasement stance was in part driven by the treatment that trades unionists in Germany received at the hands of the Nazis.

In World War II, Bevin was in Prime Minister Winston Churchill's coalition government as Minister of Labour – his second career – although he was a reluctant Labour MP and party politician. His job was to manage the 'home front' and this he did with skill. He had to ensure that labour was directed towards the areas in which it was most needed for the war effort. He had extraordinary legal powers to direct labour, and had a tough task balancing civil rights with the needs of the production economy and the military chiefs who needed a fighting force in the field.

However, it would be naïve to think that Bevin's skills were confined to the administration of the home front. From 1941, he was a member of the inner, war cabinet. This small group met almost daily – and sometimes more frequently than that. As this was a coalition government, the leader of the Labour Party Clement Attlee was the Deputy Prime Minister, and so both he and Bevin secured extraordinary insight and knowledge about the management of foreign policy, albeit in conditions of war. They were privy to decision-making at the very highest level on all matters relating to the prosecution of the war. Bevin was one of the figures in the cabinet with whom Churchill crossed swords only rarely: Churchill knew that success in the war required a sustained psychological effort to maintain confidence and a 'fighting spirit' amongst Britons, and he judged that Bevin engendered more confidence among working class people than any other member of his cabinet, despite their ideological differences and mutual but suppressed hostility. We can conclude that the art of diplomacy under unfavourable conditions was a large part of Bevin's skill as a politician, and he certainly prized his own skill as a negotiator.

Bevin expected his third career to be that of Chancellor of the Exchequer if the Labour Party won the July 1945 general election. So to be chosen to be Foreign Secretary by Prime Minister Clement Attlee was a not altogether pleasant surprise. The war had brought victory, but it was not clear what victory now meant. As Donald Sassoon has pointed out, the liberal-democratic tradition of individual civil and political rights was already being changed and developed by the progress of socialist parties with their expectations of group rights, and of social and economic equality.[2]

2. D. Sassoon, *One Hundred Years of Socialism: the West European Left in the Twentieth Century*, London 1996.

At the same time, there was an enormous expectation of political and ideational leadership from the one West European country that had confounded expectations of defeat. Britain alone of the major European powers had been unoccupied and had been a successful belligerent: every other continental state now had to re-invent itself, or be re-created by external powers. In its moment of victory, the UK would surely be an exporter of ideas, (even if the electorate had had enough of Churchill and the Conservatives). Yet there were few lodestars to guide the actions of the Labour Party in power. Wartime socialist deliberations had not delivered much practical advice to the framers of a postwar socialist foreign policy, any more than the governmental planners had been able to construct an agreed vision for European or global stability upon which a new government could draw. The Labour Party's election manifesto gave little specific guidance, beyond a commitment to the UN, and to sustaining Britain's own great power status. Given the emerging Cold War, the core problem for West European social democrats in power after the war therefore emerged as a strategic as well as an ideological one, both at home and abroad. The question was whether to stand firm against the capitalist liberal right, or against communism, or both; and how to combine both domestic and international politics in this endeavour. While the Labour Party victory in 1945 was extraordinary, the organisation of West European social democracy internationally was very weak indeed, and there were no obvious answers to this question.

So what kind of foreign secretary would Bevin be, and what ideas and aspirations characterised his tenure of this post? For the first year in office, he was learning the job and naturally fell back on his personal ideas and experiences. He had early hopes for the internationalist spirit of the UN founders. Bevin the social-democrat was, by 1945, to the right of the Labour Party. His views very largely derived from his practical experience: he learnt his rights-politics doing battle in the law courts and with employers over the conditions and pay of trade unionists; and his economics sitting on government committees with luminaries such as John Maynard Keynes. In particular, he favoured practical solutions to disputes over esoteric discussion of philosophy. (He called this his 'hedgerows of experience'). He was a very traditional working class man in many respects, although he had internalised the main ideas of European social democracy and collective rights that the trade union movement aimed for. He was nevertheless often at odds with his party. Apart from his irritation with middle class North London intellectuals, what he resented most bitterly were displays of a lack of loyalty within the party, a view that no doubt stemmed from his union days in which personal loyalty to the group cause – and class – had to override any internal disagreements (especially from communists), as the disagreements could be easily be exploited by the managerial classes. So his socialist vision was, by 1945, much tempered by experience. He was, after all, 65, when he became Foreign Secretary, and had already twice contemplated retirement.

A firm and doughty dislike of communism overseas, and at home, especially amongst trade unionists, was one feature of his thinking. Yet, experienced trade union leader that he was, he knew that communism would not simply go away after the war, that negotiation was going to be the name of the game, that quick solutions were a chimera, and that, if he could, he also had to generate political space for the promotion of social democratic ideas overseas. There is plenty of evidence that Bevin sought to promote social democratic ideas beyond the UK, and he frequently referred to the trade unions as part of the new fabric of international politics. He also sought to promote the ILO worldwide, and to use the diplomatic skills of the Foreign Office to do this.[3]

Perhaps quite naturally, Bevin saw postwar Western Europe as a venue where Britain should lead and British social democratic ideas should dominate. He knew that there was no prospect of ending the east-west division of Europe in the short term. Yet, as a victorious power, he did not think – and this view was widely shared – that Britain would itself have to change. The country had survived the

3. United Kingdom National Archives, Kew, London (UKNA), Ministry of Labour and National Service (LAB) 13/348, Bevin to Ministry of Labour representatives, 15 February 1949. Posts of Labour attachés were also established.

war, and what was needed was financial aid to allow Britain to re-cover from its own wartime financial sacrifices, and to implement the Labour Party's own economic and social domestic reforms. There was no appetite for other national constitutional reform (of the Lords, Church-State relations, or voting rights for example).

The recovery and strengthening of Britain in the world, interna-tional economic reconstruction, and a favourable balance of power against communism all required that Europe would be a critical sub-set of his thinking. Yet a specific agenda for Europe did not exist for Labour politicians: and while a hope for international social de-mocracy was uppermost in Bevin's mind, an overt civil and poli-tical human rights agenda certainly was not.

Human rights in the postwar years

The European Convention on Human Rights (ECHR) was signed in November 1950 in Rome. It derived from at least two sources: the first is the global, Universal Declaration of Human Rights (UDHR), agreed by the United Nations (UN) General Assembly in December 1948, although the pressure for the ECHR began before the UDHR was accepted by the UN General Assembly. The second source is the Council of Europe through whose offices the Convention was negotiated, and whose member states were the November 1950 sig-natories. Both the Council and the ECHR were seen as a regional contribution to a new global order.[4]

The UDHR originated from the Charter of the UN itself. The experience of human rights activity in the League of Nations after World War I was a powerful indication that a HR regime that simply sought to protect minorities was not effective. The prime drivers

4. Winston Churchill, Speech, Congress of Europe, The Hague, Plenary session, verbatim report, 7 May 1948, pp. 6–8, Council of Europe Publishing 1999. In both the creation of the UDHR and the ECHR, non-governmental organ-isations and key non-state actors played a major role. See generally, J. Morsink, *The Universal Declaration of Human Rights: Origins, Drafting and Intent*, Philadelphia 1999.

for the creation of the UDHR were thus the lessons of nazism, gen-ocide and the Second World War: a common set of norms that related to basic human rights was essential for a peaceful inter-national society, regardless of whether these rights derived from re-publican or natural law traditions. For the British, the establishment of a Declaration was acceptable, as long as it was just a declaration, and they were no more enthusiastic about the UDHR than they had been about the HR clauses in the UN Charter, although In June 1947, the Foreign Office arranged for the publication of a Bill of Inter-national Human Rights.[5] The tenor of the British discussion about the UDHR became more hostile by the beginning of 1948, when the UK view was that, while it was appropriate that internationally acceptable standards of HR should be discussed (standards which, of course the UK already fulfilled but which were frequently lacking in the colonies), the UDHR might become a political tool used against a colonial power. Christopher Mayhew, advising Bevin about grey and white political propaganda and who was intensely anti-Soviet, saw a HR regime as a double edged sword that could dam-age British interests.[6] This shift about intentions and instrumen-tality corresponded with a debate about the merits of a binding con-vention or a simple declaration, and indeed even from time to time, Bevin's consideration about whether to postpone the whole pro-ject[7] But all sides were now locked into a process from which they could not completely escape. Despite the worsening international situation, to admit failure would have undermined the UN itself,

5. *An International Bill of Human Rights*, London: Her Majesty's Stationery Office (HMSO), June 1947; UKNA, Foreign Office (FO) 371/78936, Brief for Bevin for Com-mittee of Ministers of Council of Europe, 1949, 'The United Nations and Human Rights'. For UDHR abstainers in the General Assem-bly, R. M. Hathaway, *Ambiguous Partnership: Britain and America, 1944–1947*, New York 1981, pp. 124, 135; A. Samnøy, *Human Rights as International Consensus: the making of the Declaration of Human Rights, 1945–1948*, Bergen 1993, passim; M. Mazower, "The Strange Triumph of Human Rights, 1933–1950", *Historical Journal*, Vol. 47, No. 2, 2004.
6. C. Mayhew, *A War of Words: Cold War Witness*, London 1998, pp. 16ff.
7. UKNA, FO371 /72808/UNE 2273, 8 June 1948.

and with it the already fading hopes for an internationally brokered peace.[8] By the end of 1948 it seemed that, if an global settlement was not going to be effective – and the Soviet Union had abstained in the General Assembly over the UDHR, while the US had made it perfectly plain that neither the UDHR, nor any subsequent conventions would be judiciable in the US itself – then the HR agenda would have to be reinvigorated and moved to Europe.

Council of Europe

The ECHR was the creation of the Council of Europe, and the detail was in part based upon the UDHR. The idea for a quasi or potentially federalist Council of Europe had long roots, and the war was a powerful short-term stimulus. Most of the states that were to sign up to the Council of Europe in 1948 had been occupied, and had suffered under, or participated in nazism/fascism.[9] The umbrella organisation, the International Committee of the Movement for European Unity, of which both Winston Churchill and his son-in-law, Duncan Sandys were leading members, along with other continental luminaries such as Paul Ramadier, Henri Brugmans and Paul-Henri Spaak, had decided in 1947 to organise a massive conference in The Hague to push for a United Europe.

But Bevin had other ideas. His strategic thinking only emerged at the beginning of 1948. He sought a global third world force – a grouping of European states and their empires which could eventually take on both the power of the capitalist US and that of the communist Soviet Union. This strategy was first publicly aired in his Western Union speech, ('I believe the time is right for a con-

8. UKNA, FO371/72799/362, Jan 1948, and FO371/72805/1869, May 1948; FO371/72810/3479, 72800/847; Samnøy, *Human Rights*, pp. 53, 109, 82.
9. States that signed the original Council of Europe statute were Kingdom of Belgium, the Kingdom of Denmark, the French Republic, the Irish Republic, the Italian Republic, the Grand Duchy of Luxembourg, the Kingdom of the Netherlands, the Kingdom of Norway, the Kingdom of Sweden and the United Kingdom of Great Britain and Northern Ireland.

solidation of Western Europe') to the House of Commons in January 1948. This speech fired the starting pistol for his attempt to further West European unity on his terms, and not those of Churchill. What Bevin wanted was an intergovernmental venture led by Britain but with the close support of France, to encourage closer European cooperation in political, strategic, security, and also economic and cultural matters, and somehow, to bind the empires of the major European participants to this enterprise. Only thus could the spiritual regeneration of a Western Europe, with social democratic values, and with the capacity for independent action take place.[10] As Attlee said in *The Times*, 'Ours is a philosophy in its own right. Our task is to work out a system of a new and challenging kind, which combines individual freedom with a planned economy, democracy with social justice ... giving the lead which is needed not only by this country, but by Europe.'[11]

On paper, the March 1948 Brussels Treaty (BTO) captured many of these hopes. It resolved to reaffirm the faith of the five signatories

> in fundamental human rights, in the dignity and worth
> of the human person and in the other ideals proclaimed in
> the Charter of the United Nations; To fortify and preserve
> the principles of democracy, personal freedom and political
> liberty, the constitutional traditions and the rule of law,
> which are their common heritage; to strengthen, with these
> aims in views, the economic, social and cultural ties by
> which they are already united.[12]

Its most important institutional characteristic was that it was inter-governmental in nature, led by foreign ministers of the five participating countries (UK, France, Belgium The Netherlands, Lux-

10. For extracts from the text of his speech, A. Deighton, "Entente neo-coloniale? Ernest Bevin & the Proposals for an Anglo-French Third World Power, 1945–1949", *Diplomacy and Statecraft*, vol. 17, no. 4, 2006.

11. *The Times*, 8 January, 1948.
12. Treaty of Economic, Social and Cultural Collaboration and Collective Self-Defence, (The Brussels Treaty), Cmnd.7599, HMSO, 1948.

embourg), with clauses that related to the promotion of social democratic policies through cooperation as well as those – and this was very important to Bevin – relating to security and defence to create a climate of inter-dependence and mutual confidence.[13]

Despite his efforts, Bevin failed to stop the Hague Congress, or even to prevent over 20 Labour MPs from attending the vast May 1948 event (of over 600 delegates), which gave a huge public relations platform to Winston Churchill, and which urged the creation of a HR Convention. It was agreed that the five BTO ministers should then manage the creation of the putative Council. Yet the Council of Europe's federalist aspirations cut across Bevin's Third Force, for the Hague declaration asserted that states would, over time, give up their sovereignty in the interests of creating a 'united Europe'; under 'a Charter of Human Rights guaranteeing liberty of thought, assembly and expression as well as the right to form a political opposition; [and] ... a Court of Justice with adequate sanctions for the implementation of this Charter.'[14]

Between May 1948 and May 1949, the constitution of the Council was negotiated and the Brussels Treaty powers invited five more countries – Ireland, Italy, Denmark, Norway and Sweden – to become founding members of Council of Europe. The Council of Europe would be stillborn without British membership, so Bevin now had a chance to shape it in British interests. But it was the proposed Assembly that presented the most problems. Paris was convinced that an assembly was the only way to extract France from 'the morass into which had fallen. It was essential ... for the French Government to give the French people some new ideal other than the Communist ideal, and the only ideal which had any popular appeal was that of European Union.' Although increasingly frustrated

13. UKNA FO371/89895, draft brief for House of Lords debate, 8 March 1950.

14. 'Message to Europeans', The Hague, plenary session, May 1948. The rights were 'civic and personal', Quoted in A.H. Robertson, *The Council of Europe*, London 1961, p. 3.

by French politics, Bevin was obliged to give way on this, and indeed could not even secure acceptance of a 'card' (bloc) voting system for the new Assembly.[15] But he did force through the creation of an intergovernmental Committee of Ministers which would take initiatives and which had to agree unanimously to proposals. The Assembly had no such powers, and the technically wide ranging scope of the Council of Europe (economic, social, cultural, scientific, legal and human rights) was also to exclude political and military/defence issues. Bevin was successful in other defensive moves: the 'economic and political union', and the 'merger of certain sovereign rights,' both phrases from the 1948 Hague Congress now became 'closer unity' and 'closer association of states in Europe'.[16]

It had been hoped within the Foreign Office that the BTO could head off the aspirations of the Council of Europe promoters, and that it would trump, or failing this swamp the organisation with its own intergovernmental, British-led social and cultural agenda. This was particularly true during the introduction of the ECHR, which became the principal tool for the Assembly leaders against the intergovernmental Committee of Ministers.[17]

The European Convention on Human Rights

By the summer of 1949, with the Council of Europe now established, ministers had to turn to the drawing up of a HR charter. Human rights were mentioned in Article 3 of the Council of Europe's May 1949 Statute, as all countries which wished to be members had to 'accept the principles of the rule of law and of the enjoyment by all persons within its jurisdiction of human rights & fundamental freedoms'. It was this clause that formed the basis of the subsequent

15. UKNA, FO 371/ 73095, Jebb to Sargent, 24 February, 1948; FO 371/73097, FO371/73090, Proposals for giving effect to Article II of the Treaty of Brussels, 7 June 1948; Jebb to Kirkpatrick and Sargent, read and initialled by Bevin, 24 August 1948.

16. Robertson, *Council of Europe*, pp. 12–13.

17. 'Proposals for giving effect to Article II of the Treaty of Brussels', 7 June 1948; Jebb to Kirkpatrick and Sargent, read and initialled by Bevin, 24 August 1948.

negotiation to create the ECHR.[18] Bevin and his team initially insisted that this should not include the provision of a court or right of individual petition: the Charter should be declaratory, not judiciable. He told his fellow BTO ministers that the court was a 'mistaken proposal', although he knew that a HR declaration was important, not least because the UN was now 'unlikely ever to achieve a satisfactory solution of the problem'.[19]

Thus it was that, in August 1949, the Council of Europe Assembly asked the Committee of Ministers to establish a HR convention. The Assembly's committee on Legal and Administrative questions, presided over by Sir David Maxwell Fyfe, a British lawyer and MP, drew heavily on the UDHR and proposed ten rights to the Assembly which were adopted in September.[20] Maxwell Fyfe's committee then set to work to flesh out these proposals, including individual petition, a Court of Justice and a Commission for HR, but excluding the social and economic rights mentioned in the UDHR and favoured by Bevin. This was an important issue, and one can only presume that they were dropped partly as they had proved so contentious in the UN Commission, partly given the political complexion of the lawyers doing the drafting, and partly because they were considered second-order rights that required a 'basic' human rights regime in the first instance, while also being less easily judiciable.[21]

At this point, it is worth rehearsing the differences that also existed between the lead players and which were an ongoing cause of concern for Bevin. First was his suspicion that continental federalists, egged on by the Conservatives in opposition, were actually aspiring to create a federal state in Western Europe – a supranation-

18. Robertson, *Council of Europe*, p. 18.
19. UKNA, FO371/78936, February 1949. The drafters were M. Cassin, M. Juliot de la Morandiere, Professor Scelle, Sir David Maxwell Fyfe, Professor Goodhart, Professor Lauterpacht.
20. Conservative MP and Consultative Assembly member. He was also Deputy Attorney General and day-to-day leader of the British prosecuting team at Nuremberg. Became Lord Chancellor (Lord Kilmuir).
21. UKNA, CAB134/425, Cabinet Steering Committee on International Organisations (CSCIO), Working Party on Human Rights, January 1950, para. 30.

al vision to which he was passionately opposed. Second, Bevin feared the creation of a court, as it was not clear what the relationship would then be between the ECHR and a national legal system, and how the convention could actually be interpreted.[22] Behind this was the sense that the British legal system – which had survived the War – did not need challenges of this sort and that those issues relating to rights in the empire were not the business of others, although perhaps the new continental systems did require reinforcement through an international convention. Third was the issue of whether individuals should have the right of petition: one the one hand, this idea was logical, given that the Convention was to protect individual, rather than group, human rights. However, the risk to non-compliant states was very real, and for the British, this seemed to mean that, in time, individuals from the colonies, or even those from minority areas in Europe might use the system with impunity.[23]

Bevin was nevertheless still fairly optimistic about the value of the Council of Europe, and now felt that, having shaped its structure, he could also shape its agenda. He wanted a full-employment project and to prioritise effective social equality – that is democratic socialist group and social rights and policies, rather than a quasi-constitutional individual rights approach. In this spirit the Brussels Treaty powers considered extending their multilateral Convention on Social Security of November 1949 to the Council of Europe.[24] And in a cabinet paper prepared in October 1949, he was happy to 'look favourably in principle upon the conclusion of a Convention of Human Rights' as long as further powers or encroachments upon UK sovereignty and freedom of manoeuvre were not contemplated. Bevin's approach was instrumental, hard-headed, and framed in the context of a cold war of ideas, seeing the ECHR as a contribution to his strategic Cold War vision:

22. UKNA, CAB134/425, CSCIO, Working Party on Human Rights, January 1950.

23. A.W.B. Simpson has dealt fascinatingly with the colonial dimension of the ECHR in *Human Rights and the end of Empire*, Oxford 2001.

24. Robertson, *Council of Europe*, pp. 130–3, a process not completed until the mid-1950s along with other social conventions examined in conjunction with the ILO.

Together with the Brussels Treaty, the OEEC and the Atlantic
Pact, it [the Council of Europe] is one of the major weapons
in the cold war. Whatever, therefore, may be our opinion
as to the ultimate relationship between this country and the
Continent, or between the continental nations, we should
do nothing now to undermine the general hopes of solidarity
and cooperation which the Council of Europe has aroused
in Europe. Stated in purely strategical terms, the most immediate task is to prevent war by the double method of
deterring an aggressor and encouraging a mood of resistance
in our Allies. Therefore the 'cold war' and the building up
of Western European morale must have a high priority in
our thinking. Any ostentatious weakening of British support
for the Council of Europe might have disastrous effects
on opinion in France, Italy, the Benelux countries and elsewhere. It might also destroy all hope of bringing Germany
into close political association with the West.[25]

The difficult part of this argument was how this could be achieved.
The Council of Europe Committee of Ministers' committee of legal
experts set to work in February 1950 but avoided the really contentious issues around which the Government had already drawn what
were called the 'limits of safety', and what we would now call its red
lines, including colonial applicability, and individual petitions.[26]
Meanwhile, domestic resistance within the government was build-

25. UKNA, CP 49 205, 24th October
1949; CM 50 27th October 1949;
UKNA, Records of the Prime
Minister's Office (PREM) 8/1431,
pt. 4, Dalton note to Bevin on
proceedings in Strasbourg 19–22
December 1949, and Bevin reply,
26 December 1949.
26. See, for example UKNA CAB134/
425, briefs for the experts' group.
The colonial powers which were
members of the Council of Europe
were UK, France, The Netherlands,
Belgium. See L. Moor and B. Simpson, "Ghosts of Colonialism in the
European Convention on Human
Rights", *The British Year Book of
International Law,* 2005, Oxford
2006; on Denmark, Norway
and Italy; UKNA FO371/88657,
17 October 1950. UKNA FO371/
89895, conversation between the
Swedish Ambassador and Pierson
Dixon, 10 July 1950.

ing up, so 'Bevin', only just out of hospital where he had been for nearly a month, went himself to the Strasbourg meetings of Ministers and then the Assembly in early August 1950. He knew that despite the opposition from within the cabinet, he did have the backing of the Party and trade unions. The National Executive of the Party produced a long, confidential document, in which they argued for the 'Bevin' approach to the Council of Europe, based, no less, upon both the practices of the ILO and even on the social and economic articles (25 and 55) of the UDHR: democratic socialism meant that Europe should think about full employment, social security, and proper economic planning, (in short also a direct attack upon the free market principles which they saw to underline the Schuman Plan).[27] This was the only way to give heart to those who had been 'undermined by totalitarian infection'. For

> The Labour Party's socialist principles demand that
> the movement towards European unity should be such
> as to permit the continuation of full employment and social
> justice. …. The price of economic liberalism today is class
> war and social unrest … [but] the combined resources of
> Western Europe in manpower, industrial potential and
> human skill, surpass even those which the Soviet Union
> can command against it … .If the [Council of Europe]
> Assembly succeeds in raising standards of employment
> policy and social justice it will attack the causes of Europe's
> weakness and division at its roots. Fascism and Communism
> will lose their appeal. The workers will give the movement
> for unity their full support. As social standards become
> more uniform a major obstacle to Union will disappear.[28]

27. Quoted in G. Warner (ed.), *In the Midst of Events: the Foreign Office papers and diaries of Kenneth Younger*, London 2005, p. 17; Paul-Henri Spaak, *Strasbourg: The Second Year*, Oxford 1952.
28. UKNA FO371/89895, 'European Unity and the Council of Europe: A Statement by the National Executive Committee of the British Labour Party', nd. The non-Communist trades union conference held in Rome in April 1950 agreed with this analysis. Per contra, R.W.G. Mackay, *Heads in the Sand: a criticism of the official Labour Party attitude to European Unity*, Oxford 1950.

However, in Strasbourg, led by Paul Henri Spaak, its Chairman, and egged on by Churchill, the Assembly's rage against Bevin was in full flow. British negotiators nevertheless still insisted on a cautious approach to the Convention: the Committee of Ministers itself should have a role in decision-making about complaints, and that a Commission should also process complaints before they reached the level of the court, whose creation would anyway require the specific consent of nine Council of Europe members.[29] They confirmed that the application of the Convention to colonies should be reserved for the decision of each metropolitan power, and moreover, that exceptional or emergency circumstances would allow for the suspension of the ECHR. The British members of the committee managed to secure a report in which their definitional approach, including exceptions to the application of the convention, was broadly accepted. The moral, normative pressure forced the British to stick with the wider negotiation, and the best they could do, as had been the case with the structure of the Council of Europe itself, was to accept the principle, but to try to shape the terms. The draft text was adopted by the Committee of Ministers in August 1950. Bevin told the cabinet that the text agreed was a compromise 'in order to attain our adherence' to the Council of Europe generally.[30]

There were three strands to the arguments of those who still opposed Bevin. The first was that the ECHR would damage British political interests; the second was that it was badly drafted and legally and culturally incompatible with British law, thus 'putting the cart before the horse'.[31] Underlying this was, thirdly, a strong sense expressed by Bevin that the whole Council of Europe project

29. The Commission would look at countries in breach of the Convention. They would report these to the Committee of Ministers which could then decide, by majority, if a breach had occurred, and then what to do. So the court was not given an automatic judiciary role, and the role of the Committee meant that the powers of the legal regime were directly mediated by elected ministers, and not in the first instance by judges. The report was binding on the member states. Robertson, *Council of Europe*, pp. 164–5.

30. UKNA, PREM8/1431, CP 50 236, 19 October, 1950, 'The Council of Europe', memorandum by the Secretary of State for Foreign Affairs.

31. UKNA FO371/78936, February 1949.

had actually been hijacked by the European Movement, 'an energetic and able pressure group dedicated to the objective of transforming the Consultative Assembly into a European Parliament and the Council as a whole into a European political authority', who were 'noisy but few … found within the ranks of opposition parties, whose enthusiasm might be quenched if they achieved power and responsibility in their own countries.'

Bevin argued to the cabinet that it was no longer necessary for the UK to try to lead Europe from within its institutions. After the war, there had always

> been a certain danger that a refusal by Great Britain to take a full part in the movement towards European unity might lead to the creation of a bloc of European powers inimical to our interests, especially if Germany were to get control of such a bloc … but the emergence of the Soviet Union as an overriding threat to Europe has altered the basis on which this policy was founded. …. I do not think it need any longer be regarded as necessary for His Majesty's Government to work against the creation of close groupings, even of a federal character, between Western European countries …. France and Italy … are in danger of losing the will to survive as separate independent nations; & it might be fatal to the preservation of democracy in western Europe if we were openly to discourage the conception of European unity which is reflec[t]ed in the Council of Europe …. we have to steer a course between becoming too deeply involved ourselves in European union on the one hand, and, on the other, standing in the way of greater continental cohesion.[32]

So Bevin was also now happy for smaller groups of countries to proceed with supranational integration. This was a highly significant turning point, as Bevin, now assured about the support of the US

32. UKNA, PREM8/1431, CP(50) 236, 19 October, 1950, 'The Council of Europe', memorandum by the Secretary of State for Foreign Affairs; OF 371/78131, 'Western European International Organisations', PUSC (48) Final, nd.1949.

through the North Atlantic Treaty, had now separated the Council, and its ECHR from any of the more intense federal efforts that his continental partners might try to aim for. Britain had still to help the Council of Europe as a whole to do 'useful work and to play a sensible part in the revival of Western Europe', including the admission of West Germany as an associate member. At the same time, he again pushed for the kind of work that he thought the Council should be doing: promoting group and functional rights, a European Manpower Board aiming for a declaration on full employment targets, and cooperation with the ILO and Economic Commission for Europe on these targets, as well as the handing over of the social and cultural elements of the Brussels Treaty to the Council of Europe. He wanted a Code of Social Security prepared, again with the help of the ILO complete with its tripartite mechanism.[33] Bevin's 1950 ideological counterblast reveals a hard negotiator, who knew that he could not withdraw from the Council, and could not reject a Human Rights Convention, but who was still prepared to try and shift the agenda, for domestic and ideological reasons.

The ECHR was signed by ministers in Rome on 4 November 1950. A Convention on the objective of full employment was also signed at the meeting. The ECHR was discussed in the House of Commons a week later. Bevin was now back on form, although he normally disliked speaking in the House of Commons. He told the House that he hoped that practical cooperation between the Committee of Ministers and the Assembly of the Council of Europe would drive it forward in an uncontroversial way, but that the European Movement 'killed' the atmosphere of cooperation. Thus he interpreted the whole 1950 crisis as the fault of the European Movement, led by none other than Churchill.[34] It is hard not to have some sympathy with Bevin, as Churchill's antics in Strasbourg were not matched by serious proposals at home, for example in the Conservatives' election manifesto of 1950.

33. UKNA, PREM8/1431, CP(50) 236, 19 October 1950.

34. *Hansard*, 13 November 1950, col 1413.

The upshot of this story is rather ironic, given Bevin's reluctance about the actual outcome of the ECHR and the long term consequenses of his work between 1949 and 1950 were unintended. The UK was still the first to ratify the Convention, which came into operation in 1953 when ten Council of Europe member states had ratified. The UK quickly agreed to the additional protocols relating to private property, education and free elections which had been exercising the attention of the Assembly after August 1950. In 1966, the Labour government agreed to individual petitions, and to its participation in the Court. Then, ten years after the end of the Cold War, the UK incorporated the ECHR into British Law. France, for whose stability Bevin had feared greatly, and for whom it seemed that the provisions of a HR regime and Court could consolidate their postwar democracy, did not even ratify the ECHR until 1974.

Conclusion

In the 1940s, Bevin's vision for Western Europe unity was strategic, strictly cooperative, intergovernmental – and British-led. His approach, informed by his social-democratic beliefs, as well as by the necessities of power, was not driven by the notion that 'essentially moral aspirations might come themselves to be regarded as a source of law.'[35] Yet his attitude to the Council of Europe was far more nuanced and positive than has normally been portrayed. Human rights, insofar as Bevin thought about them, were based upon his own experiences with organised labour, and lay within the social democratic tradition of those group social rights, and of economic equality.

Bevin was unable *not* to support the ECHR, given the developing global Cold War with its ideas-divide between East and West. Subjected to the intense pressures of a small group of lawyers, politicians and federalists, he had become locked into a defensive

35. Mazower, 'The Strange Triumph', p. 397.

negotiating process that had both global and regional dimensions.[36] At the domestic level, Bevin was at one with British colleagues in an expectation that an HR regime should not imply change within the UK. We can thus assume that the core articles were acceptable as part of his assumption of what Western political rights were about.[37] But a freshly minted and codified human rights regime was only for export. Without Bevin's own awareness of the importance of the UK's role in Western Europe, it is unlikely that either the Council of Europe or the ECHR – the least bad option that he could negotiate – would have been created.

The Council of Europe and the ECHR were a part of a Cold War ideational strategy to define and expose the differences between East and West. HR is classically seen in the context of global decolonisation and nationalism during the Cold War: however, we can see that there is a ideational debate and even identity narrative about the nature of the European dimension of HR in the rough and tumble of the early Cold War in Europe, and here we can identify unplanned and unpremeditated role of the ubiquitous Bevin in shaping this narrative.

36. This is a classic example of Europeanisation. Britain became a conscientious ratifier of Council of Europe conventions and protocols, (including those of the 1960s on social and economic issues); many of its colonies had post-colonial constitutions built around the ECHR; Britain was itself frequently taken to the Court; and, in 1998, did itself take the ECHR into British national law, and thereby adapted to a process of Europeanisation. Unintended consequences indeed. 37. Maurice Edelman thought human rights were 'really the fundamental problem of Europe', "The Council of Europe 1950", *International Affairs*, XXVII,/1, 1951, 29. 37. Maurice Edelman thought human rights were 'really the fundamental problem of Europe', "The Council of Europe 1950", *International Affairs*, XXVII,/1, 1951, 29.

Bodil Begtrup:
Biography and Transnational Agency in International Organisations and National Embassies, 1926–1973

Kristine Midtgaard
University of Southern Denmark

Bodil Begtrup (1903–87) is well known in the international literature on women's rights in the context of the Universal Declaration of Human Rights from 1948.[1] However, she held a number of other international occupations both before and after her engagement in the UN. Her career involved a multiplicity of positions in multilateral and bilateral, state and non-state fora: she was a student activist, affiliated with the Danish delegation to the League of Nations, an advising member to the Danish UN delegation and a chairman and vice chairman of commissions within the UN (1946–52). In 1949 she became the first Danish female ambassador with appointments to Iceland (1949–56), Switzerland (1959–68) and Portugal (1959–73). In the years in between her stay in Iceland and Switzerland she was Head of Office in the Ministry of Foreign Affairs in Copenhagen. Further, Begtrup was an active member of The Danish Women's National Council (DWNC). The DWNC was a member of the International Council of Women (ICW) and Begtrup took part in ICW

---

[1]. See for instance J. Morsink, "Women's Rights in the Universal Declaration", *Human Rights Quarterly*, vol. 13, 2, 1991, pp. 229–256; D. H. Linder, "Equality For Women. The Contribution of Scandinavian Women at the United Nations, 1946–66", *Scandinavian Studies*, vol. 73, no. 2, 2001, pp. 165–208.

meetings. In 1939 she also became a member of the Danish Social Democratic party.[2] As a diplomat Begtrup was an exception to the rule in the Danish Foreign Service in at least two ways. Firstly, she was Denmark's first female ambassador.[3] Secondly, she was not a career diplomat, but was politically nominated to her first post as ambassador to Iceland in 1949.

The article analyses Begtrup's agency in the international organisations and the national embassies in which she worked from her first visit in Geneva in 1926 until her retirement from the Danish Foreign Service in 1973. The aim is to trace how she built her network and worked to strengthen her main interest of women's rights. I will investigate how Begtrup entered and moved within the international arena, how she took part in a formal policy network of international women and built her own informal network and her resources/capitals in the arenas in which she worked.[4] Based on an analysis of Begtrup's perception of her career as a diplomat, the study is indicative of the principles and norms within the Danish Foreign Service. Furthermore, it will show how Begtrup's individual agency contributed to the shaping of the institutions in which she was involved, that a perception of institutions as closed categories should be softened and that both international and national political institutions may be seen also as platforms for other activities including the promotion of particular interests.

2. H. Damm, *På trods. 100 års kvindehistorie. Danske Kvinders Nationalråd 1899–1999*, Copenhagen 1999, p. 79.

3. The second Danish women ambassador was Nonny Wright who was a career diplomat and appointed ambassador to Ghana in 1967. www.kvinfo.dk/side/597/bio/1693/origin/170/ (1 March 2011).

4. For the distinction between policy networks and political networks, see W. Kaiser, B. Leucht and M. Gehler, "Transnational Networks in European Integration Governance: Historical Perspectives on an Elusive Phenomenon", in: W. Kaiser, B. Leucht and M. Gehler (eds.), *Transnational Networks in Regional Integration. Governing Europe 1945–83*, Houndmills 2010, pp. 1–17, p. 10.

I draw on Begtrup's memoirs and her personal papers, in particular her diaries, other private archives, the Archive of the Danish Ministry of Foreign Affairs, and the archive of DWNC.[5] Begtrup often wrote in her diary. The diary often contains thoughts before and after meetings, in particular during her years in the UN. Generally, throughout her career, it seems that she confided to her diary when she was upset or sad. Not least the Danish Foreign Ministry gave rise to a negative pen. Her negative perceptions of the Ministry may not always have been a mirror of 'reality'. However, as exactly Begtrup's perceptions are central to my analysis, the diary appears a valuable source.

I focus on Begtrup as a transnational political agent. At the same time the approach is inspired by 'life histories' in order to study 'agency in the historical process, and the global webs of connections in which people live and work'.[6] The article is organised chronologically analysing Begtrup as a student activist and in the League of Nations (1925–1938), as advisor to the Danish UN delegation and chairman of the UN Commission on the Status of Women (1946–52), as envoy to Iceland (1949–56), as Head of Office in the Ministry of Foreign Affairs including her participation in this capacity as representative in the Council of Europe (1956–59), as ambassador to Switzerland (1959–68) and to Portugal (1968–73). However, first I will briefly outline Begtrup's family background, central features of her private life and – as the analysis will center on her international activities her main activities at the national level in the DWNC.

Bodil Begtrup as an object of study

Bodil Begtrup was born in 1903 as Bodil Andreasen.[7] Her father, Christian Adolph Andreasen (1867–1941) was a judge. His family came from the Northern part of Jutland and had owned three large

5. Translations in the quotes from Danish material are all my translations.

6. J. M. Brown, "AHR Roundtable. "Life Histories" and the History of Modern South Asia", *American Historical Review*, vol. 114, no. 3, June 2009, pp. 587–595, p. 588.

7. Throughout the article I will use the name Bodil Begtrup.

farms. Begtrup's grandfather was the first in family to leave Northern Jutland to take a lease on a farm on Zealand. Bodil Begtrup's father received a law degree from the University of Copenhagen and got a legal position in Nyborg (as bailiff clerk). He applied – due to the upcoming legal reform in 1919 – too soon, it would seem, for a position as a civil judge and the position he got in the Northern part of Jutland was not very well paid.[8] Her mother, Carla Sigrid Locher (1876–1938) was a teacher. She grew up in Copenhagen as the daughter of a reasonably well know Danish painter, Carl Locher (1851–1915), educated by the famous Danish painter Holger Drachmann and belonging to the group of artist residing in the city of Skagen situated at the very 'top' of Denmark'. Begtrup spent both as a child and as an adult many summers 'on Skagen. She had a younger brother who died from epilepsy when he was around ten years old.[9]

Bodil Begtrup graduated from Aalborg Katedralskole (upper secondary school) in 1921 as the only girl in a math class. The same year, she began studying the history of arts at the University of Copenhagen. However, as a student of math, she had no knowledge in Greek and Latin. A professor of hers recommended that she went to Munich to improve her language skills. However, her father did not approve of this and as she met new friends and developed new interests, she chose to give up the history of arts and become a student of political science instead.[10]

In 1929 she married the doctor, Erik Worm Begtrup (1888–1976). He was a widower and Begtrup became the stepmother to four children. In 1931, Erik and Bodil Begtrup had a daughter, Marianne. In 1936, the couple separated because Erik Begtrup had a relationship with another woman whom he married soon after his divorce. Sadly, in 1941 Bodil Begtrup's daughter died only ten years old. She was born with a heart defect and had died due to an incurable infection.[11]

8. B. Begtrup, *Kvinde i et verdens-samfund*, Viby J. 1986, p. 18.
9. Begtrup, *Kvinde i et verdens-samfund*, pp. 11–17.

10. Begtrup, *Kvinde i et verdens-samfund*. pp. 11–25.
11. Begtrup, *Kvinde i et verdens-samfund*, pp. 30, 34, 38–39.

In 1948 Bodil Begtrup married the 66 year old Danish diplomat and former envoy to Moscow (1938–41) and Budapest (1941–44), Laurits Bolt-Jørgensen. The couple had no children.[12]

Begtrup's main interests were the social status of women and children and the societal and political status of women. It seems that she developed this interest because she met the president of the DWNC, Henni Forchammer, in the League of Nations and became a member of the DWNC executive committee in 1929, the vice president of the DWNC in 1931 and chairman during 1946–49. In 1935 she took part in the establishment of the DWNC's committee Our Children's Health (*Vore Børns Sundhed*) dedicated to provide public information about children's health. The activities of the association lay the ground for the later Danish public health care system for infants and school children. In 1939 she became a member of the Mother's Aid Council (*Mødrehjælpens Fællesråd*) which supported and subsidised children's equipment to poor mothers. Following the German occupation of Denmark in 1940 she participated in the establishment of Danish Women's Societal Service (*Danske Kvinders Samfundstjeneste*) which was both a practical service finding work for unemployed Danish women in order to avoid that they were appointed to work in Germany and an information service aiming to inform Danish women of Danish democratic institutions. In 1940 she participated in the establishment of the association Our Small Children's Clothing (*Vore Smaabørns Beklædning*) and became its president. After the end of the Second World War, Begtrup took part in the establishment of the Danish division of Save the Children (*Red Barnet*) providing humanitarian aid to children in the devastated Europe, in particular in Hungary. In 1947, the DWNC established the Danish Housewives' Consumer Council (*Danske Husmødres Forbrugerråd*), the later Consumers' Council (*Forbrugerrådet*), with Begtrup as council president for its first two years.[13] She took a special interest in the impact of film on chil-

12. Begtrup, Kvinde i et verdens-samfund, p. 80.

13. www.kvinfo.dk/side/682/article/9 (1 March, 2011).

dren and in 1939 she was appointed the first Danish women film censor, a post she occupied until 1948. Despite her international career, Begtrup in her memoires emphasiszes DWNC as her home port.[14]

Bodil Begtrup in international student cooperation and in the League of Nations, 1925–38

Begtrup maneuvered in a transnational infrastructure consisting at the international level of the League of Nations and the IWC and at the national level of the DWNC and made use of several channels political-diplomatic and lobbyists' to promote wishes for peace and demands for women's rights. With the DWNC as her platform, she established contacts within the Danish delegation to the League and with women in the ICW.

In 1925, the Confederation international des étudiants (C.I.E) established in 1919 held a student congress in the Danish city of Nyborg. Begtrup was asked by a friend of hers, Vibeke Mackeprang – an active member of the Danish Student)s Association and involved in the Danish Student)s International Committee – to be a secretary at the congress. Begtrup accepted and was one of thirty-seven secretaries.[15] In the following years she participated in the C.I.E's annual congresses in Prague 1926, Rome 1927 and Paris 1928.[16]

In 1926, the General Secretary of the League of Nations, Sir Eric Drummond, made a tour to several League member states. The Danish Ministry of Foreign Affairs asked the president of the Danish Student's International Committee, student of medicine Vincent Næser, to establish a Danish Students' League of Nations Union.

14. Begtrup, *Kvinde i et verdens-samfund*, pp. 40–52, 185.
15. Denmark's National Archive, Copenhagen (DKNA) Vincent Næser's private papers (VN). Denmark's National Archive, Copenhagen. Box 3. File: I.B.I.3.

Rappport du Conseil National des Étudiants Danois. Copenhagen, December 1922 and Box 5. File I.B.I.4.j: The secretaries at the CIE's Congress at Nyborg Strand summer 1925.
16. Begtrup, *Kvinde i et verdens-samfund*, p. 25.

Begtrup participated in the formulation of rules for the association and in the preparation of the meeting with the League of Nations General Secretary.[17]

In 1926, the Danish division of the International Intellectual Co-operation Committee made a number of grants available through the Danish Students' League of Nations Union. These funds facilitated the participation of students at the summer school held in Geneva by the International Students' League of Nations Union. Begtrup submitted a successful application. According to her application form she spoke English and German and could understand Italian and French. Concerning her economic situation, she was financially supported by her family. The latter was not, however able to pay for a trip to Geneva. She further promoted her application with reference to:

> the possibility of being able to study an issue which has, firstly, direct relevance for my university education, secondly, is closely connected to my deep interest in international student cooperation with which I have occupied myself in particularly during the last year in which I have been vice president of the Student Association of Law School and Political Science [Det rets- og statsvidenskabelige Studen-terråd]. Due to my interest in international student coop-eration I have also been a member of the Danish Students' League of Nations Union since its establishment. In addition, I have occupied myself with social issues in other ways, being president of the Student Association's [Studenterforeningen] Social Committee, member of the steering committee of the

17. Begtrup, Kvinde i et verdens-samfund, p. 26. DKNA, VN Box 5. File I.B.I.5.a.: Report of Sir Eric Drummond's visit to Copenhagen (in Danish translation in ibid. I.B.5.c.). Næser's papers include the rules of the Danish Student's League of Nations Union, but unfortunately no summaries of the meetings in which Begtrup took part. DKNA, VN. Box 5. File I.B.I.5.c.: Rules for the Danish Student's League of Nations Union.

Women Academics [Kvindelige akademikere] and a secretary at the CIE meeting at Nyborg Strand.[18]

The three other receivers of the grants – one law student and two students of engineering – were also involved in student organisations, two of them in either the Danish Student's League of Nations Union or in the CIE including the meeting at Nyborg Strand.[19]

During her stay in Geneva in September 1926 Begtrup attended Professor Alfred Zimmerns summer school and the League General Assembly (LGA) meetings. She later describes the open atmosphere of the Danish delegation and mentions in particular Finn Friis and his wife, Gabriele Rohde and Nonny and Peter Wright. Both Friis and Rohde worked in the League's secretariat.[20]

Not least, she met the president of the DWNC, Henni Forchhammer, who was the DWNC representative in the Danish delegation. It was an established Nordic principle that the national councils of women were represented in the Nordic delegations to the League. This principle of representation was later to be continued in the UN.[21] After their return from Geneva, Begtrup became Ms. Forchhammer's secretary and involved with the women who sought to influence world peace, human rights and politics.[22]

18. DKNA, VN. Box 5. File I.B.I.5.c. Announcement of grant by the Danish Students' League of Nations Union. Ibid. Letter from the Danish Commission for International Intellectual Cooperation to the Danish Students' League of Nations Union, 16 August 1926. Ibid. Application by Bodil Andreasen to the Danish Students' League of Nations Union.

19 DKNA, VN. Box 5. File I.B.I.5.c. Applications. There are twenty applications in the file. However, I cannot rule out that there were more applications. There are no documents summarising the number and characteristics of the applications. D. Tamm, *Federspiel. En dansk europæer*, Copenhagen 2005, pp. 58–60. For an English version see D. Tamm, *Per Federspeil. A Fighter for Danish and European Freedom*, Copenhagen 2005, pp. 23–24.

20. Begtrup, *Kvinde i et verdenssamfund*, p. 27.

21. N. Götz, *Deliberative Diplomacy. The Nordic Approach to Global Governance and Societal Representation at the United Nations*, Dordrecht 2011, pp. 114–140.

22. Begtrup, *Kvinde i et verdenssamfund*, p. 27.

In 1931 now married and newly mother Begtrup again received a grant and went to Geneva in September with her newborn girl and a nanny.[23] Mrs. Friis provided her with a baby carriage and in this way contributed to facilitate her stay.[24] In Geneva, she worked with the preparations of the disarmament conference which was postponed to 1932.[25] She went to Professor Zimmern's summer school with lectures on the League and international cooperation and attended League meetings on women's rights and met with Ms. Forchhammer and women from other League delegations and members of the International Council of Women (ICW). She attended C.I.E meetings on international intellectual cooperation. Further, she participated in suffragette meetings taking place in the evenings all during which she went home to breast feed her baby daughter. The main content of her diary is rapports from the meetings she went to and notes from the various speeches and lectures she attended. There is little information regarding Begtrup's perception of events and her own endeavors. It bears witness of a formative learning process during which Begtrup soaked up knowledge and information and forged professional-private connections.[26]

In 1937, Begtrup went with the DWNC president, Ms. Forchhammer, to Geneva as Forchhammer's secretary. They were among the Danish representatives in the League's Fifth Committee on social and humanitarian matters.[27] Begtrup gave a speech on the DWNC's work for children's nutrition and showed the film made by the DWNC on this topic.[28]

23. I have not been able to locate her application for the grant in 1931.
24. DKNA, Bodil Begtrup's private papers (BB). Box 27. Diary League of Nations 1931. No. date. The diary does not systematically contain dates. However, it runs forward from her departure from Denmark and sometimes she writes either the weekday or the date. Hence, it is possible to see at least approximately when her activities took place.

25. Begtrup, *Kvinde i et verdenssamfund*, p. 31.
26. DKNA, BB, Box 27. Diary League of Nations 1931.
27. *Beretning angaaende Folkeforbundets 18. Forsamling. 13. September – 6. Oktober 1937*, pp. 6, 29.
28. Begtrup, *Kvinde i et verdenssamfund*, p. 30. DKNA, BB. Box 15. File P. DWNC Report to the ICW Film Committee 1938.

In 1938, Begtrup replaced Ms. Forchhammer as the DWNC representative in the Danish delegation to the League.[29] In 1938 the issue of women's legal status was – contrary to the previous years not on the League's agenda. In 1937 an expert committee had been established to undertake a comprehensive and scientific enquiry into the political and civil status of women in the member states. The work was scheduled to take three years[30] Begtrup was a delegate to the 5th Commission and involved in discussions of the welfare of children and the prevention of prostitution.[31]

During last years of the 1930s, Begtrup was the Danish member of the Committee for Peace and Arbitration in the ICW.[32] At the Nordic level, she took part in the Nordic Women Associations Cooperation Organization.[33] Domestically, she was active in the DWNC and took part, among other things, in the Committee for the Promotion of Peace and League of Nations work in Denmark (Fællesudvalget til fremme af freds- og Folkeforbundsarbejde i Danmark). The DWNC was a member of the IWC and the DWNC often approached the Ministry of Foreign Affairs with request for international peace.[34]

29. Begtrup, *Kvinde i et verdenssamfund*, p. 38.
30. DKNA, BB. Box 15. File P. History of the Committee on Legal Status of Women Appointed by the League of Nations in 1938. Lake, 'From Self-Determination', p. 254–265.
31. DKNA, Archive of the Danish Women's National Council (DWNC). Box 4. Repræsentantskabsmøde 6 Oktober, 1938. *Beretning til Rigsdagen angaaende Folkeforbundets nittende Forsamling i Genève 12.–30. september 1938,* p. 37–38, 64.

32. DKNA, BB. Box 15. File P. Letter from DWNC to Danish American Women's Association. 2 January, 1939.
33. DKNA, BB. Box 15. File P. *Danske Kvinders Nationalråd, 1935–1938.* DWNC Reports of activities.
34. DKNA, BB. Box 15. File P. Danske Kvinders Nationalråd, 1931–34 and Danske Kvinders Nationalråd, 1935–1938. DWNC Reports of activities.

Begtrup in the United Nations, 1946–52

Begtrup was an advising member to the Danish UN delegation from 1946–1952.[35] She took part in the negotiations of the Third Committee on social and economic affairs. She was not among the Danish delegates to the San Francisco conference in 1945. Hence, she was not among the women delegates (notably from Latin America) at San Francisco who had successfully insisted that the formulation in preamble to the UN Charter concerning human rights be changed from the 'equal rights of men' into the 'equal rights of men and women'. She was informed, however, of the developments at the conference as well as internal Danish disagreements by the Social Democratic delegation member Hartvig Frisch upon his return to Denmark.[36]

Begtrup took part in the first UN General Assembly (UNGA) in London 1946 as one of seventeen women from eleven delegations. Mrs. Roosevelt, chairlady of the Third Committee and of the UN Human Rights Commission, gathered the female delegates with the purpose to discuss ways in which women could increase their influence in the UN. They agreed to an Open Letter to the World of Women presented by Mrs. Roosevelt to the UNGA in February 1946. Begtrup also approached the UN General Secretary, Norwegian Trygve Lie, to discuss equality for men and women employed in the UN secretariat.[37]

The UN Commission on the Status of Women was established as a sub-commission under the UN Commission on Human Rights (CHR) with the purpose to submit proposals, recommendations and reports on the status of women to the CHR. British women's

35. I analyse in greater detail Begtrup's role in the UN in "Bodil Begtrup and the Universal Declaration of Human Rights: Individual agency, transnationalism and intergovernmentalism in the early UN human rights", *Scandinavian Journal of History*, vol. 36, no. 4, 2011, pp. 479–499.

36. Begtrup, *Kvinde i et verdenssamfund*, p. 55. Morsink, "Women's Rights in the Universal Declaration", p. 230.

37. Linder, "Equality for Women", p. 170. DKNA, BB. Box 27. Begtrup's diary. 7 January, 1946.

association had preferred an independent UN women's commission directly under the ECOSOC. However, Mrs. Roosevelt opposed this. The sub-commission members were expert members appointed on the grounds of their expert qualifications and with an eye to ensuring a wide geographic representation. Begtrup was informed by the Danish Foreign Service that she was appointed by the UN as member to the sub-commission which would have its first meeting in New York on 29 April 1946.[38]

Soon upon her arrival to the first sub-commission meeting, Begtrup was informed by Minerva Bernadino from the Dominican Republic and president of The Inter-American Commission of Women that the sub-commission wanted her as their chairman. Bernadino herself whom Begtrup knew from London and with whom she was on a first name basis wanted to be vice chairman of the sub-commission and Angela Jurdak from Lenanon were to be the rapporteur. Gabriella Mistral from Chile withdrew, according to Begtrup's memoirs, because she had never been involved in the women's cause. The Soviet representative failed to appear, so the remaining members of the sub-commission were Fryderika Kalinovske from Poland, Marie Heléne Lefauchou from France, Hansa Metha from India and W.S. New from China. Bernadino was critised by Mistral for a lack of democratic legitimacy because she came from a non-democratic state. It may be that this was the real reason why Mistral withdrew. It may also well be the reason why Bernadino recognised that she could not be the chairman of the sub-commission.[39] Begtrup held greater democratic legitimacy. However, seemingly she was chosen to the position not only due to her own qualifications, but also because of Bernadino's lack of such.

The sub-commission completed a report for the CHR within the two weeks scheduled for the task. Begtrup characterised the work in the sub-commission as 'the most harmonious working group

38. Begtrup, *Kvinde i et verdenssamfund*, p. 60.

39. Begtrup, *Kvinde i et verdenssamfund*, p. 60, p. 61. DKNA, BB. Box 17.

'Old diary', 29 April, 1946. The diary was reconstructed in June 1982 when Begtrup wrote her memoirs.

I have ever participated in.'[40] She claimed that it managed to finish its report in the short time of two weeks because its members were well informed about the challenges to women in their respective part of the world and because disagreements among the members were discussed in a matter-of fact way. The meetings were held during the nights in order to be prepared for what Begtrup considered to be a very skeptical New York press that made fun of the sub-commissions work. Finally, she emphasised that the sub-commission 'had been left working fairly alone by the political representatives.'[41] Her evaluation of the sub-commission's work indicate that it mattered to the working atmosphere that it was an expert commission able to work without the interference from political representatives.

The reception of the report in the CHR in May 1946 was rather negative. Begtrup was disappointed in particular with the attitude of Mrs. Roosevelt who according to Begtrup represented an American policy that was not favorable to gender equality and 'did everything to kill our report'.[42] This stimulated her to seek permission to present the report directly to the ECOSOC and to have the sub-commission transformed into a full commission under the ECOSOC. Mrs. Roosevelt was initially against the women's commission as a full commission, but at the insistence of Begtrup and her supporters she accepted the idea. Begtrup had several meetings with various women's associations of which thirty were in favor of a full women's commission. She also approached and gained support for the idea from the General Secretary, whom she describes as being central to her endeavors, the chairman of the ECOSOC, Ramaswami Mudaljar, and Mr. Mezeryk, a journalist specialised in women's issues.[43] Her networking and entrepreneurship proved successful. In late June 1946, the ECOSOC recommended to the

40. DKNA, BB. Box 17. Notes on the development of the early UN human rights system and in particular the work in the UN Commission on the Status of Women. No date, but before March 1949, p. 10.
41. DKNA, BB. Box 17. Notes on the development of the early UN human rights system and in particular the work in the UN Commission on the Status of Women. No date, but before March 1949, p. 0.
42. DKNA, BB. Box 17. Old diary. 17 May, 1946.
43. DKNA, BB. Box 17. Old diary. 19, 23, 27 May, 1946.

UNGA that the Commission on the Status on Women be established as a full commission now with state representatives instead of experts. This was eventually approved by the UNGA in October 1946.[44]

In November 1946, Begtrup, after prior consultation with the Danish delegation, presented a resolution on the political rights of women to the Third Committee. It originated in the work discussed in the sub-commission and recommended that states which had not already done so adopted measures necessary to fulfill the purpose in the UN Charter concerning equal rights to men and women and it invited the General Secretary to communicate this recommendation to the UN member states. A final paragraph recommending the Security Council and the UNGA to take gender equality into account when new states applied for UN membership was omitted with reference to the fact that the question of admittance of new members had already been discussed intensively in the First Committee dealing with political and security matters. This issue was controversial because the policy of admittance of new states might, in the context of the cold war, shift the balance of power within the UN. Hereafter, the resolution was unanimously adopted.[45]

In her capacity of chairman of the CSW, Begtrup participated in the meetings of the CHR in December 1947 together with the Soviet delegate from Belarus, Mrs. Uralova. Begtrup also stayed in contact with Jessie Street from Australia, who had been in Geneva in 1930 and 1938, and who had taken part in the CSW preparation of the amendments to the draft declaration of the UDHR. Begtrup was successful in amending several articles and in securing support for a proposal according to which the CHR every time the word 'men' was used implied both men and women.[46]

44. Begtrup, *Kvinde i et verdenssamfund*, p. 66.
45. DKNA, BB. Box 17. UNGA. A/220. 7 December, 1946. Political Rights of Women. Report of the Third Committee, p. 1.

46. DKNA, BB. Box 16. Report to the UN Status of Women Commission on the work of the Human Rights Commission. Geneva 2–17 December 1947. Sign. Begtrup; Morsink, "Womens Rights at the Universal Declaration".

In the autumn of 1948 she was elected – with reference to her position as chairman of the CSW vice chairman of the Third Committee which negotiated through eighty-five meetings the final draft of the UDHR.[47] She sought to improve women's rights concerning marriage and proposed to change the reading of the draft paragraph from women's rights 'as to marriage' into 'equal matrimonial rights' which was seen as expressing the intention of the article in a better way. However, a Soviet proposal which read that 'men and women shall enjoy equal rights during marriage and its dissolution' was adopted, hence accommodating a wish from Muslim women who had emphasised also equality concerning divorce. Begtrup also supported this proposal.[48]

Begtrup continued until 1952 as advising member to the Danish UN delegation. In 1952 she on behalf of Denmark presented the Convention on Women's Political Rights which was adopted by 46 votes against 0 and eleven abstentions.[49]

Begtrup continuously filed reports on the development in the UN regarding women's rights to the DWNC and the reports of the sub-commission were incorporated in the study material of the DWNC.[50] The IWC praised her for her launch of the Danish resolution on women's rights in the UNGA.[51] She also approached the Social Democratic Party leader Hedtoft with a suggestion that active women party members be informed on a monthly basis about rele-

47. Begtrup, *Kvinde i et verdenssamfund*, p. 73; L. Coltheart, "Citizens of the World. Jessie Street and International Feminism", Hecate, Vol. 31, No. 1, 2005. pp. 186, 188, 190.
48. DKNA, Archive of the Danish Mission to the UN (DKUN). Box XIB13. Report by Begtrup. Declaration of Human Rights.
49. *Beretning til Rigsdagen. De Forenede Nationers syvende plenarforsamling. New York 14. oktober–21. december 1952 og 28. februar–23. april 1953*, p. 128.

50. DKNA, BB. Box 17. Circular letter to the presidents of women's associations within the DWNC, 1946. DWNC Archive. Box 4. Repræsentantsskabsmøde 21 March, 1946. Ibid. Repræsentantsskabsmøde 16 September 1946.
51. DKNA, DWNC. Box 43. Letter from Marta Boël, Chairman of the ICW to Begtrup. 10 January 1947.

vant developments concerning the status of women.[52] Begtrup sought to involve her friend and Social Democratic politician, Hartvig Frisch, in her women's rights activities, for instance as a speaker in the DWNC, and in making a request for having a female expert on the issue of women in the radio broadcasting committee.[53] When Denmark was elected member of the ECOSOC in 1947 she presented 'Hartvig' with her 'great anxiety that the government would nominate a diplomat instead of a socially and economically clever person to represent Denmark'.[54] Prior to the annual UNESCO meeting in Beirut, she approached Frisch in his capacity as minister for education (1947–50) stressing that 'you have to include a woman in the group being sent down there. It must be possible to do something to show that we have a young, fresh and women friendly government'.[55] The correspondence indicates that Begtrup relied to a great extent on her connections within the Social Democratic party and that she in addition to women's rights was concerned with the image and power platform of the Social Democratic party.

Envoy and ambassador to Iceland, 1949–56

Begtrup was appointed Denmark's envoy to Reykjavik from 1949–56 (from 1955 as ambassador).[56] Her way into this post was rather extraordinary. Whereas she had conducted her international engagement in various capacities, she had not had any formal affiliation with the Danish Foreign Service and had no formal foreign ministerial carrier or training. In the first place Begtrup's husband, Bolt-Jørgensen, was supposed to be nominated to the post. However, as

52. Library and Archive of the Labour Movement (Arbejderbevægelsens Bibliotek og Arkiv, ABA), Copenhagen, Hans Hedtoft papers (HH). Box 25. Hedtoft to Begtrup. 25 September 1946.

53. ABA, Hartvig Frisch papers (HF). Begtrup to Frisch. 17 February 1948. Ibid. From Begtrup to Mr. and

Mrs. Frisch. 25 Dec. 1946. Ibid. Begtrup to Frisch. 6 May 1948.

54. ABA, HF. Letter from Begtrup to Frisch. 2 October 1947.

55. ABA, HF. Begtrup to Frisch. No date.

56. Begtrup, *Kvinde i et verdenssamfund*, pp. 104–105.

he would retire in three years, he would not limit his wife's carrier opportunities by taking her to Reykjavik, and hence proposed to the Ministry of Foreign Affairs with reference to Begtrup's international experience that she instead was offered the post. Bolt-Jørgensen would then retire and go with his wife to Reykjavik. The foreign minister as well as the Prime Minister were consulted and were supportive. The Prime Minister contacted the social democratic member of the Danish UN delegation who also supported the idea.[57] The Foreign Minister informed the Foreign Policy Committee of the Danish parliament that the Ministry of Foreign Affairs 'even it is not the custom' had offered Begtrup the post as envoy to Iceland.[58]

Begtrup recalls in her memoirs that her nomination was called a political nomination. However, her own perception was that her experience in different national and international organisations had qualified her for the position.[59] Her understanding of her nomination is the first example of how she disagreed with the foreign ministerial codex and practice concerning career paths.

In Iceland Begtrup's appointment was received with surprise. However, she was pleased to know in advance a number of key Icelandic politicians who she could lean on and show familiarity with. The key politicians included the former Prime Minister Ólafur Thors (the Independence Party) and the two social democrats, Finnur Jónsson and Ásgeir Ásgeirsson, whom she had met at the UNGA in Paris in the fall 1948.[60]

The relation between Iceland and Denmark was marked by Icelandic bitterness over Denmark's colonial rule and ongoing negotiations of the final repeal of the Danish-Icelandic Federal Law of 1918 (Forbundsloven) unilaterally abolished by Iceland in 1944.[61] Begtrup aimed in several ways to work in favor of the improvement

57. Begtrup, *Kvinde i et verdens-samfund*, pp. 80–81.
58. DKNA, Archive of the Danish Ministry of Foreign Affairs (DKFA). 3 E 92. Summaries of meetings in the Foreign Policy Committee. 17 November 1948.

59. Begtrup, *Kvinde i et verdens-samfund*, pp. 80–81.
60. Begtrup, *Kvinde i et verdens-samfund*, p. 81.
61. Begtrup, *Kvinde i et verdens-samfund*, p. 86.

of Icelandic-Danish relations. One of the major controversies between Iceland and Denmark was the Icelandic request that the Icelandic manuscripts collected and left by will by Arne Magnusson (1663–
1730) to the University of Copenhagen were returned to Iceland.[62]

Begtrup, and her predecessor C.A.C Brun, sought in accordance
with the Danish Ministry of Foreign Affairs, to encourage the Icelandic press to curb their hostility against Denmark. They explained
to Icelandic journalists that it would be counterproductive and only
strengthen the position of the forces against the return of the manuscripts to Iceland.[63]

Moreover, Begtrup was keenly focused on improving Danish-
Icelandic relations – according to her own perception of how to do
this. She kept the Social Democratic opposition – not the government informed of developments in the Icelandic manuscript case.
Seemingly, she had difficulties in accepting and handling her diplomatic role. Begtrup engaged in the issue, according to Hedtoft, 'with
an almost Old Norse fanaticism and opinionatedness' and the president of the Manuscript Commission warned her not to be too
eager in this case as people had come to doubt whether she was
Denmark's envoy to Iceland or the other way around.[64]

Begtrup continued her work for promoting women's interests.
At her arrival to Reykjavik the president of the Icelandic Women's

62. The case was not settled until
1971 when the Icelandic parliament
agreed to the conditions of the return
of the manuscripts negotiated by
Denmark and Iceland after two
verdicts by the Danish Supreme
Court. The majority of the Icelandic
manuscripts were returned during
the period 1971–1997. S. Davídsdottir,
*Håndskriftsagaens Saga – i politisk
belysning*, Odense 1999, pp. 81, 87;
G. Hálfdanarson, "'Værsågod Flat-
øbogen". Håndskriftsagen og afslut-
ningen på Islands kamp for selvstæn-
dighed", in: S. Mentz (ed.), *Rejse*

*gennem Islands historie den danske
forbindelse*, Copenhagen 2008;
Begtrup, *Kvinde i et verdenssamfund*,
pp. 120–123.
63. Davídsdottir, *Håndskriftsagaens Saga*, p. 81. ABA, HF. Box 29.
Begtrup to Frisch. 18. February 1949.
64. ABA, HH. Box 25. Begtrup
to Hedtoft, 22 August 1951. Hedtoft
to Begtrup, 29 August 1951. Begtrup
to Hedtoft, 6 January 1952. DKNA,
BB. Box 28. Diary. 24 November
1958. 7 January 1959. Davídsdottir,
Håndskriftsagaens Saga, p. 85.

Association (IWA), Sigrídur Magnússon who Begtrup knew from the first Nordic Women Meeting after the war in Copenhagen in 1946 was among the persons receiving her. Begtrup participated in many meetings in the IWA. Further, she established an association for Danish women in Iceland.[65]

In January 1956 Begtrup was informed of her upcoming return to Copenhagen in June 1956. She was very surprised and displeased with this decision. She believed she had contributed positively to a better relationship between Denmark and Iceland and that she could do more good in Iceland than in a new position in Copenhagen. She was well aware that she was popular in Iceland.[66] Further, she disliked what she perceived as a very competitive culture in the Ministry of Foreign Affairs in which she was certain to become among the 'hunted' which demanded 'good nerves'. She felt that the Ministry deliberately sought to treat her badly for instance by placing at her disposal an apartment situated so far away from the Ministry that she would not have time to go home for a rest and to change clothes during the day. She also noted a striking difference between the lack of assistance in terms of renovation and interior decoration offered to her when going to Reykjavik in 1949, and the number of architects now preparing the embassy residence prior to the arrival of her successor.[67]

It is difficult to decide whether her perception mirrored the reality; i.e. if the Danish Foreign Ministry deliberately treated her badly. It seems that Begtrup – due to her political appointment – was not fully accepted in the Ministry. At the same time, her perception should also be seen in the context that she did not accept the culture and codex of the Ministry of Foreign Affairs. A discussion with her husband supports this interpretation. Her husband explained that 'she should not think in terms of having achieved something in Iceland. The post was to be handed on in a reasonably

65. Begtrup, *Kvinde i et verdens-samfund*, pp. 85, 96–97, 100–102.
66. DKFA, 1946–72. 3 G Bodil Begtrup. Box 1. Translation of articles in the Icelandic newspaper May 1956.

67. DKNA, BB. Box 28. Diary 1955–56. 8, 10, 25 January 1956, 14 February 1956. No date, but between 9 and 14 February 1956. No date. March 1956.

state of affairs, perhaps better. An envoy was not supposed to be popular, but respected, and not so popular that it would be problem for the successor'. Begtrup far from shared these observations which to her were 'nonsense'. In Iceland, Begtrup remarked in her diary, 'they knew that Denmark could not have a better representative in Iceland. Copenhagen just followed the conventional practice'.[68]

Her perception indicates that she was out of touch with the Ministry of Foreign Affairs. She saw her work in Iceland as a way to strengthen the Icelandic-Danish relation. However, others noted the eagerness with which she engaged in the matter of the Icelandic manuscripts as being in favor of the Icelandic position. Her eager engagement in the matter of the Icelandic manuscripts indicates that she did not work in accordance with the diplomatic codex. Her correspondence with in particular Prime Minister Hedtoft further indicates that her main network was not within the Ministry of Foreign Affairs, but within the Social Democratic leading politicians. These had played an important role in her nomination to Iceland and '[i]f the Ministry of Foreign Affairs had not emphasised that H.C. Hansen agreed to my return, I had never given in', she claimed in her diary in May 1955 in which she also complained that the fact that husband would like to return did not help her case.[69] Without political support she could not manage to prolong her stay in Iceland.

Head of Office in the Ministry of Foreign Affairs and Denmark's representative to the Council of Europe, 1956–59

Back in Copenhagen Begtrup was made Head of the Third Office. Its areas of responsibility included the Danish minority in Southern Schleswig, the preparation of the instruction to the Danish UN

68. DKNA, BB. Box 28. Diary 1955–56. No date, but between 9 and 14 February 1956. No date. March 1956.

69. DKNA, BB. Box 28. Diary 1955–56. 16 May 1955.

delegation, and the Council of Europe to which Begtrup went approximately eight times a year to represent Denmark in the Committee of Deputies. Furthermore, while serving in Copenhagen, Begtrup was chosen as President of the Danish UN Association (Dansk Samråd for FN). She was in charge of the organisation of several events and lectures on the UN, including the reception for Mrs. Roosevelt to speak in Copenhagen on her way to the Soviet Union in 1956.[70]

Begtrup was uncomfortable with working in the Ministry of Foreign Affairs. She missed flexible working hours and the possibility to work in favor of matters of her interest.[71] The work in the Ministry appeared to her to be of limited importance and it failed to motivate her.[72]

Moreover, she felt unappreciated and misplaced. She complained to her diary that 'while among women I was chosen to everything, these men have a thousand explanations for why I shall not be part of the team.'[73] A remark in her diary in June 1956 captures very well her perception of the Ministry of Foreign Affairs and of her political appointment:

> When the Ministry of Foreign Affairs recruits a candidate from the outside, which I can understand is a liability, it is because he has a particular background or way of thinking which is usable as in my case when a special kind of person was sought for the position in Iceland. Such people should, after having discarded their duties, be given the opportunity to withdraw to estates in the country side or to another post. They cannot accept to be placed at a subordinate position in the Ministry of Foreign Affairs in order to be adapted to a group of small men who have been trained to this work in its most antiquated form. To the extent that the ministry

70. Begtrup, *Kvinde i et verdens-samfund*, pp. 142–144. DKNA, BB. Box 28. Diary. 22 August 1956. Ibid. Box 20. File: Material concerning Dansk Samråd for FN during Begtrup's presidency, 1956–59.

71. DKNA, BB. Box 28. Diary. 28 June 1956.
72. DKNA, BB. Box 28. Diary. No date, but June 1956, 10 August 1956. 21 July 1956. 19 August 1956.
73. DKNA, BB. Box 28. Diary. 4 January 1959.

does this there is probably also an element of revenge to it. They do not want people of my class [...].[74]

She did not like the trips to Strasbourg. According to her memoirs, she had taken an interest in European cooperation since she had first heard speeches by Stresemann and Briand in Geneva in the interwar years and she had participated in the founding meeting of the Council of Europe in The Hague in 1948 in which the DWNC had taken part. She describes the work in the Council of Europe to be quite a struggle. In particular she found her task was to organise the Danish involvement in the Council of Europe difficult. At the same time, she claimed, the work was stimulating and at the ideational level in harmony with her other international work.[75]

A comparison with her diary suggests that her memoirs concerning the Council of Europe represents a post rationalisation or at least that there was a wide gap between the ideational level and her practical engagement in the Council. Her diary contains remarkable little on thoughts of and her actual work in the Council of Europe. She mentions no specific cases in which she was engaged. She mainly emphasised the discontent with which she went to Strasbourg. The reason may be that she perceived of the Council of Europe as a toothless organisation and what she stressed the most that she always caught a cold while going there.[76] In fact, in 1958, she had somewhat 'settled within the Ministry of Foreign Affairs', except for the 'terrible and tiring trips to Strasbourg' to 'this negative Council of Europe' which usually 'gave her a cold' and which 'was occupied with problems of no further importance.'[77]

It remained vital to her to hold a position with which she was capable of making a difference. When a new stationing abroad came closer, she felt frustrated by the prospect of having to 'take up a new post without any particular interest, and run a small office with

74. DKNA, BB. Box 28. Diary. 20 June 1956.
75. Begtrup, *Kvinde i et verdenssamfund*, pp. 143–144.

76. DKNA, BB. Box 28. Diary. 1 December 1958, 17 Dec. 1958.
77. DKNA, BB. Box 28. Diary. 24 December 1958. 7 January 1959. 17 January 1959.

a bad secretary. There is not much fun in a job that anyone in the Ministry of Foreign Affairs can do just as good.'[78] Begtrup was, it seems fair to argue, a fiery soul and had difficulties accepting the work as a diplomat. The diplomatic field was only a field of interest to her to the extent that she could make use of it as a platform to pursue her own primary interests.

Ambassador in Switzerland and Austria, 1959–68

Begtrup was informed during the summer of 1958 that she would be appointed ambassador to Bern with extra-accreditation to Vienna. Her stationing in Bern formed part of a larger change of posts within the Foreign Service seemingly originating in dissatisfaction with a Head of Section who had to be replaced decided in the end by the Foreign Minister.[79] The Ministry of Foreign Affairs had sought to keep her two more years in Copenhagen. She was pleased to leave the home service, but less pleased with Bern. Switzerland was displeased with a woman ambassador. Begtrup questioned 'what Denmark would at all do in Switzerland, a country in which it took no interest, and would just have 'an office of expedition'. She thought a lot about what she could make of it.[80] She found it a rather stationary post, and in particular as the Ministry of Foreign Affairs considered the establishment of an independent embassy in Vienna, she was worried that there would be little to do. Additionally, she was surprised to be sent to a country in which women had no voting right. She complained again how posts were distributed according to seniority rather than with an eye to who 'could do a good job here'. In Norway, where she would have liked to go, the Norwegian Social Democratic politician Finn Moe told her, diplomatic posts were assigned to 'outsiders', but 'we are so bureaucratic and give priority to career', she noted.[81]

78. DKNA, BB. Box 28. Diary. 1 December 1958.
79. DKNA, BB. Box 28. Diary. 7 January 1959.
80. DKNA, BB. Box 28. Diary. 7 January 1959, 28 January 1959. 15 February 1959.
81. DKNA, BB. Box 28. Diary. 1 December 1958, 18. January 1959.

She did not give up the hope of going to Oslo, where she felt she 'could make a difference for Denmark, for the government'.[82] In March 1959, Begtrup approached the Social Democratic Foreign Minister both directly and through the Social Democratic Church Minister, women's rights and peace activist, Bodil Koch.[83] Koch informed Begtrup, that Prime Minister H.C. Hansen was supportive. However, the Foreign Minister, J.O. Krag, was more reserved.[84] The Foreign Minister explained to Begtrup that Oslo belonged to another set of replacements. Begtrup noted again how the consideration of a person who had served five years in Moscow to the post in Oslo proved the conventional approach of nominations in the Danish Foreign Service and of how for her part 'it was now over'. Diplomatic appointments depended on seniority. When candidates were equal the final choice depended on personal relations and sympathies, she noted.[85] Begtrup continued to draw on contacts within the Social Democratic party. However, towards the end of the 1950s they proved less efficient. Comforting, though, in these years, were friends within the DWNC.[86]

Begtrup was consciously aware that as an ambassador she could not comment on the status of women in Switzerland as this would be an internal Swiss matter. She did manage, though, to make friends with the president of the Swiss women's associations and several of the members of these. The presidents of the Swiss women's associations were invited to her sixty-year birthday in 1963 at the Embassy. One hundred attended.[87]

As she could not officially comment on the status of Swiss women, she made use of her political contacts in order to promote women's right to vote in Switzerland. She sent newspapers excerpts

82. DKNA, BB. Box 28. Diary. 11 March 1959.
83. For Bodil Koch see B. Possing, *Uden omsvøb. Portræt af Bodil Koch*, Copenhagen 2007. See also the chapter on Bodil Koch in this volume.
84. DKNA, BB. Box 28. Diary. 21 March 1959.

85. DKNA, BB. Box 28. Diary. 3 March 1959.
86. DKNA, BB. Box 28. Diary. 15 February 1959, 31 March 1959. Ibid. Box 31. Diary. 12 April 1959.
87. Begtrup, Kvinde i et verdenssamfund, p. 162.

to a Danish female Social Democratic MP and president of the Social Democratic Women's Association 'for her to see how Swiss
women were treated and to stimulate the National Council
[DWNC], to prepare good answers to the questions from the president of the Swiss canton Zürich concerning positive experience
with women's right to vote.'[88]

Following the establishment of the EEC, Swiss women's associations in August 1961 gathered representatives from ten national
women's council in the Swiss city of Axenstein with the purpose to
establish a forum to follow the impact of European integration on
the status of women. Begtrup participated as a private person. In her
speech she claimed that during her representation in the Council
of Europe she had discovered the lieu of a European women's movement which might have an influence on the status of women in the
new Europe. She saw the Swiss initiative as the establishment of
an important novelty in this regard. Furthermore, she claimed that
Danish women should prepare for the new Europe.[89]

Begtrup also asked the organisers of the conference 'Europe and
the World' organised by the Swiss Ministry of Foreign Affairs and
the Council of Europe to be held in Basel in 1964 if she could participate. The participants were not state representatives, but 'certain
cultural personalities' and she proposed that she could participate
in her private capacity if the organisers considered the social status
of women as part of the particular phenomenon within the European culture. She referred to the participation in the conference
of Professor Hal Koch as a friend of hers who would share her prop-
osition (he was married to the Social Democratic Church Minister
Bodil Koch mentioned above).[90]

88. DKNA, BB. Box 22. File:
The time as ambassador in Switzerland, 1959–68. Material concerning
Swiss women's suffrage. Begtrup
to Grethe Hækkerup. 22 April 1966.
89. DKNA, DWNC. Box 84. Exposé
présenté à l'occasion de la reunion
d'Axenstein 21–23 Août 1961.

90. DKNA, BB. Box 21. File Z.
Begtrup to l'ancien Conceiller
federal M. Petitpierre (former
Swiss Minister of Foreign Affairs).
No date.

The potential impact of the EEC on the status of women may have contributed to the apparent change in Begtrup's perception of European integration. In the early years of the European integration process, she doubted the usefulness of it, because, the real danger, she claimed, 'was at the European doorstep: the Asian danger.'[91] She preferred European cooperation in an intergovernmental form rather than a supranational form and she was very negative of the EEC, notable of Danish EEC membership. This would 'be the dissolution and the end of Denmark. [...] Neuropa is Hitler's legacy'.[92] Later she turned more positive of European cooperation as a stabilising factor for Europe in the wider world. The strength of Swiss commonality and the concept of Switzerland internationally played a vital role, she claimed in her memoirs, in shaping her perception of European cooperation.[93] Seemingly, her participation in the Council of Europe drew her attention to the European women's movement focusing of the impact of the EEC on the status of women and her presence in Switzerland let her to affiliate with the shaping of a post-war European women's movement.

Ambassador to Portugal, 1968–73

Begtrup was informed in March 1968 that she would be replaced from Bern to Lisbon. It came as a surprise to her and she was once again displeased with her new appointment to a post 'considered among colleagues as a retirement post without much work to do or political importance'.[94] She saw it 'as a degradation after nine years of highly appreciated work in Switzerland'.[95] The Head of the Ministry of Foreign Affairs explained to her that the Danish Ambas-

91. DKNA, BB. Box 28. Diary. 24 December 1958.
92. DKNA, BB. Box 28. Diary. 18 January 1959.
93. Begtrup, *Kvinde i et verdens-samfund*, p. 161.

94. DKNA, BB. Box 22. File Æ. Begtrup to the Minister of Foreign Affairs. 26 April 1968.
95. DKNA, BB. Box 22. File Æ. Begtrup's hand written notes in her Summary of journey Lisbon-Copenhagen-Zürich. 23 April 1968.

sador in Yugoslavia for six years was entitled to be replaced to Bern, for which reason Begtrup had to be replaced. Begtrup argued, in vain, how it would be difficult for her as a single woman (Bolt-Jørgensen had died in 1967) to become established in a catholic country which was even a dictatorship and suggested that the ambassador in Yugoslavia and his wife be send to Lisbon. The Head of the Ministry, however, agreed that Begtrup could rent a new house and have better facilities than in the flat which had housed the Danish embassy in Lisbon so far.[96]

She also approached the Foreign Minister. However, he had been very busy and had argued that he had nothing to do with her replacement in particular.[97] Seemingly, she had neither sufficient seniority, goodwill within the Ministry of Foreign Affairs nor political connections who could help her.

Portugal was a member of both EFTA and NATO. However, Portugal was also seen as a dictatorship by the Danish government who further criticised the Portugal's colonial rule in Mozambique and Angola in the UN.[98] Begtrup made connections within the Portuguese Social Democratic Party who informed Begtrup about the development in the colonial areas and she received, as did the other Nordic ambassadors, representatives from democratic groups. However, Begtrup seems to have favored a stable and slow democratic progress in the overseas territories. She had a positive perception of General de Spinola, who advocated a slow process of decentralisation, but not absolute independence to the colonies.[99]

Begtrup had little contact with the Portuguese women's associations as these were of a religious kind. Instead, she made connections to a few women members of the Portuguese parliament.[100] Portugal appears to be the post in which Begtrup had the least opportunity to strengthen the status and rights of women.

96. DKNA, BB. Box 22. File Æ. Begtrup's hand written notes in her Summary of journey Lisbon-Copenhagen-Zürich. 23 April 1968.
97. DKNA, BB. Box 22. File Æ. Begtrup's hand written notes in her Summary of journey Lisbon-Copenhagen-Zürich. 23 April 1968.
98. Ibid., pp. 170, 181.
99. Ibid., pp. 172, 181–182.
100. Ibid., pp. 177.

Conclusion

By combining a transnational and a life history approach, this article has identified and analysed the multiple social worlds that Begtrup was part of and, linking to other chapters in the book, the gradually changing career structures in politics and diplomacy in twentieth century Europe; other examples of new types of transnational agency and multiple social worlds are portrayed in the chapters by Meyer and van der Harst. Begtrup entered the international arena as a student activist in national and international students' unions of the League of Nations. In this way she became acquainted with the Danish League of Nations delegation and with the DWNC. The DWNC was the basis for her way into the UN as she was the DWNC advisor to the Danish UN delegation and an expert in the status of women which led to her appointment to the chairman of the UN CSW. Following her work to promote women's rights in the UN she was politically nominated to envoy to Iceland. It was a post first to be occupied by her husband. She began her career as an activist, in an NGO and on the international stage occupied with relatively gendered activities. She then became the first Danish female ambassador in a fairly masculine diplomatic world and was appointed to diplomatic posts in small states in Europe.

Begtrup was part of an international women's policy network. In addition she formed a more informal political network centered on politicians within the Danish Social Democratic party. Her political network appears efficient in the first half of 1950s when it proved useful in order for Begtrup to be appointed as envoy to Iceland. After the generational change in the Social Democratic leadership in the late 1950, her political network proved less useable.

Begtrup had difficulties in accepting the norms and principles of the Danish Foreign Service. In particular, she opposed the principle of seniority as a basis for replacements. She was a fiery soul rather than a diplomat and believed that she should be stationed according to where she could make the most of the representations she held. Her career in the Foreign Service proved in large part to be a struggle – mostly in vain – against the conventional norms.

Begtrup took advantage of her various posts to promote matters of concern to her. Her interest in the status and rights of women was in harmony with her formal duties in the League UN CSW. In Iceland she engaged in the case of the Icelandic Manuscripts with eagerness in favor of a return of the manuscripts and informed in particular the Danish Social Democratic leadership with information of developments in the Icelandic position in the matter. During her time as ambassador to Switzerland she sought to assist informally Swiss women by taking advantage of her informal political network within the Danish Social Democratic party and she attended as a private person meetings arranged by the Council of Europe and the Swiss Ministry of Foreign Affairs. This way, Begtrup continuously managed to take advantage of her formal representations as platforms for her agency in favor of her main interest in women's rights.

A good European?
Hans-Edgar Jahn – Anti-Bolshevist, Cold Warrior, Environmentalist

Jan-Henrik Meyer
Aarhus University

The end of a career

On 7–10 June 1979, the first direct elections to the European Parliament (EP) were held. What has frequently been considered the beginning of European supranational democracy coincided with the end of Hans Edgar Jahn's long career in national and European politics. Jahn had been a committed Member of the European Parliament (MEP), promoting in particular the new European environmental policy. As vice-president of the relevant EP committee, he produced parliamentary reports on key environmental issues, such as the first and second Environmental Action Programmes (of 1973 and 1977, respectively), and fought for the supranational protection of Europe's wild birds, in particular. He vigorously supported the move towards direct elections. Even at the age of 64, he envisioned his European career to continue, campaigned for his (re-)election, and won a seat.[1] Nevertheless, Jahn's career ended in a scandal. On 23 May 1979, the magazine 'Der Stern' published a report,[2] which accused Jahn of having written the aggressively anti-semitic and anti-Bolshevist book 'Der Steppensturm. Der jüdisch-bolschewistische Imperialis-

1. E.g. H.-E. Jahn, "Arbeit für Europa", Der Okerbote no. 5, February, in: Archiv für Christlich-Demokratische Politik (ACDP), Nachlaß Hans-Edgar Jahn (HEJ) Presse 093/1 (1979).

2. A. von Manikowsky, "Christdemokraten: Ein Mann für Europa? Über die NS-Vergangenheit eines CDU Spitzenkandidaten für die Europa-Wahl", in: *Stern* 23 May no. 21, 1979, 246–251.

mus' ('The Storm in the Steppe. Jewish-Bolshevist Imperialism'),
a pamphlet of crude Nazi propaganda, published in 1943.[3]

There is a certain irony in this course of events, in three respects:
First, Jahn was one of those post-war German politicians, who felt
that they had worked very hard to help Germany make advance on
its 'long path to the West'.[4] Working as a public relations (PR) specialist for West Germany's first Chancellor Konrad Adenauer, Jahn
had been a staunch supporter of Germany's economic and political
integration in the European Communities (EC) and the North Atlantic Treaty Organisation (NATO) and a lobbyist for the domestic
democratisation of Germany – along Christian democratic lines.
Now he was brought down by a past that he seemed to have quite
actively deleted from his memory.[5] Secondly, Jahn, the PR expert,
himself now faced the media's scandalisation of his wartime writings, and found it difficult to deal with it. He even withdrew from
the public eye for a while. Apparently he underestimated the impact
of the media across the Community, those media that he was used
to handling rather skilfully. Thirdly, it was in particular the Euro-

3. H. Jahn, *Der Steppensturm.
Der jüdisch-bolschewistische
Imperialismus*, Dresden 1943.
4. H. A. Winkler, "Der lange Weg
nach Westen", *Deutsche Geschichte
vom "Dritten Reich" bis zur Wiedervereinigung*, Vol. 2, Munich 2000.
Evidence for such a self-perception
can be taken from Jahn's self-assured
letter reminding his regional head
of party, Philip von Bismarck, not
to forget that he was approaching
the age of sixty, at which politicians
of his rank were due to receive the
German medal of honour (Bundesverdienstkreuz). Hans Edgar Jahn,
Letter to Philipp von Bismarck,
CDU, on "Bundesverdienstkreuz",
in: ACDP, HEJ, 079/1 Korrespon-
denz als MEP (1974).

5. Jahn is reported to have found
the "Anti-Jewish terminology"
"shocking", upon reading the book,
and claimed that "This is not the
way I thought, this is not the way
I wrote". [My translation, JHM]
"Zwischen Mensch und Tier",
in: *Der Spiegel* 18 June 1979, 25,
p. 104. Research on the coming
to terms with the Nazi past has
frequently highlighted those psychological effects of distancing one-self
from one's action. A. Assmann and
U. Frevert, *Geschichtsvergessenheit
– Geschichtsversessenheit. Vom Umgang mit deutschen Vergangenheiten
nach 1945*, Stuttgart 1999, pp. 140f.
See also R. Bessel and D. Schumann
(eds.), *Life After Death. Approaches
to a Cultural and Social History of
Europe During the 1940s and 1950s*,
Cambridge 2003.

pean reactions, the transnational resonance of the news about his erstwhile ideas in what amounted to a veritable European public sphere[6] that made him eventually untenable for his party at the European level. At the national level, Jahn was able to retain his seat in the German Bundestag until the 1980 elections.[7]

The goal of this chapter is to approach the history of European integration and 'ideas of Europe' taking a biographical perspective.[8] The life of Hans-Edgar Jahn, his ideas about Europe more generally and European integration in particular and his political action will be at the centre of the analysis. Jahn not only makes for an interesting case because his European career ended in disgrace. Rather the scandal alerts us to questions of continuity and change in interpreting and advocating Europe. Clearly, conceptualisations of 'Europe' have a long history, that is evidently also reflected in the lives of those actors who were involved in European politics in the postwar period.[9] The biographical approach makes the interplay of con-

6. On the European public sphere in a historical perspective see: J.-H. Meyer, *The European Public Sphere. Media and Transnational Communication in European Integration 1969–1991*, Stuttgart 2010.

7. Rolf Zundel, "Nervös wie die Hühner", *Die Zeit* 4 April 1980, p. 8.

8. This article draws on information collected within the context of the larger project "Protecting the Environment. Transnational Networks in the Emergence of a New EC Policy in the 1970s". This research was supported by a Marie Curie Intra European Fellowship and a Marie Curie Intra European Reintegration Grant within the 7th European Community framework programme, as well as by the Danish Research Council (Forskningsrådet for Kultur og Kommunikation) within the project "Transnational History" at Aarhus University. It also benefitted from a fellowship at the Kolleg-Forschergruppe (KFG) "The Transformative Power of Europe" www.transform-europe.eu, hosted at Free University Berlin, funded by the German Science Foundation (DFG).

9. For an overview of the variegated conceptions of Europe which arguably influence the understanding of European integration, see e.g. M. af Malmborg and B. Stråth (eds.), *The Meaning of Europe. Variety and Contention within and among Nations*, Oxford 2002; M. Wintle (ed.), *Imagining Europe. Europe and European Civilisation as seen from its Margins and by the Rest of the World in the Nineteenth and Twentieth Centuries*, Brussels 2008; A. Pagden (ed.), *The Idea of Europe: From Antiquity to the European Union*, Cambridge 2002.

tinuity and change visible. There is no zero hour in 1945, no clean slate in the history of European integration.

The construction and deconstruction of the story of Jahn's life and ideas alert us to the structural embeddedness of actors' views, their socialisation and the historical baggage they carry around with them during their lifetime.[10] As I will demonstrate below, the key idea of Europe that Jahn cherished and promoted throughout his post-1945 career was shaped by the anti-Bolshevist worldview he acquired as a National Socialist before 1945. Even after becoming a West German Christian Democrat in the late 1940s, he continued to conceive of Europe as the positive counter-concept to Bolshevist Soviet Union.[11] Researchers of Germany's 'coming to terms with the past' have argued that the continuity of anti-Bolshevism helped integrating West German post-war society and its citizens to live with the break that the end of the war had meant to many of them, and helped externalising responsibility and consideration of personal or collective guilt.[12] This clearly applies to Jahn too, who lost both his physical and his intellectual home.

In her inquiry into European identity, the historian Ute Frevert defined a 'good European' as 'someone, who has a consciousness of his or her belonging to Europe'. She stresses its variability over time.[13] Taking up this notion, this chapter will analyse how it makes sense to think of Jahn as a 'good European'. There is ample evidence that Jahn thought of himself as a 'good European'. He regularly professed his belief in and his sense of 'belonging to Europe' – a Europe which he essentially defined as the counter-concept to the Soviet Union – even if the exact contents of his ideas and the terminology he used changed over time. However, I hold that self-perception

10. S. Lässig, «Die historische Biographie auf neuen Wegen», *Geschichte in Wissenschaft und Unterricht* vol. 60, no. 10, 2009, pp. 540–553, 551.
11. R. Koselleck, "Zur historischen Semantik asymmetrischer Gegenbegriffe", in: R. Koselleck (ed.), *Vergangene Zukunft: Zur Semantik geschichtlicher Zeiten*, Frankfurt 1995 [1979], pp. 211–259.
12. Assmann and Frevert, *Geschichtsvergessenheit – Geschichtsversessenheit*, pp. 141f.
13. U. Frevert, *Eurovisionen: Ansichten guter Europäer im 19. und 20. Jahrhundert*, Frankfurt 2003, p. 19.

is not sufficient to define a 'good European'. It is indispensable that this view is shared and accepted by the fellow Europeans. At the end of his career, Jahn's self-perception as a good European was no longer credible to the fellow MEPs and the European media which scandalised his past.

The chapter is divided in three parts. First, I will examine the scandal in the media more closely, before moving on to study Jahn's biography, divided into the three main stages of his career before and after 1945, focusing on the conceptions of Europe he first promoted as a Nazi propaganda writer, and later as Adenauer's PR expert from the early 1950s, and subsequently in the EP in the 1970s. The chapter will conclude with a few observations on the uses of a biographical approach to European integration.

A short remark about on types of sources that form the basis of this chapter: Jahn was a prolific writer, whose works include – apart from the incriminated 1943 book – a 500 pages memoir focusing on his work as a PR-expert to the Christian Democratic Union (CDU) government,[14] numerous publications produced in the context of his work in PR or related to his role as a representative of the refugees from his Eastern home province.[15] He also wrote travel books, which were quite political in tone.[16] Still, it is relatively difficult to reconstruct his life, notably the pre-1945 years. His private papers, accessible at the Archive of Christian Democracy of the Konrad-Adenauer Foundation, only contain the same biographical information that is also available from biographical handbooks.[17] For this chapter, I am mainly relying on Jahn's own publications and contemporary newspaper reports. Additional information is available from a *Festschrift* produced by some of Jahn's former collaborators

14. H. E. Jahn, *An Adenauers Seite. Sein Berater erinnert sich*, Munich 1987.

15. E.g. H. E. Jahn, *Pommersche Passion*, Preetz/Holstein 1964; H. E. Jahn, *Rede, Diskussion, Gespräch*, Frankfurt 1954; H. E. Jahn and A. Roth, *Spionage in Deutschland*, Preetz 1962; H. E. Jahn, *Vertrauen, Verantwortung, Mitarbeit. Eine Studie über* *public relations Arbeit in Deutschland*, Oberlahnstein/Rhein 1953.

16. H. E. Jahn, *Vom Feuerland nach Mexiko. Lateinamerika am Scheideweg*, Munich 1962; H. E. Jahn, *Vom Kap nach Kairo. Afrikas Weg in die Weltpolitik*, Munich 1963.

17. H. E. Jahn, "Viten – Verschiedene Lebensläufe", in: ACDP, HEJ 079/1 (n.d.).

from the Arbeitsgemeinschaft Demokratischer Kreise (Working Group of Democratic Circles, ADK), the organisation Jahn built up. It is published by what became the ADK's successor organisation, the 'Studiengesellschaft für Public Relations' (Study Association for PR, founded in 1956), and is full of praise, completely ignoring the scandal. Furthermore, there is also a critical study on the ADK, which – despite its somewhat emotional tone – is a useful source. Its author Stefan Stosch interviewed Jahn in the 1990s – before Jahn passed away in April 2000 – and consulted the files on the ADK in the Federal Archive in Koblenz.[18] Given that Jahn was a politically contentious figure, both his own writings and reports about him, frequently very critical in tone, have to be treated with utmost care.

A scandal in the European public sphere

Jahn was not only brought down in scandal because of what he was accused of, but also because the scandal created transnational resonance in Europe, which eventually made it impossible for his party to continue to support him. This makes for an interesting case, since political science research on the European public sphere has so far claimed that effective transnational scandalisation at the European level is a more recent phenomenon starting in the late 1990s.[19]

Clearly, the timing of the scandal amplified the attention the media devoted to it. It was towards the end of the first European election campaign that the left-leaning investigative Hamburg

18. S. Stosch, *Die Adenauer-Legion: Geheimauftrag Wiederbewaffnung*, Konstanz 1994; W. Grünthal, *Festschrift für Dr. Hans Edgar Jahn zur Vollendung des 80. Lebensjahres: Dr. Hans Edgar Jahn – ein Mann der ersten Stunde*, Bonn 1994.
19. C. O. Meyer, *Die Wächterfunktion von europäischer Öffentlichkeit. Das Brüsseler Pressecorps und der Rücktritt der EU-Kommission*, in: A. Klein, et al. (eds.), *Bürgerschaft,* *Öffentlichkeit und Demokratie in Europa*, Opladen 2003, pp. 231–245; H.-J. Trenz, "Korruption und politischer Skandal in der EU. Auf dem Weg zu einer Europäischen Öffentlichkeit?", in: Maurizio Bach (ed.), *Die Europäisierung nationaler Gesellschaften* (Kölner Zeitschrift für Soziologie und Sozialpsychologie, special issue), Opladen 2000, pp. 332–359.

newsmagazine revealed Jahn's past as the author of Nazi propaganda. *Der Stern's* author Arnim von Manikowsky, who was only 16 years old when World War II ended, was generally critical of Germany's coming to terms with its past.[20] First and foremost, Manikowsky scandalised the anti-semitism, and the crude and racist anti-Bolshevism which seemed less acceptable in the détente-era of the 1970s than in the 1950s. What made Manikowsky's article really resonate more broadly was that he re-contextualised what Jahn had written not only about Jews and Bolsheviks, but also about the Western nations. The author linked this to Jahn's candidacy for direct elections, questioning his suitability to act as a (German) representative in the EP. It was this particular interpretation, which was reiterated in the subsequent media and political debate, and which was crucial for triggering a scandal with broader repercussions.

Initially it was a broad spectrum of German national and regional newspapers which immediately picked up the accusations published by *Der Stern*. Some of them included a first response by Jahn.[21] Only two days after the initial publication, the French newspaper *Le Monde*, one of the internationally most widely read newspapers at the time, ran two articles on the affair, scandalising Jahn

20. G. Gründler and A. von Manikowsky, *Das Gericht der Sieger. Der Prozeß gegen Göring, Heß, Ribbentrop, Keitel, Kaltenbrunner u.a.*, Oldenburg 1967; G. Gründler, *Erinnerung an Arnim von Manikowsky* [obituary], 2010, available from: http://www.gerdgruendler.de/ Manikowsky,Arnim%v..html, [6 July 2011].
21. "'Stern': Der CDU-Politiker Jahn verherrlichte 1943 Hitler", *Die Welt*, 22 May 1979; "CDU Niedersachsen. Vorwurf gegen den Euro-Kandidaten", *Handelsblatt*, 22 May 1979; ""Juden sind Bastarde" Schwere Vorwürfe gegen CDU Europa-Kandidat", *Hamburger Morgenpost*,

22 May 1979; "Vorwürfe gegen CDU Europakandidat: "Nach Jahrtausenden: Ehrfurcht vor Hitler". "Stern" beschuldigt Hans-Edgar Jahn der antijüdischen Hetze während der Nazizeit", *Nürnberger Nachrichten*, 23 May 1979, p. 2; E. Spoo, "CDU Politiker rühmte einst Hitler. Antisemitische Propagandaschrift Hans Edgar Jahns von 1943 aufgetaucht", *Frankfurter Rundschau*, 23 May 1979; "Jahn weist Vorwürfe zurück. Braunschweiger Abgeordneter der Hetze beschuldigt", *Braunschweiger Zeitung*, 23 May 1979; "CDU-Europa-Kandidat der antijüdischen Hetze beschuldigt", *Süddeutsche Zeitung*, 23 May 1979.

also beyond German borders. A few days later, newspapers from his home constituency of Braunschweig reported about the exasperation of Belgian politicians about Jahn's wartime writings. The next day they noted that Jahn had apparently fallen sick and withdrawn from all campaign events.[22] However, while his own party did not openly call for his withdrawal before the elections, what eventually brought down Jahn were the protests of the fellow European MEPs, notably from Belgium and the Netherlands, who threatened to boycott the inaugural session of the EP unless Jahn withdrew his candidacy. Only then, under pressure from his own party leadership, who demanded clarification, and after critical comments in opinion-leading German newspapers, did Jahn reluctantly withdraw. Jahn's comment that he had to come to realise 'that there was apparently no mercy for political error' might at first sight seem self-righteous and defensive. At the same time, it illustrates that Jahn's attitude and self-understanding had increasingly become anachronistic. At the late 1970s, he was out of synch with the expectations of a (European) public sphere.[23]

Jahn's ousting from the EP did not only mark the end of a transnational political career. It was also a reflection of generational change[24] which went hand in hand with changing attitudes – both towards Europe and towards the Nazi past. Jahn's conception of Europe had been shaped by the anti-Bolshevist consensus of the early

22. "Belgische Attacke gegen Hans Edgar Jahn", *Harzburger Zeitung*, 29 May 1979; "CDU Spitzenkandidat für Europa ist erkrankt. Parteiveranstaltungen vorerst ohne Dr. Jahn", *Harzburger Zeitung*, 30 May 1979; "Angriffe gegen Jahn aus Belgien", *Braunschweiger Zeitung*, 30 May 1979; Arnim von Manikowsky, "'Wie ein Schock getroffen'. Reaktionen auf den Stern-Bericht über die NS-Vergangenheit des CDU-Europa-Kandidaten Hans Edgar Jahn", *Stern*, 31 May 1979, no. 22, pp. 228–231.

23. "Peinliche Bockigkeit", *Die Zeit* 22 June 1979, p. 1; "Zwischen Mensch und Tier"; "Beschuldigungen gegen Bremer SPD Politiker", *Frankfurter Allgemeine Zeitung*, 25 June 1979, p. 5, [quote, my translation, JHM]; "Vergangenheiten", *Frankfurter Allgemeine Zeitung*, 16 June 1979, p. 10.

24. On the contentious, but analytically useful notion of "generation", see: B. Weisbrod, "Generation und Generationalität in der Neueren Geschichte", *Aus Politik und Zeitgeschichte*, vol. 52, no. 8, 2005, pp. 3–9.

post-war period, championed by Adenauer's CDU.[25] Jahn's defensive argument that the nations represented in the EP did 'not charge their historical baggage up against each other' apparently no longer applied.[26] The attitudes Jahn invoked were largely characteristic of the early post-war period, when networks of West European Christian democrats who cooperated to bring about European integration included former members of the Nazi party, such as Kurt-Georg Kiesinger, premier of Baden-Württemberg (1958–1966) and Chancellor (1966–1969).[27]

In the context of heightened public awareness of the newly elected EP, the Nazi past did start to matter, as the transnational European critique suggests. In West Germany, the scandal about Jahn's past writings was part of a larger wave of scandalisation beginning in the late 1970s.[28] The media started holding leading politicians to account for what they had written and done prior to 1945. For instance, in August 1978, public pressure had already brought down the former Nazi judge and Christian-democratic premier of Baden-Württemberg Hans Karl Filbinger,[29] and just a few days after Jahn, a social-democratic regional minister in the federal state of Bremen.[30] To some extent, the heightened awareness for the Nazi past can be linked to the major public debate triggered by the broadcasting of the American TV programme 'Holocaust' earlier in 1979.[31] In fact, *Der Stern* author Manikowski invoked the awareness of 'a European

26. "Vergangenheiten", *Frankfurter Allgemeine Zeitung*, 16 June 1979, p. 10.
27. W. Kaiser, *Christian Democracy and the Origins of European Union*, Cambridge 2007, pp. 159, 270.
28. F. Bösch, "Politische Skandale in Deutschland und Großbritannien", *Aus Politik und Zeitgeschichte*, Vol. 53, No. 7, 2006, pp. 25–32, p. 32. See also F. Esser and U. Hartung, "Nazis, Pollution, and No Sex: Political Scandals as a Reflection of Political Culture in Germany", *The American Behavioral Scientist*, vol. 47, no. 8, 2004, pp. 1040–1071.

29. W. Wette (ed.), *Filbinger – eine deutsche Karriere*, Springe 2006.
30. "Nachtritt ohne Nachsicht", *Die Zeit* 29 June 1979, p. 1; Bischoff, Ministerpräsident a.D., "Einsam auf der Solitüde. Im Augenblick will Hans Karl Filbinger von seiner Partei nichts wissen".
31. J. Müller-Bauseneik, "Die US-Fernsehserie "Holocaust" im Spiegel der deutschen Presse", *Historical Social Research*, vol. 30, no. 4, 2005, pp. 128–140.

public sphere induced by "Holocaust'" as an argument for the unacceptability of someone like Jahn as a German representative.[32] Generational change might have mattered too. Younger journalists now scandalised the deeds of an earlier generation that had been adults during the Nazi period.[33] To what extent the scandal served intra-party competitors as a tool to bring about generational change in a quite practical sense, by getting rid of an aging incumbent unwilling to leave,[34] must remain an open question. At age 64, Jahn was clearly approaching the official retirement age.

The Anti-Bolshevist

Jahn was born some three months after the outbreak of the first year of the Great War, on 21 November 1914, in Neustettin (today: Szczecinek, Poland), a small town of about 10,000 inhabitants in the Eastern part of the Prussian province of Pomerania (Hinterpommern). In this rural backwater, the new racist anti-Semitism of the late 19th century had taken root relatively early. The region was one of the first areas to be targeted by this wave of anti-Semitic propaganda. Neustettin made the national news when the local synagogue was burnt down in 1881, a few days after an anti-Semitic agitator had held inflammatory speeches locally. The media also followed the ensuing court case: Initially five Jewish citizens were accused of arson, but were subsequently acquitted by a higher court. Local relations with Jewish citizens turned sour, including boycotts of Jewish shops.[35]

32. Manikowsky, "Christdemokraten", p. 251.

33. Assmann and Frevert, Geschichtsvergessenheit –

34. H. Tumber and S. R. Waisbord, "Introduction: Political Scandals and Media Across Democracies Volume 1" The American Behavioral Scientist, vol. 47, no. 8, 2004, pp. 1031–1040, p. 1037.

35. S.C.J. Nicholls, The Burning of the Synagogue in Neustettin. Ideological Arson in the 1880s, Centre for German Jewish Studies, University of Sussex 1999, available from: http://www.sussex.ac.uk/Units/cgjs/publications/nic.html.

Relatively little is known about Jahn's family. Like most Pomer-
anians, Jahn was a protestant. His father was a master-smith, and
– according to Jahn – a member of the social-democratic party.[36] In
the beginning of the 1930s, the protestant rural Northern and Eastern provinces of Prussia were among those places where the National Socialists gained early and strong support.[37] Possibly affected
by National Socialist mobilisation, despite growing up in a social-
democratic home, Jahn became a Hitler Youth in 1930 at age 16 and
soon joined the Nazi party.[38]

Jahn only completed eight years of 'Volksschule', which was very
common for children of his background in what was still a very
class-ridden educational system, followed by a traineeship at the
local newspaper *Norddeutsche Presse*.[39] In 1933, when the National
Socialists came to power, Jahn volunteered for military service with
the German Navy, where he served until 1938. It was only after his
military service, in 1939, that Jahn gained access to higher education.
Party connections facilitated access to the necessary financial means.
Benefitting from a generous scholarship, financed by the Chancellor's office from a special fund,[40] Jahn first passed the necessary
external university-entry exam (Begabten-Abitur) and then – inter-
rupted by a brief period of service in the war in 1939 – studied history, geography, geopolitics, political economy and international
law at the Institute for Politics (Hochschule für Politik) in Berlin
and, after its dissolution, at Berlin's Friedrich-Wilhelms-Univer-
sität.[41] All the subjects he studied were deeply shaped by current
politics and ideology, notably after the universities had been purged

36. "Hans-Edgar Jahn", *Internationales Biographisches Archiv*, Vol. 45,
2000; Jahn, *An Adenauers Seite.
Sein Berater erinnert sich*, p. 31. This
is impossible to verify, since the
party membership records are lost.
37. H. E. Winkler, "Der lange Weg
nach Westen", *Deutsche Geschichte
vom Ende des Alten Reiches bis zum
Untergang der Weimarer Republik*,
vol. 1, Munich 2000, pp. 483, 491.

38. Manikowsky, "Christdemokraten", p. 248.
39. Grünthal, *Festschrift für
Dr. Hans Edgar Jahn*, pp. 1f.
40. Manikowsky, "Christdemokraten," 248. Similarly also: "Propaganda: Wir sind schon da", *Der Spiegel*
10 July 1957, pp. 23–25, p. 24.
41. "Hans-Edgar Jahn."

from 1933 onwards. It is remarkable that Jahn – a well-trained former professional soldier – was effectively spared from military service during the first half of the war. He was only drafted into service in 1942.[42] From 1944 onwards, Jahn was appointed to serve both the National Socialist (NS) party and the military simultaneously as an officer with special propagandistic duties (NS-Führungsoffizier),[43] responsible for the political instruction of the marines.[44]

In 1943 the book 'Der Steppensturm' was published, which was at the core of the 1979 scandal. There is little doubt that Jahn had actually written the book, notably since he had claimed authorship with the official publishing office (Reichsschrifttumskammer) in 1943. During the scandal Jahn defended himself contending that he had only written a short paper during his studies and that the problematic passages had been inserted by unknown editors in the ministry of propaganda. When his party leadership demanded evidence of this, he was unable to produce it.[45] What makes Jahn's explanation most unlikely is that the entire book is written in a fairly uniform language full of anti-Semitic and anti-Bolshevist rhetoric. Given that Jahn was a long-time faithful of the Nazi party, had been trained and worked in propaganda, there is very little in the way to suggest that he could not have been the author of a propagandistic book which dealt with the geopolitical and military issues he had studied and continued to be interested in after the war.

Jahn's book reflects a context of European rhetoric that is frequently ignored and forgotten, but that provides an important line of continuity in Jahn's life and that of many people of his generation. Nazi rhetoric, particularly since the beginning of the war against the Soviet Union, frequently combined three elements: anti-Bolshe-

42. "Jahn, Hans Edgar", in: W. Becker, et al. (eds.), Lexikon der Christlichen Demokratie in Deutschland, Paderborn 2002, pp. 287.
43. On this particular institution see: A. Kunz, Wehrmacht und Niederlage. Die bewaffnete Macht in der Endphase der nationalsozialistischen Herrschaft 1944–1945, Munich 2005, pp. 240f.

44. "Propaganda: Wir sind schon da", p. 24.
45. A. von Manikowsky, "Hinters Licht geführt. Vier Wochen nach der Aufdeckung seiner NS-Vergangenheit gab der CDU-Euro-Parlamentarier Hans Edgar Jahn sein Mandat zurück", Stern 21 June 1979, no. 26, p. 133.

vism, anti-Semitism and pro-Europeanism. The Nazis presented themselves as defenders of 'Europe' against the Soviet assault. To some extent, the goal was to gain the support of the citizens even of those nations who had been subjected during the war.[46]

What was Jahn's book about and what kind of ideas of Europe did he profess? The proclaimed goal of the book was to analyse 'how the Bolshevists conducted their war against Europe and the world'.[47] The world he described was full of conspiracies and a Manichaean battle of racially defined entities. The core of the argument is that the National-Socialists were defending 'Europe' against Jewish-led Bolshevism in a battle about who is to rule the world. Applying asymmetric counter-concepts to distinguish friends and foes, the author emphasised the normative inferiority of 'Europe's' enemies.[48] Russia – inhabited by 'half-savage people' with 'cruel instincts', a 'racial blend of Europeans and Asians' – the author claimed, could only be counted as belonging to European culture due to its 'Nordic upper strata'. The country had been used by the Jews – gaining power in the country via imperialist Bolshevism – to attack Europe and destroy it.[49]

Against this imagery of all what seems foul and despicable from a racist's perspective, Hitler is presented as the 'great German, but also the great European Adolf Hitler, who takes responsibility for the future of Europe'.[50] Quoting Hitler who in turn had referred to Voltaire, Jahn emphasised European commonalities in terms of shared principles of humanism and shared laws that also distinguished Europeans from the rest of the world. He claimed that it was this tradition of humanism and laws that Germany was fighting for. The book closes with a vision for Europe: 'After the destruction of

46. M. L. Smith, "The Anti-Bolshevik Crusade and Europe", in: M. L. Smith and P. M. R. Stirk (eds.), *Making the new Europe – European Unity and the Second World War*, London 1990, pp. 46–65; D. Barnouw, "The New Nazi Order and Europe", in: M. Wintle (ed.), *Imagining Europe. Europe and European Civilisation as seen from its Margins and by the*

Rest of the World in the Nineteenth and Twentieth Centuries, Brussels 2008, pp. 73–90.

47. Jahn, *Der Steppensturm*, p. 18.

48. Koselleck, *Zur historischen Semantik asymmetrischer Gegenbegriffe*.

49. Jahn, *Der Steppensturm*, pp. 14–17.

50. Jahn, *Der Steppensturm*, p. 322.

Bolshevism, the last attempt of the Jews to dominate the world will be intercepted'. Thus Europe will be reinstated 'in its historical vocation as the centre of culture of the world'. By associating Europe with culture, laws, and humanism, the author invoked a venerable tradition dating back to the enlightenment. At the same time, glossing over the contradiction, the world was clearly perceived in racist terms. There was no doubt about who was going to rule such a Europe: With the 'Germanic people assembled around one hearth', Jahn emphasised, the German empire was going to provide protection, and 'for millennia' the entire world was going to praise Hitler.[51]

The fellow Europeans were described as peace-loving and weak.[52] They had been drawn into the war either by the 'Jewish international' playing out its 'financial dominance', or by their misguided alliance with the Bolsheviks (such as France). Thus Jahn argued that the French had to be brought back to the 'hearth of European culture' by their defeat against Germany.[53] While stressing European commonalities, the racist logic implied that the fellow Europeans were portrayed as inferior. Hence Europe was to be structured along the lines of racial hierarchies. This of course legitimised German dominance.

England and the US were not exactly considered part of the category Europe, not least due to their 'Pluto-democratic-Jewish-Freemason' leading classes, who – the author claimed – had actually prepared the Bolshevist threat to the continent. Only by overthrowing this 'world of the Jewish international', the racist argument went, would these people be able to live.[54] At the same time, not only Europe, but also the English and the Americans were to profit from the Nazi defence against the Bolshevists. Recalling the tenet that the Bolshevists were no trustworthy allies, the English and the Americans would be grateful after German victory that that they were spared from the revolution the Bolshevists had in store for them.[55] The latter argument – when taken out of its racist context – lent itself to recycling in the Cold War.

51. Jahn, *Der Steppensturm*, pp. 368f.   53. Jahn, *Der Steppensturm*, pp. 367f.
52. Jahn, *Der Steppensturm*, p. 358   54. Jahn, *Der Steppensturm*, p. 359.
(quoting a speech by Hitler).   55. Jahn, *Der Steppensturm*, p. 368.

The Cold-Warrior and Environmentalist

From 1945 to 1947, Jahn was a British prisoner of war in Schleswig-Holstein, where he had last served as a lieutenant of the German navy. This was when he broke with national-socialist ideology, as he explained in an interview with *Der Stern* in 1979.[56]

After his release to the West coast city of Husum, Jahn worked as a local reporter and political commentator for the newspapers *Flensburger Tageblatt* and *Kieler Nachrichten*.[57] Soon he became politically involved in a nationalist cause, namely the defence of Southern Schleswig against secession to Denmark. In his memoirs, he vividly recalls the activities of pro-Danish associations. They lobbied for the 'liberation' of Southern Schleswig, using the local resentment against East German refugees, people like Jahn and his family, who had arrived in Schleswig-Holstein in great numbers. To a nationalist like Jahn the idea seemed outrageous that the Schleswigers could be willing to give up German nationhood for 'Danish ham', i.e. the economic advantages of being part of Denmark. Both the CDU – which was the new party of the right, founded to overcome the political divisions between Catholics and Protestants – and the re-established Social Democratic Party (SPD) as the major postwar parties were active in the 'battle of the border' ('Grenzkampf'). However, Jahn had little sympathy for the Social Democrats' continued attachment to Marxist heritage. Jahn joined the CDU instead, which was much more committed to the nationalist cause.[58] In 1947, the CDU's membership in Schleswig-Holstein was small, consisting largely of Catholic refugees, which was not an advantage in a protestant province. The party lacked those kinds of local institutional structures, which the SPD had been able to re-establish. Thus the CDU used the 'battle of the border' to mobilise support both among refugees, most of whom tended to vote for the Social Democrats, and more importantly in the Conservative milieu among

56. Manikowsky, *Christdemokraten*, p. 250.

57. Jahn, *An Adenauers Seite*, p. 32.

58. Jahn, *An Adenauers Seite*, pp. 29–32.

locals. The border issue was also helpful to muster financial support from the new federal government in Bonn.[59] In the 1948 local elections, Jahn was elected county counsellor in Husum, and head of a committee responsible for culture. As a member of the CDU party leadership in Schleswig-Holstein, he dealt with issues of 'publicity and advertising', started training orators for the party, and held – as he claimed – more than one hundred public speeches 'for the CDU and Adenauer' during the 1949 election campaign.[60]

After the CDU's victory and Adenauer's election as first Chancellor of the Federal Republic, Jahn was able to establish contact with the leadership of the party in Bonn. Building on what he had learnt during his studies in Berlin, Jahn acquainted himself with Anglo-Saxon methods of PR which he deemed more appropriate for a democratic society than old-style propaganda. He proposed to target the pre- or non-political area of citizens' associations. His analysis was that given the wide-spread disappointment with politics after the experience of National Socialism and a reluctance to join parties, it was in this area, where citizens met. This would be the place where the government's message would fall on more fertile ground. Citizens would be much more receptive in an environment where they felt at ease. Engaging them in dialogical communication, rather than relying on one-way communication via propaganda speeches, was simply much more effective, Jahn concluded. In a proposal submitted to the federal press and information office, Jahn suggested to set up an institution to administer and organise this – undercover – PR effort, both for the benefit of the government and the CDU.[61]

59. K. Andresen, Schleswig-Holsteins Identitäten. Die Geschichtspolitik des Schleswig-Holsteinischen Heimatbundes, Neumünster 2010, pp. 83f. See also: F. Bösch, Das konservative Milieu. Vereinskultur und lokale Sammlungspolitik, Göttingen 2002, p. 207.

60. Jahn, An Adenauers Seite. Sein Berater erinnert sich, pp. 33, 46f. [quote p. 47].
61. Jahn, *An Adenauers Seite. Sein Berater erinnert sich*, pp. 69f; H. E. Jahn, *Gesellschaft und Demokratie in der Zeitwende*, Cologne 1955, pp. 338f.

The new head of the chancellor's office, secretary of state Otto Lenz, liked the proposal. Chancellor Adenauer invited Jahn for a personal meeting in 1951. Jahn was very impressed by him as a figure of authority, as he recalls in his memoirs. Adenauer complained about the bad relations he had with the press and that it was necessary to generate public support. Affiliated to the secretary of state of the Chancellor's office, Jahn was placed in charge of setting up an organisation to turn into practice what he had proposed.[62]

The organisation, the ADK – officially a private, non-profit association – was operational in October 1951 under Jahn's leadership as director, from 1957 as president. It quickly established a differentiated structure, from the federal down to the county level. Its dual goal was to report about the local situation of public opinion to the central office in Bad Godesberg, near Bonn, and to establish relations with citizens' organisations and associations, in what Jahn called the 'pre-parliamentary space' ('vorparlamentarischer Raum'). By 1967, it had set up cooperative relations with more than 700 associations.[63] Already in 1952, the ADK reported that it had organised more than 1000 events – discussion meetings, seminars, public film presentations – reaching a total audience of more than 120,000 people. By 1967, it had a total staff of more than 100 full-time employees. In the course of almost two decades, its files included some 100,000 people who had acted as orators or facilitators at least once. Speakers did not arrive unprepared: They were trained in rhetoric. A special school was even established for this purpose with ministerial support in 1954. In order to make sure that the right message was delivered, two journals were established that kept the ADK's collaborators updated about current affairs.[64] Interestingly enough, Jahn replicated those structures of disseminating information – such as specific newsletters and information services for speakers – that he was familiar with from his time as a wartime officer with special propagandistic duties for the National Socialist Party.[65]

62. Jahn, *An Adenauers Seite. Sein Berater erinnert sich*, pp. 71–81.
63. For an overview of these organisations see: Jahn, *Vertrauen, Verantwortung, Mitarbeit*, pp. 97–308.
64. They were called Politische Information Series A and B; Stosch, *Die Adenauer-Legion*, 37–40.
65. Kunz, *Wehrmacht und Niederlage*, p. 243.

The ADK did not only benefit from direct access to government information and informal support. In fact, the expensive enterprise was funded from the budget of the Chancellor's office, drawing on a title that the Chancellor was able to use at his discretion. From the mid-1950s, additional funding came from the new ministry of defence. Effectively, and this was already criticised by the contemporary press and by the opposition SPD, Jahn's officially non-partisan organisation was a government-sponsored lobbying organisation for the CDU.[66]

The ADK presented itself as an organisation of citizen education. Its official aim was threefold – generating acceptance and support for democracy, mobilising 'the people' to engage in politics and take responsibility, in order to create a firm base for the 'democratic, constitutional institutions'.[67] However, when considering the messages it promoted, it quickly becomes clear that its goal was to support the policy pursued by the CDU-led government policy, notably (West) European integration[68] and the deeply divisive issue of West German re-armament in the 1950s. For the latter purpose, the ADK closely cooperated with veterans' organisations and former officers. Many of the latter were recruited as speakers at ADK-sponsored events.[69] Similarly, Jahn had employees of the European institutions trained in Brussels to act as speakers lobbying for European integration. At many events, Jahn himself took over this role.[70] The ADK also organised trips to visit the headquarters of NATO and the OEEC in Paris and of the European Coal and Steel Community (ECSC) in Luxembourg, to inform, but also to reward and motivate their speakers.[71]

66. Stosch, *Die Adenauer-Legion*, pp. 40–45; "Propaganda: Wir sind schon da".
67. M. Kunczik, "Die Arbeitsgemeinschaft Demokratischer Kreise (ADK)", *PR-Magazin*, vol. 29, 1998, pp. 53–77, p. 54.
68. H. E. Jahn, *10 Jahre Arbeitsgemeinschaft Demokratischer Kreise. Eine Bilanz staatsbürgerlicher Bildungsarbeit*, Bad Godesberg, 1961, p. 5.
69. Kunczik, Die Arbeitsgemeinschaft Demokratischer Kreise (ADK), pp. 57f.
70. Jahn, *An Adenauers Seite. Sein Berater erinnert sich*, p. 88.
71. Jahn, *10 Jahre Arbeitsgemeinschaft Demokratischer Kreise*, pp. 16f.

As lobbyists for the CDU-led government, Jahn – and the ADK – promoted the Christian democratic pro-European federalist consensus. Western integration was the key tenet of Adenauer's foreign policy. Western defence, and West Germany's contribution to it, were considered necessary for re-gaining sovereignty. Political integration was also presented as a precondition for eventual German unity. Accordingly, from the perspective of national interest, thus defined, Jahn staunchly supported European integration.[72]

However, how did Jahn describe and promote Europe in the 1950s? In one of his programmatic books about PR in Germany, Jahn outlined his idea of Europe as early as 1953. Dismissing the idealist traditions of the interwar years as ineffective, he emphasised the importance of functional integration. As a lesson to be learnt from the history of the League of Nations, he argued that economic integration was the key to changing 'social realities'. Thus, the Schuman plan was an important 'first step' achieved by statesmen he praised as 'realists'. However, while he perceived political actors as important, his description also implied a certain structural determinism: It was 'economic and social necessities' which forced Europeans to unite. He declared Europe to be 'a reality' that people would have to 'eventually accept'. He proclaimed that Europe might even become a nation ('Nationalidee'), quoting the Spanish writer José Ortega y Gasset.[73]

This positive vision of Europe was however only the other side of the coin of Jahn's continued fierce anti-Bolshevism: 'Moscow's expansion' and its on-going attempt to subjugate 'Europe' required the (Western) Europeans to unite, Catholics and Protestants to overcome their differences, and was the key rationale for West German re-armament.[74]

The ADK was an effective organisation for the CDU government, organising citizen support, lobbying local elites and integrat-

72. Jahn, *An Adenauers Seite. Sein Berater erinnert sich*, p. 15.
73. Jahn, *Vertrauen, Verantwortung, Mitarbeit*, pp. 17f.

74. Jahn, *An Adenauers Seite. Sein Berater erinnert sich*, p. 14.

ing refugees and former soldiers. It might even have contributed to what its official goal was, namely generating political legitimacy for the new republic, something the Weimar republic had never achieved. The ADK was closed down in 1969, after the CDU had joined a grand coalition with the SPD. By that time, Jahn was already a member of the German Parliament. In 1970, he entered the EP.[75]

Up to June 1979, Jahn held a dual mandate in the EP, i.e. he was member of both the German national parliament and the EP, and, unlike some of his MEP colleagues, he became actively involved in this arena. Jahn was spokesman of the Christian Democratic faction for foreign policy, vice-president of the committee for the association of Turkey and of the Committee for the Environment, Public Health and Consumer Protection (and member of its predecessor, the Committee for Public Health and Social Affairs). He also contributed his expertise in PR as the president of the information committee, in which the EP and the Commission collaborated to prepare the first European election campaign in 1979.[76]

From 1970 onwards, Jahn was a tireless rapporteur on environmental issues. In conjunction with the report by the Dutch Social Democrat Jacob Boersma, who wrote on water pollution, Jahn's report on air pollution was instrumental in placing the novel issue of the environment on the European agenda. The so-called 'own initiative reports', reports on issues of their own choosing, were one of the few instruments the essentially powerless EP had at the time to influence the European politics. Boersma's and Jahn's initial reports on environmental issues played an important role in encouraging the European Commission to go ahead on this dossier and prepare a 'First communication'.[77] At various instances, Jahn also used the

75. "Hans-Edgar Jahn".
76. "Hans-Edgar Jahn".
77. European Commission, First Communication of the Commission about the Community's Policy on the Environment. SEC(71)2616 final, 22 July 1971, available from: http://aei.pitt.edu/3126/01/000045_1.pdf, [7 February 2011]. On the role of the EP and Jahn in particular, with detailed references, see: J.-H. Meyer, "Green Activism. The European Parliament's Environmental Committee promoting a European Environmental Policy in the 1970s", *Journal of European Integration History* vol. 17, 2011, no. 1, pp. 73–85.

plenary to call for European action on the new issue that he deemed to be 'the most important problem of the Community'. True to his federalist convictions, Jahn rejected any arguments that there was no Treaty base for action in this new area. Europe, he argued, provided the functionally most appropriate framework for environmental policy.[78] Jahn's support for the new issue was deeply intertwined with his general political goal to advance European integration.

Speaking as an MEP in the 1970s, Jahn continued to be committed not only to European integration but also to his anti-Bolshevist agenda. When a trade agreement with the Soviet Union was discussed in 1973, Jahn refuted such cooperation, arguing that the Soviet Union had always worked against European integration, trying to undermine and destroy it. In order to strengthen its influence, the Soviet Union preferred a weak array of individual states to the strong Community Jahn thought the EC actually were at the time.[79]

Jahn also lobbied for European protection of migratory birds.[80] His efforts to place this unlikely issue on the EC agenda via an own initiative report – cooperating with bird protection groups, who had submitted a petition against the killing of small songbirds – were instrumental to convince the Commission to actually include bird protection in their programme of action. Jahn's continued lobbying activities, his parliamentary questions and reports, clearly helped pushing the dossier to eventual agreement in the Council of Ministers at the end of 1978. The birds directive he pushed for provided an important precedent the EC's engagement in nature protection. However, Jahn was not able to harvest the fruits of his efforts.

78. Hans Edgar Jahn, Speech in European Parliament, 8 May 1972, in: *Official Journal of the European Communities, Annex: Proceedings of the European Parliament* (1972) May 1972, pp. 24f.
79. Hans Edgar Jahn, Speech in European Parliament, 4 April 1973, in: *Official Journal of the European Communities, Annex: Proceedings of the European Parliament* (1973) April 1973, pp. 28f.

80. A more extensive treatment of this issue can be found in: J.-H. Meyer, "Saving Migrants. A Transnational Network supporting Supranational Bird Protection Policy in the 1970s", in: W. Kaiser, B. Leucht and M. Gehler (eds.), *Transnational Networks in Regional Integration. Governing Europe 1945–83*, Basingstoke 2010, pp. 176–198.

Conclusions: Constructing and de-constructing the good European

When trying to reconstruct Hans Edgar Jahn's biography as a 'good European', we are able to observe continuity in his ideas and convictions – pro-Europeanism and anti-Bolshevism. However, there is also ample continuity in his action and behaviour. Clearly, his studies and professional experience during the war provided him with skills in propaganda – democratically reframed and renamed PR. He had become acquainted with methods and tools that he could implement again on the new job. A behavioural trait that might be more fundamental is the way he dealt with figures of authority, notably political leaders. Both his wartime book and his autobiography are full of long quotes and expressions of reverence – to Chancellors Hitler and to Adenauer, respectively. Apparently, he admired 'great men', while his ambition was to be working close to the centre of power.

However, when changing perspective and looking at Jahn's own and his contemporaries' construction, reconstruction and deconstruction of the story of Jahn's life, we can observe different – and conflicting – narrative strategies. In the 1950s and 1960s Jahn seemed to have quite actively forgotten or pushed aside some of the ideas he had cherished until 1945. Those that were suitable, he recycled for what was still considered a worthwhile cause. Jahn was assisted in this by his compatriots and fellow Europeans who preferred not to ask critical questions in the spirit of reconstruction, democratisation and European reconciliation. It is not that this aspect of his life was completely unknown: In an article in 1957 *Der Spiegel* noted that Jahn belonged to the 'wreckage of the Third Reich' ('Strandgut des Dritten Reiches').[81] However, when *Der Stern* started framing Jahn's wartime writings – and life – in terms of deviance and guilt in 1979, this caught Jahn unawares, and he found it impossible to come up with a convincing strategy of defence.

81. "Propaganda: Wir sind schon da".

The construction and de-construction of Jahn's biography by himself and different observers – as Possing makes us aware in her chapter – points to continuities as well as the reshaping of ideas of Europe by the same people in different political contexts across the main turning points of 20th century history. As a professional cold-warrior, Jahn was able to continue advocating anti-Bolshevism and Europe. Instead of the racist image of Germanic domination of 1943, Jahn now promoted Western European integration as an economic necessity and political vision. Europe, i.e. the EC, provided a supra-national institutional framework for superior policy making, for improving the 'quality of life' via environmental policy, and for pro-tecting the cute songbirds from uncivilised Italian hunters.

Constructing the narrative of Jahn's biography also alerts us to the distinction of generations in politics, which were shaped by dif-ferent experiences and promoted different conceptions of Europe. The end of Jahn's career may mark such a generational shift – even if Jahn fiercely resisted any suggestion that he had passed his expiry date – not least by getting involved in the environmental issue that was considered most innovative at the time.

Practicing Political Biography:
Reconstructing Max Kohnstamm's Europe

Jan van der Harst
University of Groningen

Dutch-born Max Kohnstamm belongs to the leading figures in the early development of postwar European integration, and could be considered one of the founding fathers of the present European Union. Recently, his life has been documented in a political biography, written by Anjo Harryvan and the author of this contribution.[1] Kohnstamm was a close collaborator to Jean Monnet, *le père d'Europe*, the renowned activist for European unity whose life and career have been subject to intense biographical politicking, as also shown in the chapter by Kølvraa in this volume.[2] Like Monnet, Kohnstamm was not a politician: they were lobbyists *avant la lettre*, at a time that lobbying was a rare, unusual phenomenon on the European continent.

In this contribution several aspects concerning the writing of a political biography will be discussed, based on the practical experience of the Kohnstamm book. We start with the rationale behind the choice for Kohnstamm as a biographical object and how this interlinks with the biographers' historiographical background and approaches to European integration history. Hence, we provide a brief overview of the archives and sources consulted for this project, sketch the state of biographical research on our main character and investigate the most crucial influences on his European life and career.

1. A. G. Harryvan and J. van der Harst, *Max Kohnstamm. A European's Life and Work,* Baden-Baden, 2011 (originally published in Dutch under the titel *Max Kohnstamm. Leven en werk van een Europeaan,* Utrecht 2008). Both authors are historians by training and are now employed at the department of International Relations, University of Groningen, Netherlands.
2. The most ambitious Monnet biography is the one written by F. Duchêne, *Jean Monnet. The first statesman of interdependence*, New York 1994.

Why Kohnstamm?

The first fundamental question every biographer has to address before starting research is: why a book on this particular individual?
Applied to our main character, the question was rephrased as: what
arguments would justify a biography of a person like Kohnstamm,
who was not a BN'er (= *bekende Nederlander*, well- and widely-
known Dutchman)? Admittedly, the authors initially had to be
made convinced of Kohnstamm's irrefutable significance, due to the
circumstance that for most of his career he has been a 'second man',
the man behind Monnet. Would it be possible to picture Kohnstamm as a person in his own right? After careful consideration, we
decided to answer this question in the affirmative, for the following
set of reasons.

Firstly, Kohnstamm stands out because of his important pioneering work. Pioneers are generally worth investigating because of their
tendency to question existing practices and their susceptibility for
change and innovation. Kohnstamm was at the origin of several
trail-blazing political developments, both at the national and inter-
national/European level. In 1949, while working for the Ministry
of Foreign Affairs in The Hague, he was charged with the task of
drafting a memorandum on the Dutch government's policy towards
early postwar Germany.[3] Kohnstamm convincingly chose the path
of reconciliation and integration, at a time that the public perception of the big neighbour and recent enemy was still outspokenly
negative. Subsequently, in 1952, Kohnstamm was appointed the first
secretary-general of the High Authority, the supranationally constructed institutional core of the European Coal and Steel Community (ECSC). Here, he was put in charge of setting up an entirely

3. Kohnstamm entered the Foreign
Ministry in 1950. From 1948–1950
he was employed at a 'Government
commission' (called Bureau-Hirschfeld), which advised the national
government on policy issues regarding the Dutch-Indies (Indonesia) and
Germany. While most of the time,
the Bureau-Hirschfeld coordinated
its activities with the Foreign
Ministry, Kohnstamm's Germany
memorandum provoked a lot of
controversy in diplomatic circles,
because of its – in the view of many
– overly-conciliatory tone vis-à-vis
Germany.

new organisation with public servants coming from different backgrounds and cultures: *es war nie da gewesen*. In the mid-1950s, he became the driving force behind the Monnet committee, the first official lobby group for European integration. Following the signing of the Rome treaty in 1957, Kohnstamm visited the United States and convinced the Eisenhower government of the need of supporting Europe's embryonic atomic energy community (Euratom) through the donation of indispensable funds and technology. Later on, during the 1970s, he was appointed first president of the European University Institute (EUI) in Florence, and manifested himself as a member of the influential Bilderberg group[4] and Trilateral Commission.[5] During the 1980s, at the end of his active career, he refounded the *Comité-Monnet*, in the form of the Second Action Committee, which actively stimulated the realization of Europe's internal or common market. Hence, at various stages of his career, Kohnstamm was 'present at the creation'.

Secondly, the choice for Kohnstamm as a biographical object was motivated by his intellectual capacity for analysing European political and organisational challenges and solutions. Probably more than Jean Monnet, Kohnstamm manifested himself as an esteemed participant in the theoretical debate on how to structure international relations after the devastating second world war. Kohnstamm graduated as an historian, but during his study and prewar visit to the United States[6], he had developed a great interest in IR theory, which brought him into contact with the works of E.H. Carr, Reinhold Niebuhr, Clarence Streit and others. The international political thinking

4. The Bilderberg group had a secret character and worked on personal invitation. Its main concern was to improve and intensify mutual relations between Western Europe and the United States.
5. The Trilateral Commission was founded in 1973 by private citizens of Europe, Japan and North-America, with the aim of discussing common problems and challenges of democratic, industrialized areas. Kohnstamm chaired this commission from 1973–1975.
6. Max Kohnstamm studied history at the University of Amsterdam. In the period 1938–1939 he visited the United States on a study grant. He used this opportunity to travel through the country and do research on President Roosevelt's 'New Deal' policy.

of Kohnstamm developed against this background had an unmistakable idealistic intonation; he rejected the 'realist' preference for balance of power politics, arguing that such a balance tended to favour the bigger states and preclude the establishment of international rules aimed to protect minorities and less privileged actors. Even more importantly, it provided a fake safety, tenable in the short run only. Kohnstamm warned against the dangers of lawlessness and emphasized instead the creation of widely observed norms and treaties to regulate interstate relations. Although he favoured federal-supranational solutions for European problems, he was not a federalist *pur sang*. Rather than schematically desiging European integration as a process with a clear final outcome, he preferred to move ahead incrementally by taking small practical steps, looking for favourable opportunities to book the best possible results. In his view, European unification was not a linear development, but a stop and go process being in constant demand of maintenance and overhaul. Rather than a realist or federalist, Kohnstamm could in IR terms best be characterized a *pragmatic* European idealist.

A third factor was academic curiosity on the part of the authors. We are – like Kohnstamm – historians by training, and aware of the usefulness of combining our empirically oriented background with theoretical approaches derived from the discipline of International Relations. Back in the 1980s, we had been educated in the tradition of Alan Milward, belonging to a grouping of historians of European integration based at the EUI in Florence and at the London School of Economics – who were rather dismissive of the classical historiographical image of the 'great men who created Europe'. Rather than studying European integration as an inevitable process, with a steering role for some important individuals ('saints'), Milward and his followers emphasized the central position of governments and bureaucracies, whose main preoccupation at the negotiating table was to defend and promote (perceived) national interests. Only when they were able to find a common denominator of their individual preferences – mostly on social and economic issues – supranational solutions were within reach, but most of the times such a denominator proved unavailable.[7] In that respect, Milward's position was close to the intergovernmentalist school of thought, represented by political scientists like Stanley Hoffmann.[8] However, unlike traditional intergovernmentalists, Milward saw European integration not as a simple zero-sum game: national states did not necessarily 'lose' what they delegated to the supranational level. Due to their involvement in the European Community, they were in the position to perform beneficial tasks for their citizens, notably in the area of economic and social welfare, which they most probably would not have been able to deliver in the absence of integration. As a result, Europe contributed to an increase of legitimacy of governmental elites whose motivation for integration was the preservation of executive capacity at the national level, not its erosion. In other words: Europe helped to 'rescue' the nation-state.[9] In this view, the founding fathers, including Monnet and Kohnstamm, played a useful supporting role, but hardly more than that.

In doing research for this biography, we wanted to find out whether the near-neglect of individuals and ideas – deriving from the eurocritical (not eurosceptical) interpretation we had been brought up with – after all proved justifiable. We started to wonder: to what extent could Milward's almost exclusive focus on the socio-economic needs of national governments be considered sacrosanct? Should Monnet indeed be seen as an overrated individual, whose prominence in European affairs had petered out by 1954, the year of the demise of the European Defence Community (EDC)? Or is it rather exaggerated and academically unproductive to belittle the influence and ideas of the founding fathers? Hence, the biographical exercise offered in some way a framework to reflect on our own academic upbringing.

7. A. S. Milward, *The Reconstruction of Western Europe 1945–1951*, Berkely 1984.

8. S. Hoffmann, "Obstinate or obsolete? The Fate of the Nation State and the Case of Western Europe", *Daedalus*, vol. 95, 1966, pp. 862–915; S. Hoffmann, "Reflections on the Nation State in Western Europe Today", *Journal of Common Market Studies*, vol. 21, no. 1, 1982, pp. 21–37.

9. A. S. Milward, *The European Rescue of the Nation-State*, London 1992; a highly accessible introduction to Milward's theoretical thinking is: A. S. Milward et al., *The Frontier of National Sovereignty. History and Theory, 1945–1992*, London 1994, pp. 1–32.

The good thing of our background as disciples of Milward and writing this book was that we never could be accused – and in fact never *have* been accused – of writing a hagiography of our main character. Which is of course a perennial danger when working on a biography, perhaps even more so if it concerns – like in this case – somebody who was still alive at the time we undertook the research.[10]

As it turned out, the work on the Kohnstamm biography had considerable instructive value for the two authors. The shift from a macro- to a micro-level historical analysis, that is involved in doing biographical research made us realise that European integration is much more than a member state-directed project on socio-economic benefits and material gains. Thus far, we had studied Europe as an interesting and important level of governance, which could be analysed impartially, but in doing so we had neglected the impact of individuals and ideas, as well as the impact of, what may be called, emotion or dedication. For Kohnstamm, Europe was not just a neutral level of governance but a question of life and death, or better said: the difference between war and peace. The biography thus taught us that *persons* should be taken into consideration as well, if we want to make a balanced investigation of the history of European integration. After all, the early postwar creation of a supranational Europe was not self-evident or unavoidable. Europe is not just a market-driven phenomenon or propelled by an automatic logic. Political ideals and inventive plans were called for to get European integration going and subsequently to prevent it from backlash. From this perspective, founding fathers are actors who deserve to be studied.

Before Harryvan and I were invited to start the work on Kohnstamm, several other candidates had been approached, among whose two prominent Dutch journalists.[11] Eventually, due to the emphasis which obviously had to be laid on the history of Euro-

10. The biography was published in 2008. Max Kohnstamm died on 20 October 2010 in Amsterdam at the age of 96.
11. One of the two is the journalist-historian Geert Mak, who had a major success with his international

bestseller *In Europe: Travels through the twentieth century*, New York 2007, which was probably the decisive reason why he could not commit himself to writing the Kohnstamm biography.

pean integration and its (institutional) intricacies, the decision was made to attribute the biographical task to two historians specialized in the topic. The biographers had got to know Kohnstamm some time before when working on an interview project with ten Dutch European policy-makers in the period 1945–1975.[12] At that occasion, an atmosphere of mutual trust had been created. The actual invitation for writing the biography came from Prof. Hans Daalder, a leading political scientist in the Netherlands, who had been a professor at the European University Institute in Florence at the time of Kohnstamm's EUI presidency. Kohnstamm had intimated Daalder about his biographical intentions, and Daalder had taken up the hint.[13]

Archives, sources and audience

The text we have written is based on a wide variety of written and oral sources. We (and our research assistant Ms. Geertje Tolsma) visited a great many archives in the Netherlands and abroad, most notably: the Ministry of Foreign Affairs, the National Archive and the Royal Family Archive[14] in The Hague; the Historical Archives of the European Union in Florence; the archives of the Dutch-Reformed Church; the Jean Monnet Foundation in Lausanne; and private archives of former colleagues and contemporaries of Kohnstamm. We held interviews with individuals who had got to know Kohnstamm in various stages of his life and career: family, friends, colleagues and contemporaries, both from national and European backgrounds. And, although the biography is unauthorized (see the concluding remarks), Kohnstamm has helped us enormously with

12. The ten interviews are collected in the volume A.G. Harryvan, J. van der Harst and S. van Voorst (eds.), *Voor Nederland en Europa. Politici en ambtenaren over het Nederlandse Europabeleid en de Europese integratie, 1945–1975*, Amsterdam 2001. The interview with Max Kohnstamm is on the pages 81–119.

13. Hans Daalder is the biographer of Dutch former Prime Minister Willem Drees (published in several volumes).

14. In the first years after the War (1945–1948), before starting his work for the Ministry of Foreign Affairs, the young Max Kohnstamm was employed as a private assistant to Queen Wilhelmina of the Netherlands (grandmother of the present Queen Beatrix). It was his first job.

executing our research. We had unlimited access to his private documents and conducted eleven two-day interview sessions with our main character. Most of the interviews took place in the study room of his home in the hamlet Fenffe in the Belgian Ardennes. To protect our academic independence, we declined the kind invitation of the Kohnstamms to stay overnight at their place and chose instead for small country hotels in the neighbourhood. This was, in fact, far from an ordeal, given the possibilities it offered to make 'reflective' strolls in the hilly surroundings of Fenffe, particularly when Kohnstamm took his daily afternoon nap.

We managed to receive funding for doing our biographical research from various sources: the Van den Berch van Heemstede Stichting (a private foundation subsidizing projects of social relevance) in The Hague, the ICOG research institute at the University of Groningen and the European University Institute in Florence.

The audience we had in mind when constructing the narrative of the book consisted of academics, policy-makers, civil servants, journalists, and every citizen with an interest in politics, history and European integration.

State of biographical research

How could the state of biographical research in relation to Max Kohnstamm be defined? Although he has been portrayed extensively in numerous newspaper articles and interviews, and despite the fact that separate phases of his life have been documented in 'letter books'[15] and annotated abstracts of his European diaries[16], the pre-

15. Collections of correspondence, in the form of edited letters sent and received by Max Kohnstamm in various stages of his life: *"Nog is er geen oorlog." Briefwisseling tussen Max en Philip Kohnstamm*, Amsterdam 2001; *Brieven mit "Hitler's Herrengefängnis" 1942–1944*, Amsterdam 2005.

16. M.L.L. Segers, *Europese dagboeken van Max Kohnstamm. Augustus 1953–September 1957*, Amsterdam 2008; and the second volume: September 1957–February 1963, Amsterdam 2011. A typoscript of the complete version of the original diaries (without annotation) can be found in the Historical Archives of the European Union in Florence.

sent work is the first – and thus far only – monographic biography on Kohnstamm. It seems safe to assume that at least in the short run another Dutch-language biography on Kohnstamm is unlikely to appear. Apart from Europe's alleged lack of popularity in the contemporary domestic arena, this could be attributed to Kohnstamm's relatively low profile as a public figure in the Netherlands. He lived here during the first 38 years of his life, until his departure for Luxembourg in 1952, never to take up Dutch residence again. Moreover, rather than a media-attracting politician, Kohnstamm was a man working behind the screens. Admittedly, after his retirement he has appeared regularly on Dutch national television to give his highly respected opinions on international and European events, but it has scarcely brought him the status of *bekende Nederlander*. As this book's introductory example of Sir Geoffrey de Freitas showed, publishing houses are not eager to commit themselves to writing without a clear national audience, most likely for cost-effective reasons. A biography on Kohnstamm in a foreign language seems a more likely perspective – as a matter of fact, an English translation has been published in 2011 with Nomos in Baden-Baden, Germany (see footnote 1).

Reconstructing Max Kohnstamm's Europe

Who was Max Kohnstamm? And what were the dominating influences on his European life and career?

What counted in the first place were Kohnstamm's family roots. On the one hand, there was the academic background of his father, an intellectual *uomo universale*, who had started as a physicist[17], had been appointed professor in thermodynamics, and later moved to the disciplines of philosophy, theology and educational theory. Even nowadays, more than fifty years after his death, Philip Kohnstamm is considered one of the most prominent Dutch education-

17. Philip Kohnstamm was a student of J.D. van der Waals at the University of Amsterdam. In 1910 Van der Waals won the Nobel Prize in Physics for his work on an equation of state for gases and liquids.

alists ever, with his pioneering research in adult and girls' education and retraining of the unemployed. On the other hand, there was the corporate background of Max' mother, the Kessler family: mother's father (Max' grandfather) was one of the founders of the Royal Dutch oil company (later to become the Royal Dutch Shell), while two brothers of mother Kohnstamm (Max' uncles) were the CEO's of Shell and the Hoogoven steel works. Max Kohnstamm thus belonged to the privileged bourgeois establishment of the capital Amsterdam. Especially his father had a profound impact on his personal thinking and development. During the interwar period, Philip Kohnstamm played an active role as a member of the 'Restore Europe' committee, a transnationally operating pressure group which had openly condemned the humiliating treatment of Germany in the aftermath of the Treaty of Versailles (1919). In the early 1920s, Max' father wrote a comprehensive report on the French reparation claims and the alleged lack of capacity of the French economy to absorb the large amount of payments demanded from the Weimar republic. Instead of countries unilaterally degrading the Germans, he pleaded for a European solution to deal with the problem on a fair, impartial and multilateral basis.[18] It was exactly the theme Max Kohnstamm would be dealing with in his own career during the postwar period, and in many respects he followed the example set by his father. Moreover, through his father, the young Max had the opportunity of meeting many prominent individuals, including the scientists Albert Einstein and Paul Ehrenfest, who came to visit the Kohnstamm family at their Amsterdam home. Max also borrowed to a considerable degree from his father's analyses and preferences concerning national political issues. Philip Kohnstamm, after having been involved in the progressive-liberal *Vrijzinnig Democratische Bond* during the interwar period, decided in 1945 to enter the newly founded social-democratic party (*Partij van de Ar-*

18. P. Kohnstamm, *Hoe mijn "Bijbels personalisme" ontstond*, Haarlem 1952, pp. 12–14.

beid), a merger of prewar socialist, liberal and progressive christian movements. These steps were followed by his son Max, who stayed on as member of the social-democratic PvdA until the mid-1970s, when he resigned out of discontentment with what he considered an overly conciliatory approach by the party leadership towards the anti-democratic regime of the German Democratic Republic.

From the above, it turns out that in terms of periodisation the year 1945 is not the typical dividing line for which it is often held in the history of European integration. Many of the ideas put forward by Kohnstamm during the 1950s and later were conceived at a much earlier stage of his life, as shows the profound impact of the Treaty of Versailles and the German reparation issue.

Secondly, there was the war experience. Notwithstanding the historical continuity observed above, the German occupation played a crucial role in Max Kohnstamm's life and thinking. During the Second World War, Kohnstamm was imprisoned twice, both times on Dutch territory, in the detention camps of Amersfoort and Haaren/Gestel. He had been a target for German occupation authorities, because of his partly Jewish origins (his father had a Jewish background) and because of 'subversive' activities he had developed as president of the students' union at the University of Amsterdam, just before the War. In this position he had made critical statements about the emerging Nazi regime and the inherent dangers it brought to Europe and the Netherlands. Especially, detention camp Amersfoort held a cruel regime and confronted him with the worst side of human beings' character. It brought him considerable physical hardship, but also taught him the lesson that lawlessness, in whatever form, had to be eradicated and that extreme nationalism – the root of the evil inflicted by Nazi Germany – had to be curtailed. Hereby, the mistakes made in Versailles after WW I should never be repeated again. Supranational institutions with independent authorities were needed to overcome the European disarray and facilitate peaceful relations between states. In Kohnstamm's view, European integration was the proper answer to war. In a supranational construction, Germany could be given a place as partner on an equal basis. Kohnstamm developed a special affinity with the German issue.

As referred to above, in 1949 he wrote an influential policy report for the Dutch Ministry of Foreign Affairs on the future of Dutch-German relations. Kohnstamm's position and excellent reputation in postwar Germany were based on his forgiving nature and his early recognition of the need of German involvement in the European construction. Later on, in the Monnet committee Kohnstamm was made responsible for the contacts with the Federal Republic. In this capacity he built up close links with the top leadership of the christian-democratic and social-democratic parties: Adenauer, Erhard, Etzel, Ollenhauer and Wehner.

Thirdly, highly influential on Kohnstamm's life and career were the years with Jean Monnet. Kohnstamm met Monnet for the first time in the summer of 1950 during the initial discussions on the Schuman plan. Monnet made an unforgettable and lasting impression on him. He had a strong personal charisma – which Kohnstamm himself lacked -, he had developed comprehensive ideas on Europe originating from his prewar and wartime experiences, and he disposed of an enormous network, both in Europe and the United States. From 1950 on, Monnet helped to finetune Kohnstamm's early supranationalist convictions. Monnet also taught Kohnstamm how to perform a successful lobby, and how to do networking and generate influence by pulling ropes behind the screens. Within the Monnet committee, the two men performed all sorts of pioneering work and introduced new techniques. For example, to prepare their meetings, Monnet and Kohnstamm held simulation games, whereby Monnet played himself and Kohnstamm the role of Adenauer or Erhard. Back then, such techniques were regarded as original and innovative. Kohnstamm learned a great deal from Monnet, but the relationship between the two also worked the other way around. Contrary to Monnet, Kohnstamm was fluent in German, which facilitated his entrée in German politics. Kohnstamm was also a better writer and organizer than Monnet, the latter being a man of ideas with minor interest in the details. Based on these observations, we may argue that Monnet was not independently the 'father of Europe', as he certainly would not have been able to do the lobby work on his own. In his memoirs Monnet wrote the following about

Kohnstamm's contribution as secretary-general to the incipient activities of ECSC's High Authority:

'Really exceptional qualities were required to interpret and give shape to the thoughts and wishes of a collegiate body made up of nine men from six different countries, speaking four different languages – not to mention their differences of character and upbringing. I had never dared to hope that we would find a single person capable of fulfilling this role, which was really a task for the European of the future – or rather, which recalled the European of the Renaissance. Kohnstamm was able to understand the French, the Germans, and the British in their own languages, as well as his compatriots in theirs; he was also familiar with their literature and their press. The misunderstandings to which we were liable owing to ignorance of each other's customs held no pitfalls for him: he was an invaluable intermediary. Everyone was impressed by his great open-mindedness and his deep moral qualities. I found in him a colleague and a friend, unshakeably and permanently loyal.'[19]

Monnet was not the first and definitely not the last to praise Kohnstamm's highstanding moral qualities and cosmopolitan outlook.

Returning to the question of which broader historical insights may be gained from practicing political biography, it is clear that the study of Kohnstamm yielded additional insights into European integration processes. A few examples may be mentioned here. During our research on Kohnstamm we discovered that the Monnet committee (also known as the Action Committee for the United States of Europe, functioning from 1955–1975) has probably been less successful than has often been assumed. The committee was certainly influential in lobbying European political circles, but influence is not the same as booking visible results. Especially after 1958, during the De Gaulle years, the committee became seriously hampered in its possibilities. Even in the early years, 1955–1958, concrete results were scarce, although Kohnstamm's personal lobby certain-

19. J. Monnet, *Memoirs*, New York 1978, p. 376.

ly helped to make the SPD (*Sozialdemokratische Partei Deutschlands*) more European-minded and to make the Treaty of Rome acceptable to Chancellor Adenauer. However, the committee's over-emphasis on Euratom, while at the same time overlooking the importance of the EEC and the common market, could be added to the debit side of the Monnet committee.

Compared to this, Kohnstamm's lesser known and lower profiled Second Action Committee (SAC) during the 1980s had some remarkable achievements. While the SAC had several prominent politicians in its ranks, such as Helmut Schmidt, Edward Heath, Jacques Chaban-Delmas and Leo Tindemans, it was Kohnstamm who manifested himself as the main driving force behind the committee. He entertained close contacts with the President of the European Commission Jacques Delors. In the research on our book, we found out that Kohnstamm played an important role in convincing Delors of adopting a comprehensive programme to revitalize Europe after the years of stagnation and eurosclerosis, by concentrating on three priority issues: 1. focus on an appealing, widely supported project: the common market (and not a monetary union or a defence community, Delors' initial priorities); 2. include decision-making procedures in the reforms: possibilities for majority-voting had to be extended; 3. fix a time schedule for creating the common market; selecting 1992 as the target year was an idea which originally sprang from Kohnstamm's mind. Of course, success has many fathers and a great many others (including the European Round Table, the Dutch multinational company Philips, Lord Cockfield, Altiero Spinelli and his Kangaroo group, the bigger European countries) claim to be the inventors of these far-reaching plans and developments, but Kohnstamm's contacts with Delors and other prominent policy-makers proved to be extremely helpful and influential. This is also confirmed by Delors himself and people around him.[20]

20. J. Delors (with J.-L. Arnaud), *Mémoires*, Paris 2004, pp. 184–185; interview with Dr. J. Vignon (Brussels, 4 May 2004).

Concluding remarks

The biographical form was in our case the only feasible option open: Kohnstamm had proved to be too much of a perfectionist (always inclined to endlessly reformulate his own and others' texts) and was probably too insecure about his own historical importance to make him consider writing an autobiography or memoirs. Interestingly, his perfectionism was also one of the reasons why we opted for an *unauthorized* form of the biography: at an early stage of the process Kohnstamm refrained voluntarily from becoming involved in the process of editing contents. This was a matter of 'self-protection' on both sides. Before we had put even one word on paper, already some insiders warned us that he would 'undoubtedly be highly disappointed with the final result', not because of us, but because of deep-seated reservations of a more general and structural nature, connected to his own mindset. After publication of the biography, Kohnstamm confided us that having read the book '[he] did not come across anything [he] did not recognize'. This was an observation which we rightly or not – at least encouraged by positive reviews in newspapers and journals – have taken as a specially worded compliment.

Controversies on matters of content and interpretation are probably the most tricky ones for biographers working on a (then) living person, but again, we have managed to avoid this pitfall by reaching a timely agreement on Kohnstamm's editorial non-involvement. This gave us the advantage of full independence in drafting our own conclusions. For the rest, the authors highly benefited from Kohnstamm's excellent memory and his unreservedness about sharing recollections. During and after the many interview sessions, he gave us the opportunity to get to know him as a person – with all his strenghts and vulnerabilities – and provided us with inside information which otherwise would have been difficult to be obtained.

The authors opted for a cradle-to-grave biography, because Kohnstamm's family background and earlier years as a young student appeared to be crucial elements in understanding the choices he made during his later career. Kohnstamm's strong European convictions are impossible to grasp without taking into account these formative experiences. A non-chronological approach like the one proposed by Birgitte Possing in her contribution to this book, would have produced a picture different from the one we wanted to sketch of Max Kohnstamm.

The choice for a *political* biography can be largely explained from our own academic background, the (history of) international relations. This does not imply that the book ignores the *person* Max Kohnstamm or his personal life, but what we have focused on is the *interrelationship* between work and personal life. This is why the subtitle of the book is called '*A European's Life and Work*', as he represents an increasing population of voluntarily expatriated civil servants who went to work for the new European and international organisations created in the post-war period.

Part III
Biography and Intellectual Politics

Europe as a Community of Values:

Hermann Heller, European Fascism and Weimar Democracy

Karl Christian Lammers
Copenhagen University

The German Social democratic constitutional thinker Hermann Heller stands out as a protagonist for the European democratic state and for defending its form as social mass democracy against upcoming fascism and fascist rule. The new democratic constitution and state in post-war Germany was placed in this broader European context. The Weimar Republic, established in August 1919, and its liberal parliamentary- democratic political system formally brought equality, universal suffrage and civil rights to the broad masses, and thus also to the Social Democratic Party (SPD) that became the largest political party. Yet Weimar democracy was, as it has been shown[1], heavily contested from the political right as well as from the political left. Contestation did not only take place politically but also physically as was the case during the Spartacus rising 1919, the Kapp-putsch 1920, the Ruhr-revolt 1920, the Hitler-Putsch 1923 and the uprising in Hamburg 1923. Weimar democracy was also contested theoretically and fundamentally by political thinkers and intellectuals who questioned this interpretation and implementation of political liberalism and pluralism, as this chapter illustrate.

---

1. Cf. above all the brilliant analysis by H. Mommsen, "Die verspielte Freiheit. Der Weg der Republik von Weimar in den Untergang 1918 bis 1933", *Propyläen Geschichte Deutsch-lands*, vol. 8, Berlin 1989; see also P. Longerich, *Deutschland 1918–1933. Die Weimarer Republik*, Hannover 1995.

This conflictual situation in many ways reflects a general tendency which might be seen overall in Europe and most European states in the interwar period. Many European democracies, especially the recently established, had since 1919 come under heavy political pressure and revolts, and this had until the year 1940 resulted in the downfall of around 16 democratic political systems.[2]

Anti- democratic and anti-liberal tendencies and ideas were flourishing in the new Weimar Germany, and the conception of 'Antidemocratic thinking' (Antidemokratisches Denken)[3] has for years been used to characterise the predominant intellectual and political climate in Germany in the interwar period. Among the well-known intellectuals of the Weimar constitutional battle were people like Ernst Jünger, Moeller van den Bruck, Othmar Spann, Oswald Spengler, as well as Carl Schmitt that all criticised the architecture of Weimar democracy and its institutions. But what is often forgotten is that this was only one dimension of the discussion among intellectuals and politicians of the new state and its political system. Democratic or pro-democratic thinking had a longer history, especially in social democratic, socialist and liberal milieus, where reforms and refinements of democracy were continuously discussed.[4]

Hermann Heller is often presented as the Social Democratic alternative to the liberal constitutional thinker Hans Kelsen and the conservative thinkers Carl Schmitt and Othmar Spann.[5] As a political and legal thinker Heller can be seen in a broad European per-

2. Cf. M. Mazower, *Dark Continent. Europe's Twentieth Century*, London 1998; K. C. Lammers, "Fascismens og diktaturets tidsalder", in: B. Fonnesbech-Wulff and P. Roslyng-Jensen(eds.), *Historiens Lange Linjer*, Copenhagen 2006.

3. Cf. K. Sontheimer, *Antidemokratisches Denken in der Weimarer Republik. Die politischen Ideen des deutschen Nationalismus zwischen 1918 und 1933* (Munich 1962).

4. Cf. Sontheimer, *Antidemokratisches Denken*, passim and H. A. Winkler, *Der Schein der Normalität. Arbeiter und Arbeiterbewegung in der Weimarer Republik 1924 bis 1930*, Berlin/Bonn 1985, pp. 367f.

5. Cf. D. Dyzenhaus, *Legality and Legitimacy. Carl Schmitt, Hans Kelsen and Hermann Heller in Weimar*, Oxford 1997.

spective defending what he saw as the European democratic state against upcoming authoritarian and fascist tendencies. In the late 1920s, he developed one of the best informed and most penetrating analyses of Italian fascism and Mussolini's state and he became acknowledged as an engaged protagonist for the democratic and constitutional state (Sozialer Rechtsstaat).[6] However, although he was a theoretician, he did not isolate himself from intervening in the political reality of the Weimar state. As this chapter will demonstrate, the biographical narrative of Heller's life allows us to capture more concretely the political struggles and dilemmas of the supporters of the social democratic constitutional order in Weimar Germany and inject this into its broader European perspective. It will do so by exploring and contextualising the political thinking of Hermann Heller as an example of the pro-democratic thinking also characteristic of the Weimar republic. Following a brief introduction of Heller's personal and ideological background, it will review Heller's analysis of European fascism and his idea of the *Sozialer Rechtsstaat* (social constitutional state). In its final part, it will map out some of the practical political aspects of these views within the context of the deteriorating Weimar state.

Personal and ideological background

Hermann Heller was born in 1891 in a Jewish family living in the province Teschen in the former Habsburg monarchy. He volunteered in the Great War on the German side and was wounded. He studied law and political science at the Austrian universities of Vienna, Graz and Innsbruck, as well as at Kiel in Germany. In 1919 he completed his preparation for a professorship qualifying Doktor habilitation under the supervision of the well known constitutional expert Gustav Radbruch at the University of Kiel. The topic of his habilitation was about G.W.F. Hegel and the national idea of power state in Germany ('Hegel und der nationale Machtstaatsgedanke in Deutsch-

6. Cf. W. Schluchter, *Entscheidung für den sozialen Rechtsstaat. Hermann Heller und die staatstheoretische* *Diskussion in der Weimarer Republik*, Cologne 1968.

land').[7] At the same time he had joined the SPD, belonging to the party's right wing. Due to this political engagement, however, he had had difficulties getting a regular professorship (Lehrstuhl) in the conservative German universities. He therefore, at first, taught at various academies and folk high schools (Volkshochschulen) relating to the German labour movement. This experience became important to him because he regarded the chances for stable democratic development in Germany as a question of education (Bildungsfrage), as, to him, politics and education were closely interlinked. Political education (politische Bildung) to democracy was a priority. He at last succeeded in getting a professorship in 1928 at the university in Berlin, where he was appointed extraordinary professor (ausserplanmässiger Professor), and later in 1930 he finally got his chair in public law at the Goethe University in Frankfurt am Main.

As member of the SPD, Heller had become part of one of the major political movements of Weimar Germany. The SPD benefited politically from the new Weimar constitution, and the party played a significant political role in Weimar Germany at least until 1930 when the party had to give up the coalition government ('Grosse Koalition'). Meanwhile, the state of democracy was discussed and contested within the SPD, where some thinkers from the left wing like Max Adler, Ernst Fraenkel and Franz Neumann criticized the democratic state and system for still being a class state. But other Social democrats engaged themselves in the struggle for democracy in its parliamentary and cooperating form. Among the few political and constitutional scholars who engaged themselves in the democratic struggle were Otto Kirchheimer and, practically unknown outside Germany, Hermann Heller.

Politically and theoretically, Hermann Heller belonged to the 'revisionist' branch, the 'Hofgeismar-Kreis' that was part of the youth organisation, the Jungsozialisten, in the SPD. Inside the party he was a rather controversial thinker because of his reflections on nation and

7. H. Heller, *Hegel und der nationale Machtstaatsgedanke in Deutschland*, Leipzig/Berlin 1921.

state and his dismissal of socialist internationalism. He had in his writings tried to reconcile socialism and nation,[8] recognizing nation and state as acceptable realities, thus contesting the traditional Marxist view of the state that was otherwise dominant among German social democrats at the time. In Heller's wording 'socialism did not mean the upheaval of the state, rather its refinement. The worker gets the more close to socialism, the more he gets close to the state.'[9]

In his writings and teaching Heller engaged himself in the struggle over the Weimar constitution, for the constitutional state and argued for its social dimensions. His principal work in this topic 'Staatslehre' – 'The doctrine of state' – was however not finished and first published posthumously in 1934.[10] During the political crisis of the Weimar Republic in the 1930s, Hermann Heller politically stood up against the authoritarian dictatorship led by Franz von Papen, and he also fought Hitler's upcoming National Socialist movement. Nonetheless, after the establishment of the National Socialist regime in January 1933, he decided to stay in Germany. That was however not possible as he was placed on the regime's list of proscription. As a Jewish Social Democrat he was, according to the Nazi regime's 'Gesetz zur Wiederherstellung des Berufsbeamtentums' (Civil servants law) from April 7 1933 dismissed from his position and professorship. He therefore chose to leave Germany and stayed in exile in Madrid in Spain. He died later that year in Spain.

European diagnosis and prescription

In the middle of the 1920s Heller began to intervene in discussions on democracy and state. He critizised Hans Kelsen's liberal concept of constitutional state (Rechtsstaat) as just formal and introduced instead his concept of 'Sozialer Rechtsstaat' (social constitutional state) as a state and government bound by the rule of law and legitimized by those who were ruled. This state was part of the social

8. "Sozialismus und Nation", 1925, printed in: M. Draht et al (eds.), *Hermann Heller, Gesammelte Schriften*, vol. I-III, Leiden 1971 (here vol. 1).

9. "Sozialismus und Staat", 1931, in: Draht et al., *Heller, Gesammelte Schriften* , vol. 1.

10. H. Heller, *Staatslehre*, Leiden 1934.

reality with its promises of equality.[11] This is not the place to continue discussing Heller's constitutional thinking in depth.[12] It is however on this background that Heller viewed European fascism as threatening the democratic constitutional state, its separation of powers and guarantee of civil rights.

The focus will be on Heller's considerations in regards to Europe, and they are mainly dealing with two topics. Firstly, his analysis of Italian and international fascism which he regarded as a serious challenge and threat to European democracy. He claimed that fascism threatened the community of values ('Wertegemeinschaft'), which in his eyes should support the 'social mass democracy' ('soziale Massendemokratie').[13]

Secondly, he operated with a general concept of European democracy in comparison with other forms of government. In his writings he was the protagonist of the 'sozialer Rechtsstaat' ('social constitutional state'), although his thoughts seemed not thoroughly consistent. He emphasised the community of values ('Wertegemeinschaft') which had to be the basis of social mass democracy in Europe, and he saw it threatened by fascism. A similar position might be found later in his criticism of totalitarianism, as he saw it represented in fascism in Italy and in bolshevism in the Soviet Union that, to him, were the two twin brothers of totalitarianism. Totalitarianism was the threat to his concept of democracy.

The politics of the German SPD to the upcoming of German fascism in the form of the National Socialist Party (NSDAP) is one of the most controversial issues in the party's history. The SPD saw itself as anti-fascist, it recognized already in 1923 the threat and danger

11. Cf. Dyzenhaus, *Legality and Legitimacy*, pp. 161f; W. Schluchter, *Entscheidung für den sozialen Rechtsstaat*.
12. Cf. also J. Blau, *Sozialdemokratische Staatslehre in der Weimarer Republik. Darstellung und Untersuchung der staatstheoretischen*
Konzeptionen von Hermann Heller, Ernst Fraenkel und Otto Kirchheimer, Marburg 1980; C. Müller and I. Staff (eds.), *Staatslehre in der Weimarer Republik. Hermann Heller zu Ehren*, Baden-Baden 1984.
13. H. Heller, *Europa und der Fascismus*. Berlin/Leipzig 1929, p. 11.

from National Socialism to Weimar's democracy[14], and it tried politically with its policy of toleration ('Tolerierungspolitik') to the bourgeois Brüning-government since the September elections 1930 to prevent the German Nazi party the NSDAP from coming to power in Germany. In 1933, the SPD however lost this fight with Hitler's ascent to the chancellorship, a fight lost almost without fighting. It opposed thereafter the new Nazi government on legal grounds, but that did not secure it and the party became forbidden already in June 1933.[15] The SPD and its leadership have been heavily criticized for underestimating the power of National Socialism and for not fighting it, among others by Danish politician Hartvig Frisch discussed in the chapter by Karen Gram-Skjoldager and Thorsten Borring Olesen in this book. Yet, although this criticism might have been valid, it seems too insensitive and unsubtle in light of SPD attitudes and politics. I shall try to illustrate this through the case of Hermann Heller.

The SPD regarded National Socialism as a German version of fascism, but also as totalitarian, anti-democratic, and the twin brother to bolshevism. Shortly after the Italian fascists came to power in 1922, the SPD criticised the Italian socialist party for not aligning itself with the liberal democratic parts of the bourgeoisie against fascism. The historical lesson to be learnt was that socialists should avoid driving liberal and democratic bourgeois parties into the arms of fascism. Rather, the SPD should compromise with them in order to regain them in the fight for democracy against fascism. It has often been overlooked that the SPD was in fact well informed about the development in Italy and thus about fascism as the most dangerous threat to democracy.

14. Cf. K. C. Lammers, "Antifascismen i SPD. Fascismeopfattelse og imødegåelse af den tyske fascisme op til 1933", in: H. Löe and J. L. Kristensen (eds.), *Kritisk fascismeforskning i Norden*, Aalborg 1982, p. 326.

15. Cf. W. Pyta, *Gegen Hitler und für die Republik. Die Auseinandersetzung der deutschen Sozialdemokratie mit der NSDAP in der Weimarer Republik*, Düsseldorf 1989.

This also holds true for Heller, who actually went to Italy in the spring of 1928 for six months to study fascism and what he called the 'false alternative' to democracy: the 'false' alternative he saw in Benito Mussolini's fascist dictatorship, established in 1925. As he viewed it, the existing democratic European state was going through a difficult and dangerous crisis where fascism presented itself as a model for a renewal of the state, and he asked himself what fascism might tell 'politically ill Europe':[16] Could the European state learn from fascism, and if so, what could it learn?

He published his analysis under the title 'Europa und der Fascismus' (Europe and Fascism) the following year, in 1929, when Italian fascism had found imitation movements in several European countries like Spain, Portugal, Greece, Poland and Hungary and when German fascism National Socialism was ascending, but politically was still a small and ignorable minority. Heller's analysis is practically unknown, but in my view it actually constitutes one of the best informed and most penetrating contemporary analyses of Italian fascism, its ideology and practice from the outside,[17] and Heller is to be looked upon as one of the few contemporaries, who very early recognized fascism, fascist dictatorship and National Socialism as a challenge and threat to the concept of the European democratic state.

Heller had visited Italy earlier and based on another visit to Italy in 1928, he – confronted with fascist rule – believed that the European state urgently needed renovation as fascism offered itself as a model and challenge: 'We therefore,' said Heller, 'have every reason to ask the question what fascism can tell politically ill Europe.'[18] What could Europe learn from fascism, asked Heller with reference to what Italian fascist leader Giuseppe Bottai had postulated in his book 'Internationaler Fascismus' (International Fascism, 1928): 'Fascism creates the new ideals, opens up new frontiers for political thinking, works out new constitutional law, accomplishes the experiment with its own programs and offers civilized nations

16. Heller, *Europa und der Fascismus*, p. 5.
17. Heller, *Europa und der Fascismus*, quote pp. 5–6, see also "Rechtsstaat oder Diktatur?" (1929), in: Draht et al. (eds.); *Herman Heller, Gesammelte Schriften*, vol. 2, p. 443f.
18. Heller, *Europa und der Fascismus*, p. 5.

a total of ideas and works that might be enough to satisfy this century and give it character and name.'[19] Heller of course did not share this view because he saw fascism and fascist dictatorship very differently. He admitted that fascism at first in some regards was of a socialist outlook; but as a ruling ideology fascism exhibited inhuman use of power.

Although Heller had the impression that a politically satisfying remodelling of social mass democracy seemed not to be successful, he dissociated himself from Carl Schmitt who had declared fascist dictatorship as the 'new and real democracy'. In Heller's view, Carl Schmitt wrongly presented dictatorship as the 'specific modern form of state'. Schmitt declared parliamentarian democracy as dead and saw in the fascist dictatorship the 'real' democracy ('wahre' Demokratie), based on the 'uniformity of will' ('Vereinheitlichung des Willens').[20]

With fascist Italy as example Heller tried to demonstrate that although pseudo-democratic institutions (parliament with Senate and Chamber of deputies) still existed, they only constituted a 'parliamentarian facade': parliament was out of foreign regards kept as 'democratic decoration' or in the words of Mussolini as 'toys'.[21] Italy was in reality a dictatorship that had determinedly destroyed all elements of a constitutional democracy. As he viewed Mussolini's fascist dictatorship that had been implemented in Italy around 1928, it had defeated and dissolved liberalism, pluralism, democracy and socialism, especially mass democracy. Instead it in reality had installed the one-party-state, the *stato totalitario* with its strict and unconstitutional control over society and people. For that reason he claimed that Europe could not expect a renewal of its political ideas from fascism. Revolutionary fascism as accomplished in the fascist dictatorship had destroyed fundamental and vital democratic issues: above all the constitutional state (Rechtsstaat), its division of powers and its guarantees of fundamental civil rights, and it had placed

19. Heller, *Europa und der Fascismus*, p. 5.
20. Quotations from Heller, *Rechtsstaat oder Demokratie* (p. 3) and Heller, *Europa und der Fascismus* (p. 30), in: Draht et al., *Heller, Gesammelte Schriften*, vol. 2.
21. Heller, *Europa und der Fascismus*, p. 80 (where Mussolini is also quoted).

action before moral standards ('bei welchem der Akt immer der Norm vorausgeht',), whereas in the constitutional state action complied with certain moral standards. In a precise sentence he distinguished fascism from democracy: 'The unresisting standard was replaced by the normless will, the powerless law by the lawless power' ('Die willenlose Norm wurde ersetzt durch den normlosen Willen, das machtlose Recht durch die rechtlose Macht').[22] To Heller fascism and fascist rule thus broke with the central democratic principle of 'through standards regulated power' ('normierte Macht').[23] This was accomplished through the power resources of the fascist state: the party, the corporations and the state bureaucracy.

Fascism and fascist dictatorship as presented in Italy thus had eliminated fundamentals of democracy and threatened the core of democracy in Europe: In his view the social constitutional state ('sozialer Rechtsstaat'). That was even a warning against Hitler and his National Socialism, who was inspired by Italian fascism and in fascism saw an ideal to be followed in Germany.

Against this background, Heller claimed that fascism was not a solution to Europe's political crisis, and he appealed to the bourgeoisie not to succumb to the fascination from fascism and fascist dictatorship. He expressed these views in his writings and even in the Social Democratic party's daily journal Vorwärts[24], where he again and again warned against rising fascism in Germany, and the title of his articles made his message very clear, such as 'The Danger from Fascism' ('Die Gefahr des Faschismus') and 'Fight Fascism' ('Kampf dem Faschismus'), both from 1930.[25]

To Heller, the solution to the political crisis in Europe was to be found in the refinement of democracy to a 'social constitutional state' ('sozialer Rechtsstaat'). To his view, democracy was not only a 'constitutional state (Rechtsstaat)' ruled by law, democracy was even

---

22. Heller, *Europa und der Fascismus*, p. 69.
23. Heller, *Europa und der Fascismus*, p. 66.
24. Cf. H. Heller, "Die Gefahr des Faschismus", *Vorwärts* 17 November, 1930.

25. Cf. K-E. Lönne, *Faschismus als Herausforderung. Die Auseinandersetzung der "Roten Fahne" und des "Vorwärts" mit dem italienischen Faschismus*, Cologne 1981, p. 302.

a political community of values (Wertegemeinschaft). If this community did not exist there was neither a community of will (Willensgemeinschaft) nor a community of law (Rechtsgemeinschaft). It was particularly the dissolution of the so-called community of values that to Heller was the real reason for the European crisis.[26]

In 1929 he had published an article 'Constitutional State or Dictatorship?' ('Rechtsstaat oder Diktatur?') where he defended the 'democratic and social constitutional state' against the threat from fascism, and he appealed to the bourgeoisie to cooperate with the SPD against Nazism, to accept the constitutional social democracy and to avoid fascist dictatorship from succeeding in Germany.[27]

Beyond democratic theory, Heller was a protagonist for the civil, social democracy and for the theory of social compromise, and politically he advocated the continuation of the Weimar-form of parliamentary democracy.[28] The economic and political crisis of the Weimar Republic that broke out around 1929/30, triggered intense political-theoretical discussions in the SPD on the eventual renovation and future of the Weimar democracy. These discussions were carried out in leftist journals like 'Sozialistische Monatshefte' and 'Neue Blätter für den Sozialismus'. Among the discussants were Social Democrats like Carlo Mierendorf, Otto Kirchheimer, Ernst Fraenkel and also Hermann Heller. When in 1932, the Weimar Republic was in a deep political and constitutional crisis, Heller saw only the alternative 'social constitutional state or fascist dictatorship' ('sozialer Rechtsstaat oder faschistische Diktatur'). In order to defend the social constitutional state, he put forward ideas on a constitutional reform aiming at an 'authoritarian' strengthening of the state towards society in order to create a working parliament and government. He imagined some form of 'authoritarian democracy', in which state and government vis-à-vis parliament had a stronger and more independ-

26. Heller, *Europa und der Fascismus*, p. 17.
27. Heller, "Rechtsstaat oder Diktatur?", in: Draht et al., *Heller, Gesammelte Schriften*, vol. 2.

28. Heller, *Staatslehre*, in: Draht et al., *Heller, Gesammelte Schriften*, vol. 3.

ent role. But it was still to be bound by law and within the context of his idea of the social constitutional state (Sozialer Rechtsstaat).[29]

Weimar political and constitutional involvement

It is worth mentioning that Heller even openly and at high personal risk defended the new Weimar democracy in two critical instances. In his younger years in March 1920, he had actively engaged himself in defence of the republic against the mutinous right-wing Kapp-putsch. He was arrested by the insurgents and was together with his teacher Gustav Radbruch at a summary court (Standgericht) sentenced to death. The Kapp-putsch was however stopped so that he escaped being executed. And later in 1932 when he was a widely recognized expert on constitutional law he was part in the lawsuit 'Prussia against the Reich' ('Preussen gegen das Reich') at the supreme court (Staatsgerichtshof) in Leipzig, after the authoritarian Reichsgovernment led by Franz von Papen had suspended and dismissed the legitimate Prussian government headed by Otto Braun (SPD) on July 20th 1932. Before the Supreme Court, Heller represented the dismissed Prussian government, while Carl Schmitt represented the Reichs-government on its unconstitutional removal of the Prussian government. In his pleading, Heller questioned the proportionality of the measures taken by the Reichs government, but the compromise offered later by the Court in part supported his arguments, but did not reinstall what he saw as the legitimate Prussian government.[30]

29. Heller, „Ziele und Grenzen einer deutschen Verfassungsreform" (1931), in: *Draht et al., Heller, Gesammelte Schriften,* vol. 2, pp. 413–417.

30. On Heller's life and career, see S. Albrecht, *Hermann Hellers Staats und Demokratieauffassung,* Frankfurt am Main 1983; W. Schluchter, "Hermann Heller. Ein wissenschaftliches und politisches Portrait", in: ed. C. Müller and I. Staff (eds.),

Staatslehre in der Weimarer Republik. Hermann Heller zu ehren, Baden-Baden 1984, pp. 24f.; S. Albrecht, "Rechtsstaat, autoritäre Demokratie und der europäische Faschismus. Hermann Hellers Grundlegungen einer starken Demokratie", in M. Schmeitzner (ed.): *Totalitarismuskritik von links. Deutsche Diskurse im 20. Jahrhundert,* Göttingen 2007, pp. 83–102.

In this court case, Carl Schmitt was Heller's adversary, and in some ways Heller stands out as the defender of democracy in contrast to Carl Schmitt. Even if he did not regard the democracy of the Weimar Republic as the ideal model, it was the preferable form for society theoretically as well as politically. The Weimar constitution was to him a flexible model in which social democracy could be realised, if the political will and power was present. Yet he criticised the lack of political will. The two experts on constitutional law, Heller and Schmitt , also had some controversies on state and democracy. Heller criticized Schmitt's theory of the total and uniform state, and objected to Schmitt's view of the Reich-president (Reichspräsident) as 'sovereign dictator' during the political crisis of the Weimar Republic after 1930 where he had stuck to his idea of the parliamentary road and a social democracy.[31]

Hermann Heller seemed to have lost the ground to Carl Schmitt in the 1930es, as Schmitt became the leading theoretician of the authoritarian and totalitarian state. He should even promote Hitler's Führerstate (Führerstaat) and in 1934 legitimise the Führer's unlimited power: 'Der Führer schützt das Recht' ('The Führer protects the law').[32] But Heller's theories on state and democracy survived the National Socialist regime which is why he needs to be seen as an important thinker on democracy and constitutional state, whose significance exceeds his historic period. His thinking has indirectly but clearly through social democratic constitutionalists influenced the constitution of the new German Federal Republic Grundgesetz, established in 1949. That applied especially to his notion of the social constitutional state ('sozialer Rechtsstaat') in the sense of the equality of citizens before the law.[33]

---

31. Cf. I. Staff, "Staatslehre in der Weimarer Republik", in: Müller and Staff, Staatslehre, p. 19.
32. Quoted with W. Michalka, Das Dritte Reich. Dokumente zur Innen- und Aussenpolitik, vol. 1 (Munich 1985), p. 54.

33. Article 3 in the Grundgesetz: "Gleichheitsgrundsatz", cf. D. Gosewinkel, Adolf Arndt. Die Wiederbegründung des Rechtsstaats aus dem Geist der Sozialdemokratie (1945–1961), Bonn 1991, p. 85.

Conclusions: European democracy and Fascism

It is through the biographical approach that we see how Heller stands out as a protagonist of the new European mass social democracy, and in this context, his vision of Europe was first and foremost that of a constitutional and democratic Europe. He believed that fascism not only challenged, but also threatened the essence of constitutional and democratic Europe, and fascist rule as implemented in the Italian state meant the destruction of European democracy and democratic standards. Heller is however not to be looked upon as a European federalist or unionist advocating some form of a political or united Europe. A European federation or union was no topic in his thinking. Although he in 1926 had asked if the 'national idea should not be supplemented by a more comprehensive substratum Europe, in whose name alone the contemporary state crisis might be overcome'[34] Heller should be regarded as a political theoretician to whom Europe was an idea, Europe was seen as a set of values and standards ('Wertegemeinschaft') that were under threat in his day from authoritarian and fascist tendencies – the very values and standards that had been eliminated in fascist Italy. His reflections on Europe were still within the context of the nation and the national state. But he was European in the sense that Europe to him primarily was seen as a community of values, Europe was constituted of democratic states with common values, constitutional law and common human or civil rights. He was visionary and modern in the sense that Europe constituted a non-formalized community of such democratic states. The biographical approach thus offers a way to grasp what was progressive in Heller's thoughts concerning the core of Europe.

34. "Die politischen Ideenkreise
der Gegenwart", 1926, in: Draht
et al., *Heller, Gesammelte Schriften*,
vol. 1, p. 374

Promise or Plague?

Hartvig Frisch, Denmark and the European Challenge 1920–1950

Karen Gram-Skjoldager and Thorsten B. Olesen
Aarhus University

Historical narratives about Danish attitudes towards Europe and European cooperation in the 20th century are generally centred on the break caused by the Second World War. The war is seen as a turning point in at least two regards. Firstly, it is portrayed as a point where old policies of neutrality and anti-militarism were substituted for new policies of collective security, multilateralism and military defence. Even if there is a strong understanding of the neutralist traditions that fed into the foreign policy decisions after the war, the emphasis is on the immediate post-war years as a period in which old modes and means of foreign policy were superseded by fundamentally new ones. Secondly, and more implicitly, the post-war years are portrayed as a period in which a shift occurred away from the dominance of social liberal foreign policy towards social democratic foreign policy. In the 1930s, Danish foreign policy was effectively monopolised by the antimilitaristic centrist party, the Social Liberals and its party leader, P. Munch, who was foreign minister from 1929 to 1940. The post-war years, on the other hand, were characterised by the dominance of social democratic foreign policy.

This article proposes to take a biographical approach to studying this development. While not fundamentally challenging existing interpretations, it will sketch the intellectual development of one of the key transformative figures in social democratic foreign policy thinking in this period. Its subject is Hartvig Frisch, who was one of the leading intellectual and political characters in the Danish Social Democratic Party from the 1920s. A Member of Parliament from 1926 and political spokesperson from 1935, he was one of the political heavyweights of the Social Democratic Party at the outbreak of the war. And as one of the first academics to reach a central position in the party, and the ideological mentor for the generation of social democrats who charted the new course for Danish foreign policy after the Second World War, he was a key figure in the ideological development of his party from the inter- to the post-war period.

In charting this development, the article highlights one of the strands of gradual evolution that runs through the Second World War and ties together inter- and post-war foreign policy thinking. It will explore this continuity by scrutinising Frisch's understanding of three central and mutually constitutive, geographical and political categories in social democratic foreign policy thinking: Denmark, Norden[1] and Europe. In so doing it will show how these concepts developed in the context of and were shaped by two general developments: 1) the international political developments of the inter-war period, the World War and the early Cold War, and 2) the transformation of the Danish Social Democratic Party from a socialist proletarian – and potentially revolutionary – party into a broad, reformist people's party that was integrated into – and a dedicated champion of – national parliamentary democracy. However, a central point of the article is also to demonstrate how Frisch's personal circumstances and disposition, shaped at the same time by his personal experiences of national and international politics and by his own original political ideas, contributed to the shaping, timing and articulation of his foreign policy ideas and to the kind of reception they achieved inside his party. In other words this chap-

1. Throughout this article the Nordic word *Norden* (as opposed to *Scandinavia*) is used to designate the combined area of Denmark, Finland, Iceland, Norway and Sweden, although it was not until 1944 that Iceland became fully independent from Denmark. *Scandinavia*, on the other hand, only comprises Denmark, Norway and Sweden. However, in the inter-national literature the terms have often overlapped, such that Nordism and Nordic cooperation have been employed to refer to the specific cooperative framework of Scandinavia. Thus, in the Nordic languages, as opposed to English, Scandinavia and Scandinavian are often less comprehensive but more precise terms than Norden and Nordic.

ter is not biographical in the sense that it wants to explore Frisch as a complete human being. Rather it is interested in the point at which Frisch as an individual political and academic agent interacted with the society surrounding him, thus illuminating both the general and unique aspects of his political and intellectual profile and the political structures and processes he was enmeshed in.[2]

Hartvig Frisch

Hartvig Frisch was born on 17 January 1893 to middle-class parents. His father was a school headmaster and his mother the daughter of a headmaster and trained classical philologist. After finishing high school in 1910, Frisch went on to study history and classical philology at the University of Copenhagen. During his first year in university he broke with his bourgeois upbringing: he declared himself an atheist, joined the social democratic party and engaged in social democratic student activities. After a hiatus from political activities during and immediately after the First World War, in which he finished his university education and found employment as a high school teacher, he re-engaged in political activities in the early 1920s. In 1926 he won a seat in the Danish parliament and in 1935 he became its political spokesperson and Danish representative to the League of Nations.

In 1940, shortly after the German occupation of Denmark, Frisch was forced by the Germans to withdraw from national politics, although he still kept close links with the party leadership and not least with the young generation of Social Democrats who were to run the party – and to a large extent also Denmark – during the first fifteen years of the post-war period. In 1945 he resumed his international activities when he was appointed to be one of the three delegates to represent Denmark at the founding General Assembly of the United Nations. Frisch was in play as foreign minister when

2. This understanding of biography is inspired by O. Handlin, *Truth in History*, Cambridge, Mass. 1979, p.279 as quoted in D. Nasaw, "AHR Roundtable: Historians and Biography: Introduction", *American Historical Review*, vol. 114, 2009, no. 3, pp.573–8, here p.574.

Hans Hedtoft formed the first post-war Social Democratic government in 1947, but in the end Hedtoft appointed the career diplomat
Gustav Rasmussen to the post and let Frisch take the portfolio of
Minister of Education. In his later years Frisch often suffered from
illness, and he died in early 1950, just after turning 57.

Transcending the nation: Denmark and Europe in Hartvig Frisch's early socialist thinking

From the outset, Frisch was a Marxist with a clear, dogmatic belief
in historical evolution and progress pushed forward by the working
class and in the Social Democratic Party as a purely class-based party promoting working class interests. These views placed him on
the left wing of the comparatively pragmatic and reformist Danish
social democratic party. In the 1920s he still interpreted the party
within a transnational socialist framework and was highly critical
of its ideological moderation and gradual integration into the national political system. In his view the political aim of a social democratic party should be to unite all left-wing forces, including communists and radical left thinkers, around the party.[3]

This ideological standpoint obviously entailed a certain ambivalence towards the nation-state and the national parliamentarian
system. Though the First World War drew Frisch's attention to the
possible positive role of the state for the socialist project,[4] he maintained an ambivalent attitude towards national parliamentarian
democracy for the first decade of the inter-war period.[5] At the same
time, and at the broader, cultural level, he was critical of what
he perceived as narrow-minded and self-sufficient Danish national
sentiments. In particular he dismissed the fusion of late romantic
ideas and Christian beliefs that formed the basis of national ideas in
liberal and conservative quarters.[6]

3. N. F. Christiansen, *Hartvig
Frisch – mennesket og politikeren.
En biografi*, Copenhagen 1993,
pp. 30–6, 120–4, 141–3.
4. Christiansen, *Hartvig Frisch*,
pp. 51–2.

5. Christiansen, *Hartvig Frisch*,
p. 88.
6. Christiansen, *Hartvig Frisch*,
p. 41, p. 136.

Frisch's primary political frame of reference was Europe. While his political activities as a Member of Parliament in the second half of the 1920s centred on domestic political issues, he had a strong interest in – and an extensive knowledge of – European cultural and political matters which translated into two major book publications in the late 1920s and early 1930s. *Europas Kulturhistorie* [A Cultural History of Europe] published in 1928 and *Pest over Europa* [Plague over Europe] from 1933. Frisch's European interest was closely tied to his professional training in history and philology and it was nurtured through two research postings in Rome in the first half of the 1920s, where, among other things, he gained a firsthand impression of the Italian fascist movement.[7] Therefore, Frisch's European writings are a distinctive fusion of sophisticated academic analysis and political agitation.

Frisch's four-volume cultural history of Europe, published in 1928, became hugely successful. The book was an impressive piece of scholarship spanning 1246 pages and covering European cultures from the earliest times to the present. In accordance with his view of the national political entity, the book presented a transnational interpretation of different European cultures, tracing them across states and races and relating them to a general – though not particularly rigid – materialist argument. At the end of the book a short chapter was included on the situation in Europe after the First World War. This chapter put the European working classes at centre stage. Europe was an aging continent, so Frisch argued, squeezed between capitalist, imperialistic USA on the one hand and the communist dictatorship of the Soviet Union on the other. Economically and politically, Europe was losing ground and European culture was deteriorating: "... at present [it] stands in the sign of decay in as much as complex after complex of established traditions are disintegrating".[8]

The symptoms of this decline were many according to Frisch: the resurgence of nationalism in Central and Southern Europe, the new socio-political construction of fascism in Italy, which fused nationalism with a reactionary fight against the proletariat; and the Euro-

7. Christiansen, *Hartvig Frisch*, pp.64–8.

8. H. Frisch, *Europas Kulturhistorie,* Copenhagen 1928, vol. 2, p. 563.

pean bourgeoisie reacting to the turbulent post-war world by turning to remote romanticism and cultural pessimism while science
and arts were undergoing chaotic changes, ruthlessly rejecting
existing scientific and cultural conventions.[9] However, to Frisch,
Europe was not only a negative and regressive political and cultural concept. The progressive force of change, so he believed, was the
European working classes headed by the young workers of Germany
and Austria who were consciously working towards: "... moulding
the norms for the culture of the classless society in all areas of life".[10]

However, this transnational, socialist interpretation of national
and international politics was rapidly abandoned by Frisch in the early 1930s, as became clear when he published his next major analysis
of the political and cultural situation in Europe in *Pest over Europe*
in 1933.

Norden vs. Europe: Plague over Europe 1933

The substantial change in Frisch's political thinking in the early
1930s was the product of two different political developments. Of
crucial importance was the rapid rise of fascism across Europe and
the Nazi seizure of power in Germany, which paralysed what Frisch
had perceived as the spearhead of European socialism. Equally important was the changing status and role of the Danish Social Democratic Party: in government for the second time in 1929 and rapidly
growing, the Social Democratic Party was turning into a mainstay
of Danish political democracy and beginning to achieve substantial
results in the areas of economic and social policies.[11] In combination
with the Danish communist party's growth and its increasingly
confrontational attitude, this led Frisch to make a definitive choice
of social democracy and parliamentarian democracy over communism and the dictatorship of the proletariat.

9. Frisch, *Kulturhistorie,* vol. 2,
pp. 557–63.
10. Frisch, *Kulturhistorie,* vol. 2,
p. 563.
11. On this aspect, see T. B. Olesen,
"A Nordic *Sonderweg* to Europe.
Integration History from a Northern
Perspective", in H. Høibraaten and
J. Hille (eds.), *Northern Europe and
the Future of European Union,*
Berlin 2010.

These changes were evident in Frisch's European analysis in the form of a fundamentally new conceptual relationship between class, nation and state. In particular they were evident in the Nordic countries – as the primary, progressive, collective political actors in Europe, rather than in the European working classes.

At the diagnostic level, *Pest over Europa* developed and expanded the pessimistic interpretation of the European political situation Frisch had introduced in the last chapter of his cultural history of Europe. The book was basically an analysis of how communism, fascism and Nazism had emerged and spread and how these different totalitarian regimes exercised power. Compared with his 1928 analysis, he drew a grimmer picture of Soviet communism. But unlike many social democratic interpretations of the day he maintained that there were principled differences between the new totalitarian ideologies and regimes. While stressing the parallel patterns of development in which party organisations gained absolute power and then sustained their power by integrating party organisations and state structures into brutal regimes, he pointed in particular to the different attitudes taken by communism and fascism/Nazism to the working class.

This somewhat more nuanced view of communism also showed in his explanation of the growth of fascism. Unlike most social democratic intellectuals he did not see the growth of fascism as the result of communist attempts to split the international socialist movement. Rather, he pointed to the lack of political self confidence among European social democrats, their insufficient trust in democracy and their failing willingness to defend it. In particular, he leveled criticism against the German social democratic party for not having engaged in efforts to defend the Weimar republic against reaction. At the core of this critique lay a new, positive view of the political significance of the state. Thus, Frisch's key point of criticism towards German social democratic politicians was that they had disregarded the nation-state "... which in the present European system is the defining reality, politically as well as economically".[12]

12. Frisch, *Pest over Europa,*
pp. 11–12.

They had failed to use the state to achieve the necessary major economic reforms and taken a pacifist stance which effectively undermined their will to power.[13] It was exactly by virtue of their attitude towards the state that the Nordic social democratic parties stood out as positive examples. In the Nordic countries, so he argued, the social democratic parties had gained a strength which allowed them to actively shape national policies and as a consequence these states were fundamentally changing from liberal to social democracies. In making this point, Frisch articulated a new consensual view of the relationship between Danish – and Nordic – farmers and workers: Both had played a positive role in the development of the present parliamentarian and increasingly social democratic state and both should actively defend it. As he put it:

> It was the peasants of Norden who led parliamentarism to victory and created political democracy – for this they should be credited. It is the labour movement which has built on this basis and cast the foundation for *social democracy*. The building has not yet been erected and there is plenty of hard work for the rising generation, but the foundation has been cast and every Nordic worker and farmer, craftsman and office worker, academic and artist has reason to protect and defend this effort against any attempt at imposing dictatorship and violent rule, whether coming from East or South.[14]

Frisch's positive emphasis of Nordic similarities and unity was not entirely new. Since the beginning of the 1920s, he had argued in favour of Nordic cooperation pushed forward by the Nordic social democratic parties.[15] However, it was only with the rise of totalitarianism and the emerging Nordic social democratic welfare states that he developed a vision of the positive political role of the state and established a clear conceptual juxtaposition of Norden and Europe.

13. Frisch, *Pest over Europa,* p. 12.
14. Frisch, *Pest over Europa,* pp. 13–4 (italics in original).
15. Christiansen, *Frisch,* p. 74.

The ideas developed by Frisch in *Pest over Europa* were to become central to Danish social democratic international analysis and national self-understanding. It not only marked a decisive turning point in his personal intellectual development; it also pinpointed – and accelerated – a general ideological shift in the Danish Social Democratic Party's international attitude. Frisch's book became very influential among the young generation of social democratic politicians who entered the political scene in the 1930s and who would be in charge of Danish foreign policy after the Second World War – for instance, the coming Prime Ministers Hans Hedtoft and H.C. Hansen. Partially inspired by Frisch's analysis, they dissociated themselves from the traditional antimilitaristic stance of the Social Democratic Party and argued in favour of an active defence of the Danish state and its parliamentarian political system, if necessary by military means. Frisch's analysis also marked the beginning of an era in which the Social Democratic Party's primary international points of reference would be Norden and universal international intergovernmental cooperation – rather than Europe.

Intergovernmental internationalism: Frisch and the League of Nations

Hartvig Frisch's changed perception of the state was reflected in his attitude towards international intergovernmental cooperation. From the beginning of the 1930s, he developed a new and more positive attitude towards the League of Nations which also included a new view of the Nordic states as catalysts of peaceful international development.

In his cultural history of Europe from 1928, Frisch had effectively dismissed the League of Nations as an organisation of any relevance to the political developments in Europe. Pointing to the basic weakness that neither the USA nor the Soviet Union were among the League members, and stressing how its primary objective was to safeguard the Treaty of Versailles – "a slap in the face of reconciliation" – he concluded that: "... the League Assembly becomes a forum for dissatisfied nations without influence, while the League Council is a cabinet for the Great Powers of the Old World, for whom nothing is more alien than the idea of a united and harmonious Europe".[16]

However, this changed in the 1930s – even if the growing international tensions set very narrow limits for his active involvement in the League. In 1933 he showed the first signs of interest in the peace issue,[17] and in October 1935 he argued strongly in favour of Danish participation in the League's sanctions against Italy after Italy had invaded Abyssinia. As the Social Democratic Party's spokesperson in the parliamentarian debate over the issue, he stressed how his party supported sanctions because it viewed the League "... as the sole international means for maintaining peace ..."[18] He pointed out that security for small states could not be achieved through armament and alliances and that Denmark's only aim was peaceful coexistence and competition. Therefore, it was in Denmark's interest and the aim of the Social Democratic Party to contribute to all initiatives that strengthened the League and international peace.[19]

In 1936 Frisch also became actively involved in Danish League of Nations politics when he was appointed member of the Danish delegation to the League Assembly, a position he held for three years.[20] In the League, Frisch involved himself in its efforts to promote international 'moral disarmament'. When the League's sanctions against Italy had failed in 1936, some member states, including Denmark, attempted to create a role for the League as a dynamo for democratic and liberal internationalist information campaigns against totalitarian and expansionist ideas.[21] Frisch represented Denmark on this matter and held a seat in the committee dealing

16. Frisch: *Europas Kulturhistorie*, vol. 2, p. 556.
17. Minutes of Parliamentary Proceedings, Lower Chamber (Folketinget), 1933/34, 513–14.
18. Minutes of Parliamentary Proceedings, Lower Chamber, 1935/36, 89.

19. Minutes of Parliamentary Proceedings, Lower Chamber, 1935/36, column 222–23.
20. K. Gram-Skjoldager, *Fred og folkeret. Dansk internationalistisk udenrigspolitik 1899–1939*, Copenhagen 2012, p 533.
21. Gram-Skjoldager, *Fred og folkeret*, pp. 393–96.

with the question in the 1936 League Assembly.[22] The fact that Frisch engaged in this particular League activity was obviously closely linked to the shift in the League's focus in this direction. But his involvement in international efforts to shape public opinion also stands out as a striking replica of his position in national politics where fighting totalitarian ideologies with intellectual and cultural means had become a cornerstone of his political thinking. This belief in the importance of moral disarmament was reflected in a noticeable bitterness when efforts in this field failed. In an article on Denmark and the League of Nations published in 1937, he pointed out that while fascist and national socialist propaganda was spreading, the League of Nations still stood "... aloof in a cool air of so called neutrality. All publications issued from Geneva bear on their front the stamp of tediousness and anxiety lest any glimpse of the original ardour of its idea should irritate the tyrants and dictators of the world."[23]

Nonetheless it was evident that Frisch's view of the potential of intergovernmental – as opposed to transnational socialist – cooperation had fundamentally changed. Thus the 1937 article included a comparatively positive view of the League's political potential in the 1920s and in particular of the situation in 1924 when Great Britain and France, headed by two social democratic governments, had negotiated the Geneva Protocol – a treaty which combined arbitration, disarmament and collective security. When the protocol failed, so Frisch argued "... an opportunity was lost for democratic Europe to unite".[24]

This revaluation of international intergovernmental cooperation also entailed a new understanding of the international role for the Nordic countries. Frisch still believed that the working class and the social democratic parties had a positive role to play in the development of peaceful international relations. In the Danish parliamen-

22. H. Frisch, "Denmark and the League of Nations", *The International Observer: A Popular Quarterly*, 1937, pp. 92–107, here pp. 105–06.

23. Frisch, "Denmark and the League of Nations", pp. 106–7.
24. Frisch, "Denmark and the League of Nations", p. 101.

tarian setting, he stressed the particularly strong support of the social democratic party for the League project and – not entirely fairly – confronted the Danish conservative party with the role played by European conservatism in the deteriorating international situation.[25] But the primary collective political subjects in the promotion of international peace and cooperation were now, in Frisch's mind, the Nordic states. Just as Frisch had come to see these as role models of national political organisation, so he claimed for them a position as model states in international relations. As he put it in a speech in parliament in 1933 "... the three Scandinavian countries have been countries of peace and [...] in relation to the rest of the world, they have argued the case of peace".[26]

He developed this view on several occasions,[27] and it was at the centre of his 1937 article on Denmark and the League of Nations. Here he argued that one of the primary reasons why the League had failed was the great powers' unwillingness to consider the views held by the Nordic countries and other small neutral states about how the League of Nations was best organised. The Scandinavian states, he pointed out, had argued in favour of a League with a universal membership and without any provisions for international sanctions, two features that would have ensured from the beginning that the League could not be used as a political tool by the victorious powers as was now the case.[28] In developing this point, he was in tune with the small-state internationalism that was already widely accepted in the Danish parliamentarian milieu and which claimed that due to their impartial international position and their purely defensive national interests, the small states, and the Nordic countries in particular, had a strong interest as well as a an important role to play in developing a peaceful international world order.[29]

25. Minutes of parliamentary proceedings, lower chamber 1933/34, column 633–4.
26. Minutes of parliamentary proceedings, lower chamber 1933/34, column 513.
27. Minutes of parliamentary proceedings, lower chamber 1935/36, column 222–3; Minutes of parliamentary proceedings, lower chamber 1936/37 column 4890–91.
28. Frisch, "Denmark and the League of Nations", pp. 94–5.
29. Gram-Skjoldager, *Fred og Folkeret*, pp. 175–92.

In conclusion, even if the rapidly deteriorating international political situation had reduced Denmark's foreign policy to a question of securing Danish survival in the late 1930s, Frisch had by then developed a coherent national and international political ideology in which Denmark, Norden and – to a lesser extent – international intergovernmental cooperation stood out as positive points of reference in partial opposition to Europe.

Pro Memoria: War and Occupation

The German occupation of Denmark on 9 April 1940 and the following five years of occupation moved Frisch's political attention away from the international level and back towards the national political context and the conflicts which arose there on how to handle the German occupation.

To Frisch, the German attack was not unexpected, but still it shocked him profoundly. In many ways it was his nightmare come true in the sense that the Danish social democratic labour movement was now likely to suffer the same blows as those dealt to its Italian and German counterparts after Mussolini's and Hitler's takeovers in 1922 and 1933. In other words, the *plague* had arrived in Denmark.

But there was a further reason for Frisch's desperation in the days after 9 April. He was also very uncomfortable with the way the German occupation had been accomplished, and not least by the Danish government's handling of the situation leading up to it. Overall, Frisch did share the view that Denmark neither could nor should engage in a "war of existence", but he was also so much of an internationalist and realist that he was acutely aware of the powerful symbolism in having demonstrated a will to resist. The international norm was that a neutral position had to be defended, but due to the rather immaterial foundations of international law, it was the political repercussions of not fighting back which preoccupied him most. As he put it during a crisis meeting on 8 April with the king, government and leading party spokesmen: Seen from abroad it was not the result that counted, but "the way in which a potential attack was met". Giving orders to Danish forces to halt fighting, as the government did after only a few hours with no more than scattered clashes at the Danish-German border, did not send the right signal, according to Frisch.[30]

This view was spelt out by Frisch when on 13 April, four days after the German attack and the Danish government's de-facto acceptance of the German occupation, he detailed his frustration in an extraordinary, private reflection titled "Pro Memoria".[31] In this Pro Memoria Frisch was especially critical of the foreign policy conducted during the latter part of the 1930s as masterminded by the Social Liberal Foreign Minister of the Social Democratic-Social Liberal coalition government, Peter Munch. But quite interestingly, he did not temper his criticism of the SD position and especially of Prime Minister Thorvald Stauning's falling in line behind Munch and the Social Liberal Party's "defence nihilism".

The centre piece of Frisch's criticism was the government's "policy of confidence" towards Hitler Germany. It was this appeasement policy (not a word actually used by Frisch) which had prevented Denmark both from long-term preparation against an attack and even the necessary short-term manning of the military posts when it was obvious that an attack was imminent on 8 April. Frisch, as he stated, shared the view of the government taken on the morning of

30. Quoted from H. Frisch, "Pro Memoria", 13.4.1940, reproduced in *Betænkning til Folketinget fra Den parlamentariske Kommission*, Copenhagen 1945, pp. 517–524 (quote from p. 522). See also H. Kirchhoff, "Foreign Policy and Rationality – The Danish Capitulation of 9 April 1940. An Outline of a Pattern of Action", *Scandinavian Journal of History*, Vol. 16, 1991, pp. 237–268, and N. F. Christiansen, *Den politiske ordfører. Hartvig Frisch 1935–1940*, Copenhagen 1999, pp. 57–61.

31. Another fragment of the "Pro Memoria" not published by the Parliamentary Commission is reproduced in Christiansen, *Den politiske ordfører*. To distinguish between the two extracts, we will refer to the one published by the Parliamentary Commission as "Pro Memoria", 1945, and the one reproduced by N.F. Christiansen as "Pro Memoria", 1999.

9 April to cease fighting, but he would have liked the Danish forces to have been prepared for and in fact to have undertaken a more persistent and visible battle before surrendering. As he put it: "The policy of confidence we conducted had the result that we avoided major destruction. But we lost something which will be difficult to regain in the coming days: *the sound of the word Danish*. Finland and Norway has suffered, but the words *Finnish* and *Norwegian* will fly in the air like singing birds. That sound of our name we cannot pass on to our descendants, and they will not recapture it unless they win it back themselves".[32]

Frisch's biographer, the historian Niels Finn Christiansen, argues that the Pro Memoria bore witness to Frisch's "anger of impotence" by not being able to influence international politics, the national government and his own party, and that Frisch felt co-responsible for a foreign policy that he disagreed with but knew no alternative to.[33] This is highly plausible, but Frisch's mental imprisonment can also be seen as a product of his unwillingness to oppose the Stauning line in the government and in the party, and as a sign that ultimately Frisch was more a man of his party than of his beliefs.

Such an interpretation gains further substance when viewed against the background of Frisch's political behaviour during the occupation period. Frisch was disliked by the Germans, who were well-informed about his anti-Nazi attitudes and writings, and as early as 1940 he was forced to disengage himself from national politics, albeit allowed to sit in Parliament as a lame duck. However, behind the lines, Frisch was a staunch supporter of what was known as the policy of negotiation towards the Germans practiced by the traditional political establishment. The policy aimed, on the one hand, at preventing the local Nazis from being allowed into power sharing, and, on the other, at securing a benevolent occupation rule. Both aims were successfully accomplished until at least

32. "Pro Memoria", in: Christiansen, *Den politiske ordfører*, p. 75.

33. Christiansen, *Den politiske ordfører*, p. 61.

August 1943, when a combination of strikes and street revolts and German repressive countermeasures forced the end of this policy. But it would be difficult to claim that it was the political establishment which spearheaded this – from a future perspective – lucky break. The break opened a period lasting for the remaining part of the war, during which the Danish resistance became militarized and the resistance movement challenged the now underground power of the political establishment.[34]

The policy of negotiation had a defendable rationale, but very few of the politicians behind it were keen to defend it after the war. Frisch, however, did not cower and supported the policy openly remaining faithful to the party line. However, seen in the context of his very critical position in 1940 towards the Stauning/Munch pre-war policy of confidence, which must be regarded as the direct forerunner of the policy of negotiations during the war, a clear contradiction is evident. During the war it would even have been easier – at least after August 1943 – for Frisch to set himself free from his "anger of impotence" by joining the resistance movement and thus contributing to recapturing the right sound of the word *Danish*. He did not do this and proved once again to be more loyal to the party than to his world views.

But the main point to stress is probably that national concerns rather than his world views dictated his behaviour. If we accept this interpretation, it is also possible that in 1943 Frisch still felt himself caught in an anger of impotence, albeit of a different sort compared to that of April 1940, due to the fact that the resistance movement was largely dominated by the radical left- and right-wing groups (Communists and ultra-conservatives like *Dansk Samling*). Frisch

34. For a succinct account of the interdependence between the Danish policy of negotiation and the resistance period, see H. Poulsen, "Denmark at War? The Occupation as History", in S. Ekman and N. Edling (eds.), *War Experience, Self-Image and National Identity. The Second World War as Myth and History*, Stockholm 1997, pp. 98–113.

was not particularly interested in fighting one totalitarian ideology by directly or indirectly siding with another and by doing this even contributing to undermining the power of the democratic political establishment. Thus, there are many indications that in the last phase of the war and the early post-war period Frisch considered the greatest challenge to democracy to emanate from these ideological currents rather than from the bilateral, intergovernmental relationship Denmark upheld with occupying Germany. In the last years of the occupation, the ideologies that Frisch had associated with totalitarian 'Europe' before the war were gaining ground in the national political setting; in his own words, "Something un-Danish" had entered Danish political culture".[35]

The United Nations: Alliance and Neutrality

Despite Frisch's national pre-occupations at the end of the war, he nonetheless soon found himself in a situation where he could resume his international engagement from the League and transfer it into the new world organization, the United Nations. Combining an internationalist with a national agenda was not an easy task, and therefore during the period 1945–1947/48 one can observe Hartvig Frisch balance on a tightrope between an internationalist approach to Danish foreign policy and a very national one, with the latter gaining prominence in step with the outbreak of the Cold War.

35. C.B. Christensen, J. Lund, N.W. Olesen and J. Sørensen, *Danmark besat. Krig og hverdag 1940–1945*, Copenhagen 2005, p. 309 and 685f., and N. Christiansen, *Hartvig Frisch*, pp. 218–238. The expression "Something un-Danish" is from OWI (Office of War Information & Operation) memo titled "Inside Denmark", Paul W. Johnson to Eric C. Bellquist, 31 May 1945, recording a conversation between Johnson and Frisch in the State Department (SD), Washington DC, on the political situation in Denmark, in RG59 (State Department), Lot files: Europe; Lot 54D 224; Folder Denmark Political-General, box 12, US National Archives and Record Administration (USNARA).

Frisch took part in the Founding General Assembly in San Francisco as one of the three members of the Danish delegation. He did so as a representative of the political establishment, whereas the professor of medicine Erik Husfeldt was the designee of the resistance movement, and the third person, Henrik Kauffmann, Danish Ambassador to the United States, represented both camps (and the Foreign Ministry). Kauffmann had been admitted into the new transition Government of Liberation, jointly appointed as a Minister without Portfolio by the political establishment and the resistance movement.[36]

The appointment of Frisch to the delegation was no surprise. As demonstrated above, he had experience from the League, and since the actual number of Danish politicians with international expertise and an international outlook was remarkably low, Frisch was an obvious choice. He supported the UN wholeheartedly for international and national reasons: he saw that the world needed stability and peace, and to him a collective security system like the UN was the only way to try to secure that; and he saw UN membership as a vital means to "recapture Denmark's international position" and as a platform allowing a small state like Denmark a direct line of communication with the great powers independent of the channels of bilateral diplomacy.[37] As may be sensed, Frisch was more of a pragmatist than an unreserved idealist in his approach to the UN. This becomes fully clear in an examination of his position in the debate on the veto clause of the Charter, a debate in which he took active part both at the founding General Assembly in 1945 and in the years to come.

36. T. B. Olesen and P. Villaume, "I blokopdelingens tegn 1945–1972", *Dansk udenrigspolitiks historie*, vol. 5, Copenhagen 2005, pp. 24 ff; C.B. Christensen, J. Lund, N.W. Olesen and J. Sørensen, *Danmark besat*, pp. 435f., B. Lidegaard, *Defiant Diplomacy. Henrik Kauffmann, Denmark and the United States in World War II and the Cold War,* *1939–1958,* New York 2003, pp. 155–179.

37. See Frisch's delegation report from San Francisco published in H. Frisch and E. Husfeldt, *Rapporter fra De Delegerede ved De Forenede Nationers Konference i San Francisco,* Copenhagen 1945, pp. 12 ff (quote, in translation, from p. 13).

Frisch's position on the veto (and also more generally on the UN) was largely shaped by his interpretations of the shortcomings of the League of Nations. As we have seen above, several of his points were already present in his discussions of the League in the late 1930s.[38] Frisch (and Denmark) thus supported the introduction of the veto in the Security Council because the great powers wanted it and because it stood a chance of remedying a couple of the major problems which had paralyzed the League: on the one hand, the veto would prevent great powers from leaving the organization if they risked being voted down on vital issues, and on the other, it would ensure that small states could not be taken prisoners in the battle between the great powers by being forced to take part in collective punitive actions. By adopting this line of reasoning, Frisch recognized that he sided with a power realist point of view rather than with the idealist-democratic point of view represented by a number of western states like Australia, New Zealand, Belgium and the Netherlands. However, according to Frisch, the democratic argument was based on a false analogy that placed the principles of national or state organization on a par with those of an international organization, or, in Frisch's own words, a false analogy "between state members of a world organization and subject members of an individual state".[39]

At the same time, Frisch was adamant that more decision-making had to be transferred from the national to the international level, making international conciliation and arbitrage the norm. This point was so fundamental to him that he was willing to accept the introduction of some kind of supranational organization in an effort to reach this goal. Again, it seemed to be the League experience

38. For Frisch's views on the veto, see ibid, and Frisch's intervention during the UN ratification debate in the Danish Folketing on 6 September 1945, in *Rigsdagstidende*, "Folketingets forhandlinger" 1945, col. 1179–1191, and "The Veto", manuscript for a speech to be delivered by Frisch during the Cairo Conference of the Interparliamentary Union 1947, in Hartvig Frisch's (HF) archive at the Library and Archive of the Labour Movement (Arbejderbevægelsens Bibliotek og Arkiv, ABA), Copenhagen, box 9, file 46.

39. Frisch, "The Veto", p. 3.

which prompted his reasoning, not least the effort to make the UN so binding in character that it would not disintegrate in the way the League had done.[40]

In his biography, Niels Finn Christiansen argues that Frisch's understanding of the new post-war requirements for Danish foreign and security policy was characterized by a mixture of realism and optimistic illusions. This is probably true, but on the other hand it is also obvious that it was the realistic dimension that dominated. Christiansen is right in stressing that Frisch argued that membership of the UN meant the deathblow to neutralism, but he forgets to add that Frisch always accompanied this view with the proviso that the moment a conflict erupted between the great powers, who were the real guarantors of the new pact, the neutrality dilemma would impose itself on the small states again.[41]

In the summer of 1945, Frisch was well aware that the international power structure had been fundamentally changed and, seen from Denmark, the geo-political balance shifted from a European North-South axis to a potentially unstable Atlantic-Eurasian East-West axis. And in the following years, he, like so many other national and international analysts, became increasingly apprehensive about the durability of the war alliance and the UN's ability to cope with the growing tensions. In that light, perhaps it should be no surprise that as early as May 1946 we find Frisch active in defending a traditional Danish neutrality position. He did so in an article written for the Danish foreign policy magazine, *Fremtiden,* an article responding to an article from the previous issue written by Per Federspiel, Minister of Special Affairs in the Liberal Knud Kristensen Government.[42]

40. See Frisch's UN delegation report, 1945, p. 9 and "Conversation with Viggo A. Christensen" (1947), in HF, ABA, box 9, file 39.
41. Christiansen, Hartvig Frisch, pp. 252 f. The neutrality dilemma is stressed by Frisch in his intervention in parliament during the UN ratifi-cation debate 6.9.1945; see Minutes of parliamentary proceedings, lower chamber, 1945, col. 1188.
42. P. Federspiel, "Aktiv neutralitets-politik", and H. Frisch, "Hvad er aktiv neutralitetspolitik?", both in *Fremtiden,* vol. 1, no. 7, 1946, pp. 7–9, and vol. 1, no. 8, 1946, pp. 11–12.

What is most interesting in the article is not Frisch's recommendation of a neutrality position, but his more or less open defence of a traditional Stauning-Munch neutrality policy.[43] Without being exceptionally clear, in his intervention Federspiel had supported a UN-based neutrality policy with an active element allowing Danish diplomacy to openly pursue and take advantage, both politically and economically, of an international situation characterized by increasing bloc-building tendencies. But Frisch disagreed sharply. History had, as he put it, made him "extraordinarily sceptical towards even well-intentioned proclamations about (the need for) a change of orientation in Danish foreign policy". Peter Munch could hardly have agreed more.

NATO, Norden and Europe

> Interestingly enough, Frisch was a committed internationalist like Kauffmann, rather than a traditional neutralist. If Frisch had become Minister of Foreign Affairs in 1947, Hedtoft would have signalled a shift from the low profile, accommodationist policy inclinations of Gustav Rasmussen. The continuation of Gustav Rasmussen's tenure meant a foreign policy entirely on Hedtoft's terms without the complications and challenges that Frisch or Kauffmann would inevitably have offered.[44]

This quote from the English version of Bo Lidegaard's biography of Henrik Kauffmann is interesting for at least two reasons. First, it intimates that Frisch was a potential choice for Foreign Minister when the Liberal Knud Kristensen Government was replaced by the Social Democrat Hans Hedtoft Government in the autumn of 1947. For years Frisch had been a kind of political mentor for the ten-year

---

43. It is unclear from Frisch's article in *Fremtiden* if he was willing to take the full consequence and also rehabilitate Danish neutrality policy in its traditional low-militarized version.

44. B. Lidegaard, *Defiant Diplomacy*, p. 232.

younger Hedtoft, but in the end Hedtoft opted for Gustav Rasmussen as Foreign Minister, who, being a career diplomat, had also served on that post in the outgoing government. However, Hedtoft did recruit Frisch into his government as Minister of Education.

While Lidegaard's description of Gustav Rasmussen seems apt, the picture he paints of Frisch is more doubtful because, as we have shown, Frisch was not only an internationalist; he was also a (national) neutralist. This picture is reconfirmed when analysing Frisch's attitude to Danish membership of NATO, which he, to the surprise of many, could not support. When he announced his decision during a ministerial meeting on 22 February 1949, no pre-warning had been given, Frisch having kept a low profile in the tense security debates over Danish alignment with a Nordic defence union or a Western defence alliance (or some combination of the two) in 1948–49. But despite his NATO reservation, he never went public with it, not to say engaged in a campaign against NATO membership. During the parliamentary debate on membership he did not speak up, and only ten days after his critical intervention at the ministerial meeting he gave a speech supporting NATO membership on the official party platform.[45] It was similar to the Pro Memoria situation in 1940. Frisch did not like what he saw, but he did not actively fight it.

The motivation behind Frisch's opposition to NATO membership is only known from the eleven handwritten pages in note form that he drafted prior to the meeting. According to these notes, four main elements fuelled his scepticism. Firstly, "the empty heroism" which had conquered Danish political mentality since the resistance period and which had cast Munch's foreign policy into contempt. Secondly, NATO membership would encourage the Soviet Union to attack Denmark on day one in a conflict, an easy task since Denmark, from a geo-political perspective, was nothing but "an open city". Thirdly, in keeping with his pre-war Nordic inclination, Frisch praised Hedtoft for having tried to create a Scandinavian defence un-

45. Christiansen, *Hartvig Frisch*,
pp. 304 ff.

ion as an alternative to NATO membership because this solution would have been able to unite the nation while NATO would only divide it. And finally, the collapsed Scandinavian negotiations left only one acceptable option: to try to strengthen the UN. Therefore, Frisch suggested, Denmark should use the UN as a platform to issue a declaration making it clear that neutrality was dead, that we and all other peace-loving countries wanted to act in solidarity against an aggressor, and that the Security Council must take the initiative to advise and request member states to fulfil the military obligations necessary to safeguard collective security.[46]

There is not much will to power left in this document; in reality it is much closer to its opposite, a will to impotence. It is full of inconsistencies: the rehabilitation of traditional Danish neutralism on the one hand, and the declaration of the death of neutralism (in a well-functioning UN setting) on the other; the priority for only a Danish show defence at one end and the willingness (again within the framework of the UN) to militarize in a joint effort to safeguard collective security at the other end. It is torn between national Realpolitik and internationalism to a degree that only allows Frisch to come up with the vaguest of policy solutions: an idealist appeal to solidarity in a UN that does not work, and which Frisch, with his insights, should have known never would come to work under the existing Cold War conditions.

In this situation the less intellectually minded and less internationally experienced Prime Minister, Hans Hedtoft, demonstrated a far superior political instinct. He was not delighted about NATO alignment either, and had therefore worked hard to achieve a Scandinavian alternative instead. But contrary to Frisch, Hedtoft drew an active political lesson from the 9th of April experience, namely that Danish democracy should be defended and that Denmark could not defend herself. When this lesson was coupled with

46. Hartvig Frisch, notes for "Ministermøde 22/2 49", in HF, ABA, box 10, file 51. See also Niels Finn Christiansen's analysis of the document: Christiansen, *Hartvig Frisch*, pp. 304 ff.

the realization that the UN was powerless and the Scandinavian option exhausted, and that politics often consisted of choosing the best possible solution, Hedtoft did not shore himself up in the same kind of political impotence which was the Frisch habit.[47]

Another difference is apparent between Frisch and Hedtoft. As demonstrated above, like Hedtoft in 1948–49, Frisch had called upon Norden as a bulwark against outside threats in 1933. But in the post-war period we do not see Frisch flagging the same kind of Nordic idealism and being active in promoting Nordic cooperation just as Hedtoft did. Sometimes, when Frisch did call upon Norden in this period, it happened because he had been urged to do so by Hedtoft, for instance in the debate with Federspiel in *Fremtiden* in 1946. Frisch's intervention in the debate was a direct result of an appeal by Hedtoft in which the latter had stressed that it was the Nordic aspect of Federspiel's argument that needed critical attention.[48] In his response, Frisch also addressed this problem, but only as a kind of appendix in the last sections of his article. Despite Frisch's praise for the Nordic way, Nordic Socialism and Nordic democracy, he engaged very little in the day-to-day construction of Nordic cooperation. As Niels Finn Christiansen has touched upon, the Nordic appeals probably functioned differently for Frisch, as a kind of ideological reference rather than as a tangible political and security project.[49]

A similar parallel can also be observed concerning Frisch's reference to Europe, albeit his doing so to pave the way for a better future was certainly a new phenomenon compared to the 1930s. He was well aware that Europe of the post-war period was a crippled Europe, an 'Indianized' Europe, as he put it, because Europe, or at least Central Europe, had now experienced the same kind of dominance and subordination that India had experienced. Europe was the central stage for great power rivalry, but Europe was no longer among the main protagonists in that struggle.[50] In many ways this analysis represents an echo of the one he presented in his 1928 cul-

47. Olesen and Villaume, *I blok-opdelingens tegn*, pp. 91–125.
48. Letter from Hedtoft to Frisch (s.d) in HF, ABA, box 34, file: Hans Hedtoft-Hansen.

49. Christiansen, *Den politiske ordfører*, p. 61.
50. Hartvig Frisch, manuscript, February 1946, "Tanker omkring U.N.O", in HF, ABA, box 9, file 25.

tural history of Europe, although his pessimism concerning Europe
had grown even stronger. Nevertheless - just as in 1928 – Frisch had
hopes for Europe and European Socialism which became obvious
when he wrote an epilogue for a new, otherwise unrevised edition
of *Plague over Europe* in May 1949.

In the epilogue Frisch made it clear that the split and division of
European socialism and labour was bigger that it had been after the
First World War, and that therefore humanism and democracy were
once again threatened. The problem was worse because, on the one
hand, the Socialist split was now even visible at the conceptual level
with Eastern socialism (communism) and Western socialism using
the same concepts, but with a different meaning, and because Europe,
on the other hand, was no longer master in her own house. In this
light, Frisch concluded that "solving this problem is the world challenge for the free democratic Socialism, and that it can only be solved
from within by the European people's own will to a democracy set
equally apart from totalitarian dictatorship and reckless capitalism.
Without this Europe will fall easy prey to foreign interference".[51]

There is a strong reminiscence in this statement of an understanding of Europe as representing a Third Way, and as such taking
over the role that Frisch had envisioned for the Scandinavian states
in the inter-war period. What is equally interesting is that the Frisch
epilogue was written in the spring of 1949, at precisely the time
when Danish social democrats agreed not only to join NATO, but
also to participate in the creation of the Council of Europe, having
pressured for a more relaxed and positive approach to European federalism inside the British Labour-dominated socialist organization
Comisco for some time.[52] On the other hand, we have no indications
that Frisch engaged himself in the practical unification of Europe,
not even as a writer, prior to 1949. Despite the European awakening
in the spring of 1949, that struggle was left by Frisch – and generally
by the democratic socialists of Britain and Scandinavia – to their
continental European socialist friends.

51. H. Frisch, "Epilog", in *Pest over*
Europa, (2nd ed.), Copenhagen 1950,
p. 329.

52. Olesen and Villaume, 2005,
pp. 244 ff.

Conclusion

Through the lens of biographical narrative, this chapter has analysed the development in Hartvig Frisch's ideas about international politics in general and his views of the nation-state, Norden and Europe in particular during the period from c.1920 to 1950. At the general level, Frisch's conceptions of international politics in the 1920s moved from a transnational, socialist European perspective to a universal internationalist one based on multilateral cooperation in the League of Nations and supplemented with more specific ideological calls for Nordic mobilization against the totalitarian *plagues* of the 1930s. This view, which was first presented in *Plague over Europe* in 1933, was based on a new perception of the state. The state was no longer considered a bourgeois tool of suppression, but a bastion for the struggle against radical extremism and for the defence of (social) democracy and working-class rights. The lesson from Germany was that democrats and socialists would have to demonstrate a will to power to meet the challenges of totalitarian movements and states.

Based on such views and in the face of the increased threats to national security posed by Hitler's rearmament and aggressive foreign policy in the later part of the 1930s, Frisch became the central figure among the defence revisionists of the Social Democratic Party. They felt uncomfortable with the low-militarized Danish neutrality policy of the Social Democrat-Social Liberal government and seemed to accept a stronger military posture. The most potent and yet at the same time most impotent expression of Frisch's criticism of the Stauning government's appeasement policy towards Germany was his Pro Memoria, in which he directly criticized the low-level Danish defence capability and early surrender on 9 April 1940 – and which, however, never left his own desk drawer.

If Frisch's political inter-war journey took him from being a transnationalist with a European inclination to being an intergovernmental internationalist with strong national and Nordic underpinnings, his political travel coordinates of the post-war period became even more complex, if not politically incoherent. On the one hand, Frisch engaged himself strongly in the debates on the set-up of the UN. On the other hand, he and Denmark supported the power realists who defended and continued to defend the Veto institution which limited the powers of the new organisation significantly. This stand was evidently inspired by a reading of both the history of the League and recent Danish foreign policy, including an unwillingness to clash with the big powers, especially the Soviet Union, to whom Denmark 'owed' her invitation to the Assembly. Thus, Frisch may be said to have fused his previous internationalist ideas with the low-key, Danish tradition of neutrality and scepticism towards defence, as evidenced by his attempted rehabilitation of the Stauning-Munch legacy in his 1946 contribution to the foreign policy magazine *Fremtiden*.

Seen against this background, it should perhaps not come as a surprise that Frisch declined to support Danish NATO membership a few years later, opting instead for the unsteady combination of UN idealist internationalism and isolated Danish neutralism. On the other hand, it *is* puzzling how an acute analyst and power realist like Frisch could come this close to proposing a re-enactment of the League and isolated neutrality play of the 1930s. Equally puzzling were his ultimate appeals to the European people to unite and fight for European democracy to fend off foreign domination in the shape of either reckless capitalism or totalitarian dictatorship. What is puzzling here is not the vision of Europe as a Third Way inherent in these appeals, but that they seemed to derive more from his original visions from the 1920s than from the real political attempts by socialists and non-socialists at federating Europe in the late 1940s.[53]

However, not only did Frisch's intellectual profile change; so did his position within the party. From the inter-war to the post-war period, Frisch's position as the international ideological lodestar for the party, or at least its young up-and-coming leaders, was fading as these young leaders took over both party and country while faced with the immense international challenges of the Cold War. In

---

53. However, Frisch's rhetoric had been 'modernized' compared to the 1920s, which can be seen in his substitution of "the European working classes" with "the European peoples" and in his lack of references to the leading role of Germany.

1948–49 Frisch had little to offer in terms of analysis and political direction. Ironically, however, the distance between him and the new generation of leading social democrats was in part created because Hedtoft drew the consequence of the critical dissociation from the Stauning-Munch formula which Frisch had originally spearheaded inside the party.

While it seems fairly evident that Frisch's intellectual development in the inter-war period was the result of the new dominant role of the Social Democratic Party in the national political system and the totalitarian threat that spread across Europe, many factors must undoubtedly be mobilized to explain the rather extraordinary post-war trajectory of his international thinking. One of these is the war-time experience, which convinced him that the most immediate threats to post-war Danish democracy would not be external, but rather internal, with the main one being 'totalitarianism from within' in the form of left-wing (Communist) and right-wing (*Dansk Samling*) movements. Another factor was his failing ability to grasp the challenge and rationale of the Cold War, possibly brought about by a certain socialist doctrinaire inertia in his thinking. But probably the most salient aspect to stress is in fact Frisch's academic and intellectual inclination and perspective. Thus, Frisch repeatedly found himself in "an anger of impotence" which prevented him from acting politically – be it in relation to the pragmatic Social Democratic Party line of the 1920s, the Danish defence policy of the 1930s or the struggle over Denmark's international orientation after the war. He held this position, not because he shied away from controversy (despite being overly loyal to his party at times), but because he realized the potential dangers in all choices and because his domain was the book and pen, not the sword or organizational routine. Nonetheless, Hedtoft himself never tired of recognizing Frisch's enormous influence on his political up-bringing and on his world view. In this indirect way, one may argue that Frisch not only left a substantial theoretical and analytical, but in fact also practical impact on Danish international politics.

The Thread of a Political Life?
Biographical Reflections on the Political Career of Jens Otto Krag

Niels Wium Olesen and Johnny Laursen
Aarhus University

On 3 October 1972 at the opening of the autumn session of the Danish parliament the Social Democratic prime minister, Jens Otto Krag (1914–1978), entered the rostrum for a special statement. The day before a hard fought referendum on Danish membership of the EC had rallied a 63.3. per cent majority for entry and a resounding success for Krag's campaign to bring his Euro-sceptical country into the Communities. With a slight smile Krag glanced at the queen's box and informed the stunned MP's that although the result of the referendum meant that the government would remain in office, this did not mean that the prime minister would do so. At the following press conference the hitherto unapproachable, controlled politician enchanted the gentlemen and the few women of the press explaining that he wanted to devote his life to writing, reading and painting. The TV broadcast dramatic clou of the then 58–year-old Krag marked the apex of a remarkable political career in the Danish labour movement and international politics. The sensational ending of his career was destined to provide future historians with a dramatic mis-en-scene of their narratives of a biography entwined with the nation's slow and tortuous path towards membership of the European Communities. Even without this dramatic clou of a long political career the trajectory of Krag's life had literary qualities already before the first biographer put his pen to the paper.

Jens Otto Krag's status as one of the most influential politicians in the political history of post-war Denmark has made him an obvious object for historical and biographical studies. Moreover, the narrative qualities in Krag's personal character and political career have probably contributed to boost the scholarly interest in his life. This actualizes Pierre Bourdieu's reflections on the nature of the biographical genre in his essay *The Biographical Illusion* where he demonstrates how biographies tend to duplicate the narrative of the novel of formation (*Bildungsroman*).[1] When writing about Jens Otto Krag, and even more so when writing his biography, historians are easily drawn towards a narrative of linearity and cohesion seen from the vantage point of his dramatic exit in 1972 at the zenith of his power and at the moment of his great achievement: Denmark's decision to join the EC. Moreover, Krag's crucial role over his 18½ years as cabinet minister in shaping the modern Danish welfare state also tends to lend a certain impression of purpose and order to his political strive – an impression underpinned by Krag's compulsive strive to plan and control the political process. On this background the student of Krag's life must resist a certain impression that this was a life trajectory shaped by destiny.

In this chapter it will be argued that the time have come to question this well ordered narrative. The argument will be founded on an outline of Krag's political career, a survey of the historiography regarding Krag and on a discussion of three core episodes in Krag's career (as well as in Danish political history). Each of these three episodes constitute examples of different historical contexts and roles of our historical actor: as an ideologue and strategist of post-war planning in 1944–45, as participant observer to the decision to join the Atlantic Pact in 1948–49, and as policy maker shaping Denmark's position towards the Treaties of Rome and European integration in 1957. Each of these roles and episodes are discussed in order to illustrate diverse threads and interpretative challenges in Krag's life. The episodes are selected also because they have been accentuated in the historiography of Krag's political life. In the literature they appear, so to say, as reference marks of epochal significance in the current of political events that carried the political career of Jens Otto Krag forward.

1. P. Bourdieu, "The biographical illusion." *Working Papers and Proceedings of the Centre for Psycho-* *social Studies,* University of Chicago, vol. 14, Chicago 1987.

They are the reference points on welfare, the cold war and Europe from which the common thread of Krag's life so often are woven.

The examples will question the interpretation of the three episodes and their place in Krag's biography. They will serve to demonstrate how unguarded assumptions of linearity – common threads – in Krag's political life risk to narrow the interpretative range of the episodes in question. Seen within the framework of a comprehensive, long term view of Krag's life, the ambiguities of the episodes and the frailness of the often fragmented source material risk to be forced into an interpretative Procrustes Bed. This is not least the case for the source material and for interpretations produced by Krag himself. The inherent methodological risk is that the motives and actions of the actor appear more singular, orderly and determined than they should and were – and that suggestive scraps of source material pointing to more ambiguous interpretations of any given episode are not valued. As a result, aspects of other causations, conflicting motives and potential outcomes, might be lost out of view.

Jens Otto Krag's Political Career

Krag was born in 1914 in the provincial industrial city of Randers. At the age of 17, he joined the Social Democrat youth movement. He was trained as an economist at the University of Copenhagen during the 1930's. During the war he worked in the economic planning directorate in the central administration while also establishing close ties to the trade unions. In 1945, he contributed to shaping the post-war programme of the Social Democratic party. At the general election in 1947 at the age of 33 he was elected as an MP and appointed Minister of Trade in the new Social Democrat government, a key position in the management of Denmark's post-war reconstruction process

Apart from his rise to political influence, Krag's career was at this point quite similar to other young academics trained during the depression and war economy and coming of age politically at a time where Europe was facing the task of economic reconstruction and the increasing tension between the Western powers and Communism. In terms of the contemporary European context he was facing the same challenges as many other intellectuals of his own age. Indeed, Krag's life could be described as part of a collective biography of an elite of economists, who came to place their mark on Danish and Scandinavian European and foreign economic policies. At the eve of the Common Market in the mid-1950s these men dominated the Danish Foreign Ministry's department for European economic co-operation.[2] Thus, in terms of the structural determinants and contemporary ideas of his time Krag was one of many European politicians grappling with the nexus between domestic policies and European integration.

During 1947–50 Krag was frequently the Danish emissary to meetings on the Marshall Plan and on the creation of the OEEC. In 1950–52 he worked as economic advisor at the Danish embassy in Washington. He came back to Copenhagen in 1953. After the return to power of the Social Democrats later that same year he was appointed Minister for Economic Affairs with special responsibility for European economic co-operation. From 1953 till 1962 he participated in practically all important meetings on ministerial level in the Organisation of European Economic Cooperation (OEEC) and in the European Free Trade Association (EFTA), while developing an intensive diplomacy between the capitals of the Six and the Seven in the years of the European market split 1959–60. In 1960 Krag was known as the most well-connected and influential Danish politician on the European scene. He was also known as the Scandinavian statesman with the closest contact to the EEC.

Looking at the long presence of European affairs in Krag's biography from his early contacts to European 'pioneers' such as Jean Monnet up till the role played by Krag in Denmark's entry into the EEC in 1972 it is a tempting assumption that a continuity in actions and in ideas should exist creating a certain order in Krag's life and biography. There are, however, still many unanswered questions in this respect. If anybody among the Danish politicians and civil serv-

2. J. Laursen, "De nye mandariner i dansk markedsdiplomati. Jens Otto Krag og embedsmændene, 1953–1962", *Vandkunsten*, vol. 9/10, 1994, pp. 132–144

ants should harbour a vision for European integration it was indeed Krag who, in 1966, was honoured with the Charles prize in Aachen and in 1974 became the European Commission's permanent representative in Washington. However, the question is whether Krag's political aims for European integration and for Denmark's role in it corresponded to those of the supranational EEC, to less committed intergovernmental forms of co-operation or whether he preferred a more regional Scandinavian orientation in Danish foreign policy. Much has been said about Krag's European commitment, but the fact remains that he during the 1950s and 1960s continued to steer his country in zig-zag between closer Scandinavian co-operation and closer co-operation with the Six.

Moreover, Krag's career was through the 1940s and 1950s characterised by his close and complicated relationship to two of the giants in the history of the Danish Social Democratic labour movement – prime minister, Hans Hedtoft (1903–1955), and his successor prime minister H.C. Hansen (1906–1960). He was closely connected to party chairman and Prime Minister Hedtoft, and for a long time opposed the more centrist H.C. Hansen's growing dominance in the party and in the government. However, after the death of Hedtoft in 1955, Krag nevertheless became one of the closest collaborators of H.C. Hansen's premiership and a key actor in creating the conditions for balanced economic growth and the establishment of the affluent welfare state Denmark was turning into in the 1960's. In 1958–62 Krag was foreign minister. In 1962 he became prime minister, a post he held until 1968. Paradoxically, in terms of policy, Krag, the academically trained social democrat and adversary of the traditional Labour leader H.C. Hansen, came to provide the continuity after H.C. Hansen when he, himself, assumed the premiership from 1962. After a few years as leader of the opposition, he returned in 1971–72 as prime minister to conclude the Danish accession to the European Communities and carefully orchestrate the referendum. As prime minister his political method was discipline, stability (dotted with inspired tactical *coups*) and pragmatic reform policies. However, can such characteristics of Krag's past modus operandi also be applied as characteristics of the life and biography of the man?

Historiography and Self Representation

In 1952 a Danish socialist songwriter, Oskar Hansen, irked Krag with a poem published in the party monthly urging him not to forget the 'red thread' (common thread), i.e. the socialist tradition, in his rapid political career.[3] The hint that career oriented opportunism had prevailed over Krag's socialist idealism was tangible. In many ways the historiography on Krag and on his biography seems pervaded by the search for the threads of Krag's life and career – threads not in Oskar Hansen's socialist meaning, but common threads understood as themes binding Krag's life together as a coherent and meaningful whole. However, several of such threads seeming to run through the life of Krag do not necessarily add up to a meaningful and coherent whole. A certain tension can be found between, on the one hand, interpretations focussing on pragmatism or even opportunism as dominant features and, on the other hand, interpretations giving more weight to the man's ideology and political visions. On the whole, Krag's political career seems to have exerted contradicting influences on the writings of historians. Many have seen the exclusiveness of this clever and skilled politician as a challenge and tried to search for the true nature of the man behind the politician. At the same time, most political historians have agreed that the quest for the welfare state with full employment and membership of the European Communities are indeed distinctive threads running through the political life of Jens Otto Krag. This ambivalent combination of the picture of a sphinx and a rational, long term strategist, and between an opportunist and a visionary – even idealist – politician is characteristic of many biographical descriptions of the man.

The historian attempting to evaluate Jens Otto Krag's political career is confronted with considerable further challenges. The main one being how can he or she escapes becoming an involuntary hostage of Krag's own writings and self-representation? In his time Krag was one of the most productive analysts and writers among his contemporary commentators and colleagues.

3. O. Hansen, "Til min ven den unge nationaløkonom", *Verdens Gang* 1952.

From 1945 until 1971, Krag wrote several articles and books about – and on behalf of – the Danish labour movement and the Social Democratic Party. As early as 1955, Krag was de facto the unofficial party historian.[4] His considerable talent as a writer combined with an ability to fuse narrative and historical analysis in an easily read account of events made him very influential in shaping the party memory and identity and, not the least, his own legacy.

Krag was, in fact, his own first biographer. In 1969 and 1974 he published memoirs in two volumes covering the period 1914–52. The memoirs convey an insight into Krag's life until his early 30s. The memoirs exposes his personal life more than is usual for memoirs of Danish politicians. His political ideas and career is narrated as a seemingly haphazard, but when looked upon more closely, quite consistent development from the young wild-blooded socialist who in the wake of Hitler's take over of power was tempted by left wing radicalism and Popular Front rhetoric – to the educated young economist, who had wisened up and become a loyal, reformist Social Democrat with new ideas of welfare democracy and a strong belief in European integration and transatlantic partnership. But, the memoirs implicitly make the reader understand, personal and political maturity arrived without the protagonist becoming 'square'. In fact, it was a constant ambition of Krag never to be identified with petty-bourgeois attitudes and values, and always to be on the side of the new, the young, the modern. This could be part of the reason for the memoirs' revelations of Krag's tormented marriage with his first wife. He showed off: I dare write this. The portraits of fellow Social Democrat politicians and trade unionists and the description of the history of the party are written with respect and empathy for the party tradition. But when one digs beneath the surface, there are

4. J.O. Krag, "Manddomsgerning", in: H.C. Hansen and J. Bomholt (eds.), *Idé og arbejde. En bog til hans Hedtoft på 50-årsdagen*, Copenhagen 1953, pp. 147–154; J. O. Krag, "H.C. Hansens politiske indsats indtil hans gerning som statsminister", in: V. Kampmann and J. Bomholt (eds.), *Bogen om H.C. Hansen*, Copenhagen 1961, pp. 86–172; J.O. Krag and K.B. Andersen, *Kamp og fornyelse*, Copenhagen 1971.

also subtle hints and criticism of the people portrayed, most of them fellow Social Democrats.[5]

The memoirs were welcomed by the media with generous reviews and by the public with a considerable sale. They are, indeed still, a fascinating read. It is a two-volume life-and-times autobiography by a mature man, who, while writing, tries to understand his past. By virtue of a subtle form of self-ironic understatement the memoirs present Krag himself as a really charming acquaintance. When published, the books represented an almost provocative contrast to his public image as a shy, cold and controlled figure. The political substance of the memoirs depict the main character as a loyal Social Democrat, who worked hard to modernize the ideas and policies of the party, thus also supplying the memoirs with a somewhat concealed plot that puts Krag on centre stage as the modernizer of the party while still being loyal to its ethos.

For lack of other sources Krag's memoirs and his other historical writings were used extensively by historians in the 1970s. Research into the origins of the Danish post-war welfare state focused on Social Democratic crisis management in the 1930s and on economic regulations during the war years. These experiences of state interventionist policies, so the research of the 1970s told us, became the ideological foundation of the post-war Danish welfare state.[6] In this research Krag constituted the man who transformed the class party of the pre-war years into the modern Social Democratic party creating the welfare state. The conclusions were quite close to the underlying narrative of Krag's memoirs, but they will be problematized below.

The first biographical portrait of Krag was that of the chief of the National Archives Vagn Dybdal in the national biographical dictionary. It outlined Krag's remarkable political career and his close alliance with Hedtoft, while characterising the conflict between Krag and H.C. Hansen as one between the young modern Social Democrat and the older traditional Social Democrat. According to Dybdal, the successful quest for EEC membership earned Krag the status

5. J.O. Krag, *Ung mand fra trediver-ne*, Copenhagen 1969; J. O. Krag, *Travl tid, god tid*, Copenhagen 1974.

6. K. Hansen and L. Torpe, *Social-demokratiet og krisen i 30'rne*, Aarhus 1977.

as one the country's major statesmen in the 20th century.[7] In 1982 the historian Erik Rasmussen challenged some of the basic assumptions pointing to the close relationship between the biographer and the person in question. In a fine exercise of source criticism Rasmussen demonstrated that Krag himself through his writings and interviews had contributed to this predominant interpretation.[8] For a long period Rasmussen's insights were largely ignored or forgotten in favour of the 'visionary modernizer' school of interpretation. In 1992 the political historian Tage Kaarsted characterized Krag's role in the same vein as Vagn Dybdal had done.[9] Krag's world views, as portrayed in these contributions, were characterised by long term visions for economic modernization, full employment, welfare and Danish membership in the EEC. The line from Krag's early engagement with European co-operation over the Charles Prize to Denmark's accession to the EEC in 1972 was drawn very clear.

Krag's own legacy for and imprint on the historians was indeed also substantial. His archive in the Archive of the Labour Movement in Copenhagen contains extensive collections of private and official papers. Apart from Krag's correspondence and papers, the archive contains his complete diaries kept at brief intervals throughout his political career. One of the puzzling aspects of working with source material from Krag's hand is that during his work as minister, he continued to produce a number of central and substantial pieces of historical research. Some of these works were written in the immediate aftermath of the events described in them, while others – especially the later – increasingly bore the imprint of the authors' use of his own diaries. Krag had an eloquent pen, leaving his texts constantly changing between clarity, veiled meanings and clues. Especially disconcerting for the historian is the politicians' ability to engage in clear historical analyses of his own immediate past, while simultaneously leaving a paper trail of source material on the same matters. From the mid 1960s this turns into a methodological

7. "Jens Otto Krag", in V. Dybdal (ed.), *Dansk Biografisk Leksikon*, Copenhagen 1978–83.
8. E. Rasmussen, "H.C. Hansen, J.O. Krag og udenrigsministeriet. Kommentarer omkring efterkrigs-

tidens socialdemokratiske leder-skikkelser", *Historie*, N.R., No. 3, 1982.
9. T. Kaarsted, *De danske Ministerier 1953–1972*, Copenhagen 1992.

challenge for the biographer as the diaries not only change – with a shift in focus and in the frequency of entries – but also engage in dialogue with the process of Krag's writing of his memoirs for the decades up till the mid 1950s. Krag's awareness of the relationship between politics and his own historical legacy was never far away. In 1973 he published parts of his diaries from the period during the referendum campaign for EC membership 1971–72.[10] A further challenge adds to the complexity: Krag's diary was often kept at irregular intervals. Some entries were written at night at the heat of political battle, while other more extensive entries were written retrospectively. Moreover, in some cases Krag is as much searching for meaning in the events described by himself as the historian.

In 2001 and 2002 followed Bo Lidegaard's monumental two-volume biography of Krag.[11] Lidegaard was the first historian to mine the rich source material among Krag's papers. Lidegaard outlined Krag's life story as an epic tale – to a large extent based on the diaries – about a visionary and highly skilled politician, who from early on pursued his vision about combining the quest for full employment and welfare with Danish membership in the EC. Based on the diaries as the key source to Krag's thinking, Lidegaard was able to let the reader see the man as a man of strong emotions and the man as a disciplined and cunning politician with long term plans and visions. In this sense Lidegaard's biography is a study of the two lives of Jens Otto Krag – the man of strong emotions and ideals on the one hand and the rational, disciplined politician on the other. In terms of methodology it subscribes to a view of Krag as an analytical mind with a strong sense of mission and a vision of European commitment and welfare for his nation.

A thematic study by Johnny Laursen on Krag's diplomacy during the 1st round of negotiations about the enlargement of the EEC, 1961–63, and during the 2nd round in 1967 is inclined towards depicting Krag's policies in the nexus between domestic and foreign policies,

10. J.O. Krag, *Dagbog 1971–1972*, Copenhagen 1973.

11. B. Lidegaard, *Jens Otto Krag 1914–1961*, Copenhagen 2001; B. Lidegaard, *Jens Otto Krag 1962–1978*, Copenhagen 2002.

as determinedly pro-EEC and caught in strong structural confines owing to a number of external factors. Prominent among these were the possible nexus between market and security policies, the double dependency on the German and British markets and social and economic concerns for EEC-membership in industry and trade unions.[12] Although in some respects related with Lidegaard's interpretation this line of inquiry harbours ambivalence. On the one hand the complexities of the two-level games between domestic politics and exterior policies tend to underscore the intellect and tactical cunning of Krag. On the other hand it is also an interpretative framework that places the individual's room of action and independent decisions within the strict structural confines of the small state and gradualist politics. Thus, the interpretation contains an unresolved tension in terms of causality between the actor and the national and international context. In this sense it reflects a more nuanced view compared to an earlier study on Krag as one of the 'new Mandarins' of Denmark's policy making elite on European affairs.[13]

Niels Wium Olesen's more recent study of Krag's young years, 1914–1950, added a new and complex perspective to the making of Jens Otto Krag with an interpretation of his ideas and worldviews strongly rooted in the man's political education in the Danish labour movement in the 1930s and 40s and with an emphasis on the transnational influences on Krag by the Scandinavian, German and British labour movements.[14]

The study of Krag's political career is an exemplary case for a study of the complexities of historical-biographical analyses. His life is well suited to function as a historical laboratory for the study of the role of a centrally placed individual. In the following a number of such key situations and decisions will be studied in more detail.

12. J. Laursen, "Denmark, Scandinavia and the Second Attempt to Enlarge the EEC, 1966–67", in W. Loth (ed.), *Crises and Compromises: The European Project 1963–1969*, Baden-Baden 2001, pp. 407–436.

13. Laursen, *De nye mandariner.*
14. N. W. Olesen, *Jens Otto Krag. En socialdemokratisk politiker. De unge år 1914–1950*, PhD dissertation, University of Southern Denmark 2002.

The Architect of the Danish Welfare State?

In the biographical portrait by Dybdahl, Krag is termed the 'ideological leader of the Danish welfare state'. Dybdahl links this statement to Krag's role in developing the Social Democratic Party's postwar plans in 1944–45. Dybdahl's evaluation is both implicitly and explicitly shared by other scholars and politicians reflecting on Danish political history and has gained status as one of the master narratives in Danish popular history.[15]

Since graduating from the University of Copenhagen in 1940 Jens Otto Krag had spent the war years as a civil servant in the influential Supply Office (Direktoratet for Vareforsyning), which was the centre of the entire Danish economy of wartime regulations. Like many of his contemporaries on the European post-war political scene Krag was deeply influenced by the economic crisis of the 1930s and the subsequent World War. At least two lessons were learned by Krag and his fellow Social Democrats around Europe: Firstly, unemployment, economic crisis and war destabilized societies and brought with it political radicalization, either to the benefit of fascism or communism. Secondly, World War II had proved that the state – when mobilized for a cause and to its full potential – could fix the maladies of Liberalist capitalism leading to economic growth and the elimination of unemployment. What it took was not the breakdown of the capitalist system, but fixing it by way of state interventionism.

Krag was in November 1944, asked by the leadership of his party to act as secretary of a 'Committee of Socialization' (Socialiseringsudvalget) set up to draft a programme for the first parliamentary elections. After the liberation, in August 1945, the committee issued a manifesto called 'Denmark of the Future'. It consisted of

15. J. Torfing, "Velfærdsstatens ideologisering", in: T. B. Dyrberg, A.D. Hansen and J. Torfing, (eds.), Diskursteorien på arbejde, Roskilde 2000; A. Jørgensen, "Velfærdsstatens arkitekt", in: S. Hansen (ed.), Krag – som vi kendte ham, Copenhagen 1978.

a combination of Keynesian control of demand and employment, and corporatist regulation and planning of the entire economy, which for Danish standards was very tight. 'Denmark of the Future' did not provide a victory for the Social Democratic party in the elections in October 1945. The rival Communist Party won a big election victory, rewarded for its leading role in the Danish resistance and the very recent but widespread respect for the Red Army.

The poor fate of the Social Democratic election campaign in 1945 could have swept 'Denmark of the Future' into obscurity. Quite the opposite has happened, though, and for the last 40 years the manifesto has been hailed by different politicians of the day – both by the left and the right – as a milestone in Danish political history with something of a mythological tinge about it. Social Democratic politicians have praised it for its modernist foresight claiming it to constitute the welfare state in embryo.[16] Bourgeois politicians and commentators have criticized it for its rigid interventionist policies deeming them a step in a non-democratic direction.[17] But no politician or commentator with a historical view of his metier will question its monumental character. And even though Krag only was the secretary of the committee behind the programme and the party leadership carried the formal responsibility of the manifesto, it was considered an unquestionable truth in the Danish political debate of the late 1940s that Krag was the creator and writer of the manifesto. As late as in the spring of 2011 the leading liberal politician and cabinet minister, Søren Pind, in a profiled interview claimed that Krag in 1945 had made the exact blueprint for the next 50 years of Denmark's political development. This was a rhetorical steppingstone to lament the lack of intellectual quality of present-day Social Democratic politicians.[18]

16. "Velfærdsstatens arkitekt"; *Danmarks Radio, P1,* 18 May, 2000, radio interview with Danish Social Democratic politician Jytte Hilden.
17. H. Fonsmark, *Historien om den danske utopi. Et idepolitisk essay om*

danskernes velfærdsdemokrati, Copenhagen 1990.
18. *Politiken,* 21 March, 2011, "Jeg vil have kulturkamp", interview with Danish liberal politician Søren Pind.

For historians these assumptions have been a subject of heated controversy. How should 'Denmark of the Future' be interpreted, what was its content and general idea? Was the manifesto, if truth be told, that important and in any way linked to the development of the Danish welfare state? Is it really possible that the Social Democratic Party in the extremely precarious transition period from war to peace would hand over the responsibility of drafting an election manifesto to a thirty-year old economist? No doubt, Krag's memoirs sparked a revisionist suspicion among historians. Twenty-five years after the events and after the passing away of most of the then-leading party members, Krag casted himself in the role of the Danish prophet of Keynesian demand management policies and the modernizer of yesterday's Social Democratic policies.

Since the 1980s, historical studies of the manifesto have been divided on the interpretation of the content of 'Denmark of the Future' and its sources of inspiration, on the political purpose, on its significance in a historical perspective, and on the role and importance of Krag. Some argued that the proposed Keynesian fiscal policy was the most important element of the programme.[19] Others put more emphasis on the proposed strict interventionist planned economy with politically decided physical allocation of resources as the most prominent aspect of the manifesto.[20] Some claimed that the fiscal policy in the programme really was not Keynesian but inspired by the Swedish Stockholm School and the interventionist measures were 'stolen' from manifestoes of the Norwegian and Swedish sister parties.[21] Others, again, argued that these questions mattered little because the only purpose of the programme was to produce a cosmetic radicalization of the party line in order to stem the anticipated advance of the Communist Party.[22] On the role of

19. K. Hansen and L. Torpe, *Social-demokratiet og krisen i 30'rne*, Aarhus 1977.

20. N. O. Finnemann, *I Broder-skabets Aand. Den socialdemokrat-iske arbejderbevægelses idehistorie 1871–1977*, Copenhagen 1985.

21. N. Bredsdorff, *Fremtidens Danmark, socialdemokraterne og keyne-sianismen. En doktrinhistorisk under-søgelse*, Roskilde 2000.

22. J. Engberg, *I minefeltet, Træk af Arbejderbevægelsens Erhvervsråd historie siden 1936*, Copenhagen 1986.

Krag, some declared that he was only the messenger boy and that he had no significant say in the process, which was controlled and guided by heavy weight politicians as Hedtoft and the de facto wartime party leader and *eminence gris* Vilhelm Buhl.[23]

By combining both elaborate studies of the manifesto itself and the working process behind it on the one hand and scrutiny of Krag's role in it on the other, Niels Wium Olesen has argued that the programme has to be seen as more than just political cosmetics in order to stem the anticipated Communist tide. It was meant for real. He has also maintained that Krag played a significant role and on some crucial issues actually manipulated the committee in order to change the proposed policies from a traditional socialist line of thought to more modern, technocrat ideas of a managed capitalist economy focused on full employment policies, industrialization and growth. Thus, the question of the relative importance of planned economy policies or Keynesian demand management was not an either-or, it was a both-and.[24]

Anyway, 'Denmark of the Future' proved to be the wrong programme for the time. The manifesto's very national perspective and its highly *dirigiste* measures were not what was on the international political agenda of the immediate post-war years. The new leading power, the USA, demanded free trade, liberalisation and European cooperation and division of labour. Still, the idea of monitoring the economy with a Keynesian analytical model and Keynesian employment policies proved appropriate in managing the Marshal Plan in Denmark and elsewhere and later, in the 1950s and 1960s, in developing the local Danish variant of the modern 'mixed economy'. In a narrow Danish perspective, 'Denmark of the Future' is the first elaborate political text that conveyed a detailed understanding of

23. Bredsdorff, *Fremtidens Danmark*; Aa. Hoffmann "»Fremtidens Danmark«. En analyse af Socialdemokratiets efterkrigsprogram, dets tilblivelse, indhold og formål",

Årbog for arbejderbevægelsens historie 1993.
24. N. W. Olesen,"Jens Otto Krag og Keynes", *Arbejderhistorie*, no. 1, 2001.

Keynesian macroeconomics. But to claim the manifesto is a blue-print for the Danish welfare state or anything similar is misleading and obscures the essential character of 'Denmark of the Future'. This point is important for understanding the role of Krag in the further development of the Danish welfare state. Until the beginning of the early 1960s, Krag was not occupied with the social policy dimensions of the party's political strategy. From 1944 and 20 years on, his key concern was employment policy.

Compared to other election manifestoes of 1944 and 1945, there is hardly anything original in 'Denmark of the Future'. By all standards, it presents itself as a detailed, elaborate, elegantly written and shrewd political text – but bit by bit, the political substance and the particular suggestions are discernable in other European political texts of the time, that were available to Krag. No other Danish politician or political operative, though, were on such a detailed level sensitive to the international currents and ideas that inspired Krag when writing 'Denmark of the Future'. Occupied Denmark was extremely parochial but Krag stands out as the only Danish person of his time capable of combining an elaborate understanding of international and Danish politics with a sensitivity to the developments of international political and economic thought and, on this basis, making a coherent and appealing political text out of it.

The early Cold War

During the process of formulating 'Denmark of the Future' and creating the party's political platform in liberated Denmark, party chairman Hans Hedtoft had eyed the talents of Jens Otto Krag. Hedtoft made him his closest political counsel, and Krag thrived in the attention of the party chairman. In November 1947, Denmark went to the ballot for the second time after the war. The Social Democratic Party was strengthened. Krag, too, had run for election and won a seat in the Parliament. Hedtoft formed a minority government that lasted until 1950. Krag was appointed Minister of Trade.

The young minister went to the job with lots of ideas and enthusiasm. High on the agenda was the question of how to implement the Marshall Plan in Denmark. Krag was very much engaged in forming the Long-term Programme and he took part in the OEEC sessions. He was now playing on the big scene and enjoyed it. Foreign policy had been an interest of his since the early war years. Krag's later reputation among historians as a cosmopolitan and an internationalist could, however, lead to an exaggeration of his foreign policy influence in the Hedtoft government 1947–50 and to an amplification of his Atlantist inclinations. Bo Lidegaard, for instance, seems to do both. In a biographical study from 1996 of the Danish Washington ambassador, Henrik Kaufmann, Lidegaard portrays Krag as an 'internationalist' with Atlantist ideals already in the spring of 1948.[25] Allegedly, these ideals were honed by the development of international politics from the Prague coup and onwards. More local experiences also made an impact. In February to April 1948, rumours were swirling around in Denmark about an imminent communist coup and a possible Soviet invasion. The police and military were put in a state of readiness. The events were later termed 'the Easter Crisis'.

The dramatic escalation of tensions between the East and the West from the Prague coup in February 1948 until the decision to form the Atlantic Alliance in the spring of 1949 was observed with immense concern by the Danish government and political observers in the country. In February 1949, Prime Minister Hedtoft acknowledged that his favourite security arrangement – a Scandinavian Defence Pact – had failed. He therefore quickly embraced the Atlantic solution and turned his party in favour of this. Lidegaard is very keen to place Krag in the middle of this decision-making process, but the evidence is sketchy and calls for a general methodological evaluation of Krag's foreign policy role and views in the early Cold War and the pitfalls of the source material, especially his diaries.

In an article in 1978 in a Danish weekly, Krag recalls the Easter Crisis 30 years back. In the article, Krag cites his diaries and characterizes his younger self as a 'young man, not accustomed to think

25. B. Lidegaard, *I Kongens navn.*
Henrik Kauffmann i dansk diplomati
1918–1958, Copenhagen 1996, p. 450.

along these lines' and more occupied by other political problems. This is, in fact, a very precise reflection of his diaries before 1950. When writing about situations with Hedtoft and H.C. Hansen discussing foreign policy matters he referred their discussions, but in general he abstained from analyzing the topics involved. When writing about economic policy he analyzed the topic in its economic context and always with an eye to the possibilities of 'spinning' the issue in a domestic power battle with the opposition.

When reading such source material as the diaries of Jens Otto Krag, it is crucial to consider whether Krag actually was taking part in the decision-making or only observing it. The perspective – as seen by Krag – emphasizes the element of agency, but read carefully and in combination with other sources this emphasis can be counterbalanced. In foreign policy matters before the Danish decision to join the Atlantic Alliance, he was, in general, an observer.

If one addresses Krag's views on foreign policy in this period, it is evident that he in the early Cold War years was less of an Atlanticist than H.C. Hansen and maybe even Hedtoft. In his diaries in March 1948, he wrote *'I am on guard against an accession to a Western bloc.'*[26] Since Krag was very reluctant to convey clear positions on security policy in his diaries before 1950, the evidence is mostly indirect. But if he held any stance on the subject of alliances he was close to Hedtoft, probably with a propensity in the direction of a more traditional Danish neutrality position. In the critical days of February 1949 when the decision to join the Atlantic Alliance was reached, his diaries showed no passion for the Atlantist idea but he went along with his party chairman as a matter of necessity and loyalty.[27] Later, as foreign minister and prime minister his convictions and motives remains obscure in many instances. It was seldom clear whether Krag's line of action in security politics should be explained by deep convictions, domestic parliamentary tactics or as a simple adaptation to Cold War realities. His relationship to the US is a fair example of this ambiguity. He knew and respected American views.

26. Olesen, *Jens Otto Krag*, p. 352
27. Olesen, *Jens Otto Krag*, p. 380.

On numerous occasions he offered valuable support to US diplomacy – especially by muffling social democratic criticism of the Vietnam War. Yet, Krag was also keenly aware of the trappings of dependency and did not hesitate to manifest independent views or to withhold support on matters of principle or on questions of sovereignty. An example of this is his swift move after the crash in 1968 of an American B52 bomber plane carrying four hydrogen bombs at Thule Air Base in Greenland to reassert the principle that nuclear weapons were not to be accepted on Danish territory in peacetime.[28]

Facing the Common Market

In 1955 Krag and a senior civil servant from the Foreign ministry visited Luxembourg. Krag, then minister for economic affairs and the government's envoy to the OEEC, met with the head of the High Authority, Jean Monnet, and the prime minister of Luxembourg Joseph Bech. The chief intention with the meeting was to sort out Denmark's current dissatisfaction with the trading conditions with the ECSC on steel, coal and coke. The Danish government was – with Krag as the main protagonist – at this point deeply engaged in Scandinavian talks on a Scandinavian common market, a venture not least based on plans for a common Scandinavian market for steel and steel products – a potential conflict area with the Six. The meeting in Luxembourg served as a possibility to prod the possible reactions among the Six, but also to reconnoitre among the Six on what had transpired at the meeting in Messina just a week earlier.[29] At this point of time Krag had previously had much experience with the Coal- and Steel Community and with the High Authority and was

28. T. B. Olesen and P. Villaume, "I blokopdelingens tegn". *Dansk Udenrigspolitiks Historie 1945–1972*, Danmarks Nationalleksikon, Copenhagen 2005, p. 641.

29. Denmark's National Archive (DKNA), Copenhagen, Cabinet Economic Committee 3/8: Ministry of Commerce (MC): Note on Minister of Economic Affairs Jens Otto Krag's visit to Brussels and Luxembourg 12–13 June 1955.

beginning to draw his own conclusions with regard to the dis-
advantages of not being member of the co-operation among the Six.
It is especially tempting for the historian to see the eventual signing
of the Treaties of Rome in 1957 as the beginning of Krag's European convictions – in the sense of a beginning realisation of the
necessity to join the supranational co-operation of the Six – and the
first step in a journey that ended on the rostrum of the Danish parliament on the 3rd of October, 1972.[30]

The years between 1955 and 1959, from the Messina meeting to
the West European market schism between the Continental Six
EEC-countries and the Seven EFTA-countries, marked a decisive
formative period for Krag's understanding of the nature of the European Community. As it, in 1956 and early 1957, became clear to the
members of the OEEC that the Six were moving towards the signing of what was to become the Treaties of Rome, Krag tried desperately to bridge the market schism between the UK, the Scandinavian partners and the Six. With the emerging Common Market and
the preferential trade regimes for food exports Danish farmers
risked to loose their export markets in especially West Germany to
the Netherlands. At the same time powerful industrial and labour
interests had strong reservations with regard to joining the Common Market and abandoning the Scandinavian plans for a joint
Scandinavian market arrangement.

During these negotiations Krag gradually advanced from Minister of Economic Affairs – then a junior cabinet post – to Minister for
Foreign Economic Affairs and, eventually, in 1958 to Foreign Minister. The European question shaped Krag's career at the same time
as Krag shaped Denmark's European policy. The crucial year 1957,
the year of the Treaties of Rome, is symptomatic for this transformation. Early 1957 Danish politicians confronted the coming of
the Treaties of Rome. At the end of the year the government had
formulated its European policy. Early 1957 Krag was struggling for
his position in the Social Democrat leadership. At the end of the

30. A quite nuanced example in:
Lidegaard, *Jens Otto Krag 1914–1961*,
pp. 541, 544–547.

year his position as his country's main European spokesperson was unchallenged. Here the biographer is grappling with difficult questions of information, motives and causation. Seen through the prism of the events of this crucial year Krag's role in the shaping of Denmark's balance between Scandinavian solidarity and close relations with – bordering to applying for membership of – the Six signatories of the Treaties of Rome appears much less clear than when looking at the assumed long term continuities. The assumption of continuity in European aims does not seem to stand unchallenged in such a light. Neither does the assumption of a relatively clear understanding of the nature of the emerging European institutions and policies in the EEC.

Despite the massive source material available on this period, we know little about Krag's European convictions and about his position to supranational integration of the kind shaped by the Treaties of Rome. Reflecting on the danger for Denmark in the case of the breaking up of the OEEC, and the prospect of a Common Market with protectionist traits Krag noted in his diary 10 february 1957: *'The reality must presumably be an arrangement between Denmark and the Six. But that is a revolution'.*[31] In the Board on Foreign Policy meeting on the 28th of February, Krag equivocated and declared that the government intended to conduct an 'in-depth orientation' with regard to the plans of the Six. The intention was among other to block the pressure of the opposition for a scramble towards membership of the Six.[32] Yet, later in February Krag noted: *'We will most likely end with the Six. In certain cases the most radical changes seem to be easier to take'.*[33] During springtime 1957 on behalf of the parliamentary majority Krag made overtures to the EEC Interim Commission about the conditions for a full or partial Danish membership of the EEC. It was in an airplane on his way to the signing cer-

31. Library and Archive of the Labour Movement (Arbejderbevægelsens Bibliotek og Arkiv, ABA), Copenhagen, Jens Otto Krag's archive (JOK), Diaries, 10 Feb 1957.

32. DKNA, Archive of the Danish Ministry of Foreign Affairs (DKFA), 73.B.66.a./V: Minutes of meeting in the Board on Foreign Policy and Parliament's Committee on Supplies 28.2.1957.

33. Ibid. 28 Feb 1957.

emony of the Treaties of Rome that Paul-Henri Spaak learned about the Danish desire to meet with the Six in order to investigate the conditions for closer ties.[34] This coincidence should, however, not lead to an overestimation of the Danish government's intentions vis-à-vis the Six. At the same time Krag tried to rally the Scandinavians behind a compromise with the Six on an OEEC-wide free trade area. Much of this, of course, had a certain element of tactical bargaining in order to push for a tolerable solution to Denmark's agricultural export problems. In the spring of 1957 Krag told the British ambassador to Copenhagen that Denmark would seek some kind of association with the Six, stretching from full membership to a looser connection.[35] Krag was also one of a small group of Danish diplomats and politicians with in-depth knowledge about what was then still only a fuzzy outline of the Common Market. We also know that Krag had met men like Jean Monnet, Robert Marjolin etc., but the sources on his reflections on the European problems are few, non-committing or at times even contradicting.

The seeming linearity of the biographical approach to historical events might be misleading when looking at this crucial point in Danish history – especially seen in the long term perspective of the referendum on the 2nd of October 1972. Moreover, many dimensions of politics blended into each other in Krag's biography: During 1957 Krag fought for his position in the Social Democrat leadership. In May 1957 a general election was held resulting in a new coalition government. At the same time as Krag negotiated with the UK government, with the Scandinavian partners and the Six, he was increasingly drawn into issues of a security dimension in the Atlantic Alliance and discussing security matters with major European partners – especially West Germany. The question is thus, not only whether there is a clear continuity between 1957 and 1972. Even more, as this discussion shows it is debatable whether the eventful year 1957 can be brought on a formula of foresighted, rational policy making on European affairs in Denmark. Krag's views and aims on Denmark's rela-

34. DKNA, DKFA, 73.B.66.c: Rome delegation to E. Kristiansen, 8 April 1957.

35. United Kingdom National Archives (UKNA), Kew, London, Foreign Office (FO) 371/128287: Barclay to FO, 1 May 1957.

tionship to European integration during certain periods of this significant year were indeed inscrutable and at times also ambiguous.

Krag eventually led Denmark into EFTA, but he remained one of
the EFTA representatives with closest political ties to the capitals
of the Six. Just a few years after, in 1961, Krag led his country in a
quick and firm decision to follow the British application for EEC
membership. Thus, seemingly, began the thread of the story leading to the debacle in the Danish parliament 3 October 1972 after the
referendum on EEC membership.

Conclusion

The historiography on Krag and his own contributions in terms of
writings, diaries and archive material does constitute a case of the
methodological complexities with working on the biography of
a historical actor with a growing sense of, on the one hand, his own
historical significance and, on the other hand, of the significance of
the future historiography to his political legacy. Writing on Jens
Otto Krag's political life is in many respects ghost writing in the
sense that Krag's presence is felt in the source material, in his historical writings and – subtly – in the writings of others. Historians
consulting source materials related to Krag almost get the feeling
that he or she is expected. This raises questions about not only
the relationship between the early phases of Krag's diaries and the
later phases, but also about the impact of his growing awareness of
his historical legacy on the source material preserved after him.
Most importantly: if the awareness of his place in the future historiography indeed did tempt Krag – consciously or sub-consciously
– to gloss diary entries and retrospective writings with hints at
grand designs, clever stratagems and visionary strategies, then the
orderly narrative built on this source material comes into question.

Seen through the lens of the three episodes selected for discussion above the common thread of Krag's political life does seem to
be woven more loosely than often assumed. This is not to say that
welfare, the Atlantic Alliance and Denmark's European policies did
not loom large in Krag's mind during many of his political pursuits.

The point being made here is rather that the role of the three crucial episodes are in need of new interpretation in themselves, and that the threads spun from these three recurrent themes in Krag's political work might well be less linear and more ambiguous than we historians, the present authors included, have tended to assume. This raises questions about the understanding of the historical actor in question, of individual key episodes and of the nature of the protagonist's role in determining the outcome of such key episodes. Moreover, it touches upon questions of motive and causation in the shaping of crucial historical events. If, say, Krag's perception of the long term perspective of the welfare state were more foggy than we have tended to believe, then the political history of the 1960s with the expansion of welfare policies and institutions might be seen in a new light. If his support to NATO and the Atlantic ideology in general was more reserved than hitherto perceived, this should be part of the historical evaluations of his foreign policy decisions – in combination with his concerns of trivial domestic politics and sheer pragmatism. If Krag's priority for Denmark's accession to the EEC at times wavered in favour of internal warring between factions in the Danish labour movement, coalition tactics or election campaigns, then strands of the finely woven order of his political biography will unravel.

For the historian to evoke a certain interpretation on a historical subject or on past lives is always to impose order and meaning. Nowhere among the genres of historical writings is this more the case than in the art of writing biography. On the other hand, the best ambience for the historian to unfold his full analytical capacity in working with the source material and keeping a sensitivity to the potential and openness of concrete historical situations is that of the disorder of the past as it was and of the ensuing source material as it is. We have suggested that more attention should be given to capture this original openness and that the balance between imposing order and meaning on the one hand and on the other hand analytical openness to ambiguities might be shifted however slightly in favour of the latter. The past – also the lived past – is sometimes almost as chaotic as a historian's desk.

E.H. Carr

Changing the Intellectual Milieu

Mark F. Gilbert

Johns Hopkins University, Bologna

> In Europe some of the small units of the past may continue
> for a few generations longer to eke out a precariously
> independent existence ... But their military and economic
> insecurity has been demonstrated beyond recall. They can
> survive only as an anomaly and as an anachronism in a world
> that has moved on to other forms of organization.[1]

Denying that individuals count in politics would seem absurd outside the Academy. As citizens, if not always as scholars, we grasp that
major issues are decided differently according to who is 'in charge'.
This commonsense awareness of the centrality of individual politicians for political decision-making explains why political history
continues to be taught in history departments and why historical
approaches are once again reasserting themselves in departments of
political science. With intellectuals, the question is less straightforward. Studying the ideas and beliefs of public intellectuals and political thinkers is undeniably interesting for its own sake, but it is rare
to find an intellectual's book, article or lecture altering policy with
the immediacy that any strong-minded minister can command.

The case of E.H. Carr is actually rather a good illustration of this
observation. For if ever an intellectual was in a position to exercise
a direct influence on events, he was. As deputy editor and chief leader writer of *The Times* between 1941 and 1946, he was in a position
to provide Britain's political élite with food for thought over their

1. E.H. Carr, *Nationalism and After*,
London 1945, p. 37.

breakfast tables. But while his articles and books unquestionably influenced the analysis of his fellow intellectuals (including some who
had sharply disagreed with his pro-appeasement tendencies before
the war), his pronounced pro-Soviet views generated considerable
irritation among professional policy makers, who were alarmed that
the prestige of Carr's pulpit might lead foreigners to think that the
British government agreed with the stark realism of his sermons.
Certainly, Carr's editorials did not impinge on how Churchill, Eden
and, later, Bevin made decisions, though they did move Churchill,
after an attack by Carr on his policy towards Greece, to condemn
their 'spirit of gay, reckless, unbridled partisanship' in a House of
Commons speech on 18 January 1945.[2]

So why write about Carr? This chapter suggests that Carr's influence was not on immediate events but in the way that intellectuals
usually do have most effect: through the contribution he made to
eroding established mental structures (a.k.a. 'ideas') and through his
dissemination of new concepts which would become part of the
patrimony of political discourse over the next thirty years. This is
not a reference to his copious work on Soviet Russia, though Carr
was one of the chief originators and purveyors of the view that the
excesses of Stalinist Russia were a concomitant of its modernization,
rather than an integral part of communist ideology. This chapter
argues that Carr was also one of the thinkers in wartime Europe who
most thoughtfully contributed to the creation of the historical rationale for European integration (that is to say, to the construction
of the narrative that informed the intellectual climate surrounding
the politicians who actually took the decisive political steps).

E.H. Carr: Life and Works

Carr's stock has been rising lately in the intellectual market, after
a twenty-year hiatus in which his reputation suffered from the almost indecent vehemence of some of his obituarists. When Carr

2. J. Haslam, *The Vices of Integrity:
E.H. Carr 1892–1982*, London 1999,
p. 116.

died in November 1982, he was immediately attacked as a 'grey eminence' (Norman Stone) whose work had been chiefly concerned with lauding the strong and damning the weak. Carr's classic work from the 1930s, *The Twenty Years' Crisis*, was dismissed as a subtle theoretical justification for appeasement and more generally for the doctrine that 'might is right'; his massive multi-volume study of the Russian revolution was remembered above all as an apologia for Stalinism. In retrospect, his conception of the nature of history was seen, as Isaiah Berlin had insisted in a notorious exchange of letters and reviews in the early 1960s, as the writing of narrative from the point of view of the winners and with callous disregard for the fate of the losers.[3] There is much truth in these charges – it is worse than pointless to defend Carr where he cannot be defended – and yet there is some simplification too. Carr was a much bigger figure in the intellectual history of our times than some of his graveside detractors would admit. As his not always sympathetic biographer argues, 'his was a fascinating mind, even in its darkest interiors'.[4]

The breadth of his interests alone suffices to qualify him as a writer worthy of reappraisal and investigation. Between 1919 and 1936, Carr worked for the Foreign Office, a period which included a long posting in Riga between 1925 and 1929 that qualified him as a specialist on the 'small states' of Eastern Europe and on relations with the USSR. His earliest published works were on Russian literature, most notably his studies of *Dostoevsky* (1931) and *The Russian Exiles* (1933), a work that depicted Alexander Herzen and other intellectual refugees from Tsarist persecution. In 1936, Carr became – with one of those adroit translations of career that were possible before universities were professionalized – Woodrow Wilson professor of international politics at Aberystwyth and began an intense period of publication on the theory and practice of international relations, the high point of which, of course, was *The Twenty Years' Crisis* (Carr 1939). During the war, he first worked for the Ministry

3. M. Ignatieff, *Isaiah Berlin: A Life*, London 1998, p. 236.

4. Haslam, *The Vices of Integrity*, p. 299.

of Information, where his attempts to clarify Britain's 'Peace Aims' for propaganda purposes led to a breach with the Foreign Office, which disliked his attempt to promote what amounted to an independent foreign policy, before moving to *The Times*. His dozens of wartime articles were controversial for their outspoken conviction that the 'twin scourges' of war and unemployment could only be superseded by the establishment of a planned economy in imitation of and in cooperation with the USSR.[5] Carr developed his ideas in more extended form in his short book, *The Conditions of Peace* and in a dense but brilliant essay, *Nationalism and After*. As Charles Jones says, these two works were the 'more studied oils' for which his articles in *The Times* were the 'water colour preparatory sketches'.[6]

Carr resigned from *The Times* in 1946. He subsequently immersed himself in his studies on the development of the USSR (fourteen volumes, for twelve of which he was sole author; in all, over 6,500 pages of narrative) and had an astonishingly prolific career as an influential literary journalist and scholarly reviewer, publishing some 900 contributions to the *Times Literary Supplement* between 1930 and 1980.[7] He was elected to a research fellowship at Trinity College, Cambridge in 1955, when he was already in his sixties; the last volume of his opus on the Russian revolution was published in 1977 when he was eighty-five.

Between January-March 1961, Carr gave the Trevelyan lectures at Cambridge, which were broadcast over the radio and subsequently published as *What is History?* This brief book of pungently expressed argument, which has since become the standard introductions to the nature of historical study in English-speaking countries, is notable for its conviction that the true historian is one who has the 'future in his bones'; one, in short, who is capable of grasping history's direction and who knows how to 'project his vision into

5. C. Jones, *E.H. Carr and International Relations: A Duty to Lie*, Cambridge 1998, pp. 72–80.
6. Jones, *E.H. Carr and International Relations*, p. 76.

7. S. Collini, "The Intellectual as Realist: The Puzzling Career of E.H. Carr," in: S. Collini, *Common Reading: Critics, Historians, Publics*, Oxford 2008, pp. 156–174, here p. 159.

the future in such a way as to give him a more lasting insight into the past than can be attained by those historians whose outlook is bounded by their own immediate situation'.[8] Such a conception of the historian's task almost inevitably leads the contemporary historian into politics, since such a scholar is bound to judge current affairs in the light of his broader scheme: in short, to find particular political decisions historical, unhistorical, or even anti-historical.

Forms of European Organization

By the standards of his contributions to the contemporary history of Russia, international relations theory and historiography, Carr's ideas on European integration are small beer: a few drops in his oceanic overall production. The starting point of his analysis was the quotation with which I have prefaced this chapter. For him, the 'small units' of Europe were anachronistic. It was time to build Europe anew. Carr would have agreed with G.D.H. Cole's dictum that '(I)t is man's moral duty to be good: it is further his rational duty to be sensible and not to pursue courses of action that do not harmonise with the objective facts that he has to deal with'.[9] For Carr, it was simply not sensible to continue with a form of organisation so historically untenable as the nation state. As Carr famously asserted at the end *Nationalism and After*, it was possible to make two 'negative predictions' about the future international state system:

> We shall not again see a Europe of twenty, and a world of more than sixty, 'independent sovereign states', using the term in its hitherto accepted sense; nor shall we see in our time a single world authority as the final repository of power, political and economic, exercising supreme control over the affairs and destinies of mankind ... the world will have to

8. Edward Hallet Carr (Richard Evans (ed.)), *What is History?*, London 2003, p.117.

9. G.D.H. Cole, *Europe, Russia and the Future*, New York 1942, p. 90.
10. Carr, *Nationalism and After*, pp. 51–52.

accommodate itself to the emergence of a few great multi-national units in which power will be mainly concentrated ...[10]

The issue, therefore, was how the *European* multi-national unit should be constructed when the Nazis were defeated. Carr's answer to this question is to be found in *The Conditions of Peace*, which was written, in 1942, when German tanks were still driving across the steppes of the Ukraine, but which interestingly – given Carr's pre-war record as an appeaser – did not betray any hint that a compromise peace with Germany might be a solution to Europe's problems. Carr basically advanced five key conditions to make a workable European unit possible.

First, the *big powers should define the settlement*. Unlike in 1919, there should be no futile post-war squabbling over whether Yugoslavia or Romania should occupy the Banat or whether Poland or Czechoslovakia should claim the suburbs of Teschen: the minor powers should do as they were told. As Carr said in the conclusion to *The Conditions of Peace*, '(n)o durable peace can be made unless those who have the power have also the will in the last resort, after having tried all methods of persuasion, to take and enforce with vigour and impartiality the decisions which they think right'.[11] For both security reasons and for reasons of ideological attraction, the countries of Eastern Europe were likely to look to the USSR (and even if they did not, it was 'essential...to reserve for Russia a determining voice in the eventual organisation of that region').[12] Britain, by contrast, was the natural leader of Western Europe and could not 'wash her hands' of her duties to her neighbours.[13]

Second, *it was vital for own national interests that Britain should take the lead in post-war reconstruction*. Not the least reason for Carr's advocacy of European integration was his fear that unless Britain could find itself a way of expanding his strategic importance, it would be squeezed between the Soviet Union and the USA and

11. E.H. Carr, *The Conditions of Peace*, New York 1943, p. 280.
12. Carr, *The Conditions of Peace*, p. 201.
13. Carr, *The Conditions of Peace*, p. 193.

would see its status diminish. Carr feared, moreover, that a renascent Germany would emerge in the absence of a British initiative. It would be 'reckless folly' to leave a 'vacuum' in Western Europe.[14] Carr's 1945 book *Nationalism and After* concluded with a postscript that argued for the 'establishment of more intimate links, couched in terms appropriate to the Western tradition, between Britain and the nations of Western Europe'. These links, Carr suggested, would be essentially economic in character, rather than political, and would derive from a 'solid basis of common interest.' All the countries of Western Europe, Britain included, would face common problems of economic adjustment, balance of payments, a high degree of dependence on foreign trade and a shortage of raw materials for their highly developed industrial economies. All of them would face the same demand for social justice. Several of them faced the risky challenge of decolonization. For Carr, 'common economic planning, as well as joint military organization, will alone enable western Europe, Britain included, to confront the future with united strength and confidence'.[15]

Third – and here Carr continued his polemic with the liberal 'utopians' he had condemned so roundly in *The Twenty Years' Crisis* – *federal forms of post-war political organization for Europe were aberrant*. In this regard, he was in sharp contrast to the many British and emigré intellectuals resident in Britain who were advocating the construction of a federal European state, usually, though not invariably, together with a declaration of democratic socialist principles. Carr believed – and expressed his belief with characteristic frankness – that such people were wrong- (or muddle) headed, as were the many intellectuals who advocated world government:

> One popular approach is to plunge immediately into the elaboration of some constitutional framework for the whole world or entire continents ... There is a kind of naïve arrogance in the assumption that the problem of the government of mankind, which has defied human wit and human experi-

14. Carr, *The Conditions of Peace*, p. 199.

15. E.H. Carr, *Nationalism and After*, pp. 73–74.

ence for centuries, can be solved out of hand by some neat
paper construction of a few simple-minded enthusiasts.
... the supporters of projects like Federal Union exercise a
pernicious influence by grossly over-simplifying the problem
and by obscuring the need to study with patience and
humility the historical perspective and the economic organization of the world for which they prescribe.[16]

In Carr's view – fourth – what was necessary was *functional cooperation in 'European Reconstruction Corporations'* (ERC): transnational
institutions for reconstruction that would deal with transport,
agricultural and industrial production, employment and public
works. Above all, what was needed was a European Planning Authority (EPA), with oversight over all the reconstruction efforts,
which would specifically co-ordinate 'those fields of economic life
where the misconceived and unqualified independence of the national unit has proved so fatal to peace and prosperity in the last
twenty years', namely production choices, trade and finance. The
EPA would need to have a 'Bank of Europe' as one of its core institutions. Carr explained (here in some detail) that the Bank would
float loans, finance trade, settle claims, and, above all, establish and
maintain a common currency system through which the various
national currencies could be exchanged at a fixed rate for sterling or
for one another.[17]

All Europe's peoples, including the defeated Germans, should be
represented in the EPA's deliberations and policy making. 'The only
way', Carr insisted, 'to make young Germans into good Europeans
is to give them a role to play in the reorganisation of Germany and
Europe which will restore and enhance their self-respect'.[18] Individuals working for the EPA, however, would be functionaries who 'from
the outset' would 'represent the interests of Europe as a whole and
not any one section of it'.[19] Inevitably, however, Britain and Soviet

16. Carr, *The Conditions of Peace*, p. 167.
17. Carr, *The Conditions of Peace*, p. 274.
18. Carr, *The Conditions of Peace*, p. 240.
19. Carr, *The Conditions of Peace*, p. 260.

Russia, as the two European superpowers *in situ*, would have to take the lead and would likely provide a disproportionate contribution to its development. Carr was adamant, however, that there can be 'no branding of those of different nation or race as inferiors and no exclusion of them from the councils of the Authority'.[20] All in all:

> The European Planning Authority should therefore be regarded as the master-key to the problem of postwar settlement. If such an authority can be established and made effective, there is hope for the future of Europe. If it cannot, the prospect is almost unrelievedly dark ....[21]

Fifth, Carr believed that *post-war rivalry between the three wartime allies would be attenuated (indeed, could only be attenuated) through this collaboration in the planned reconstruction of European civilization*. Rebuilding Europe would give a 'moral purpose' that could substitute the struggle against Nazism as a force able to bind three such ideologically distinct civilizations together. However, Carr's thought on this question went rather beyond diplomatic utility. One of the most interesting aspects of *The Conditions of Peace* is Carr's essay within the essay on the subject of 'the moral crisis', which acts as an intellectual foundation for the whole book. Unlike any other British thinker of his time, at any rate on the left, Carr was prepared to recognize that war had an 'essential social function'.[22] War provided, Carr argued, 'a sense of meaning and purpose widely felt to be lacking in modern life'.[23] Indeed, it may not be entirely fanciful to extrapolate from Carr's work the belief that war is a valuable agent of the historical process: a driving force of progress and social improvement. Carr certainly thought that Hitler's war (although it should by now be clear that any historical figure, even Hitler, was thoroughly relativised in Carr's scheme of things) had at the very least provided the basis for a new leap forward. Carr, in his wartime articles and books, was sketching for British policy

20. Carr, *The Conditions of Peace*, p. 261.
21. Carr, *The Conditions of Peace*, p. 259.
22. Carr, *The Conditions of Peace*, p. 117.
23. Carr, *The Conditions of Peace*, p. 119.

makers the form he thought this leap forward should take. European integration was, in this regard, a central idea for him.

An English Historicist

Carr's advocacy of an EPA, with its obvious similarities to the EEC model that emerged in the 1950s and 1960s, is undeniably interesting, but is arguably also less important than the process of reasoning that led him to this conclusion. Carr only sketches this reasoning in *The Conditions of Peace*: One has to wait for *Nationalism and After*, in 1945, to grasp fully the sophistication of his understanding of the significance of the historical moment in which he was writing. The point is that for Carr, European integration was a *potential future* in harmony with history's deepest positive trends.

Carr saw modern European history as being driven by two motors: the rise of the masses and the rise to primacy of the concept of social justice, an intellectual development that was linked to the rise of the masses, but which was not a mere narrow function of greater mass participation in political life. The political forms of the European state, and hence the configuration of inter-state relations, had been progressively shaped by the growing hegemony of the masses and by their demand for welfare.

Carr identifies four phases in this historical process, which began after the dissolution of the 'medieval unity of empire and church and the establishment of the national state and the national church', in other words, with the Reformation.[24] The 'essential characteristic' of the first phase 'was the identification of the nation with the person of the sovereign'.[25] European states in short were the personal property of their rulers, and what states did was decided by a single individual and his or her advisors. In this phase of development, war was the instrument by which sovereigns solved their differences of opinion, but its use was circumscribed by convention and, to some extent, by nascent international law. The populations of nations at war might suffer famine and rapine as a result of war,

24. Carr, *Nationalism and After*, p. 2.
25. Carr, *Nationalism and After*, p. 2.

but this was a side-effect, not certainly a deliberate goal of policy. Civilians from warring states could 'pass to and fro and transact their business freely with each other while their respective sovereigns were at war'.[26] Economic affairs, in this international order, was at the service of politics. What we today call mercantilism was 'the economic policy of a period which identified the interest of a nation with the interest of its rulers'.[27] It was a policy directed at the acquisition of the financial wherewithal to conduct war.

This model was superseded in the turmoil that followed the French revolution by a second phase that is 'generally accounted the most orderly and enviable of modern international relations'.[28] Carr's description of the 'second period' is a sophisticated compressed account of the economic and political structure of nineteenth century Europe (and, perhaps even more, of its *mindset*) and to compress it further inevitably risks caricature. In essence, however, Carr contends that after the liberal bourgeoisie had emerged in the mid-nineteenth century as the dominant economic class, politics was subordinated to the pursuit of what would be today called economic growth. Political power was in the hands of the propertied classes and they were, to a remarkable extent, cosmopolitan in outlook and 'united by common ideals and interests', above all respect for the freedom of private property. The chief defining feature of the 'second period' in fact was 'two salutary illusions'. These were, first, that the 'world economic system was truly international'; second, that 'economic and political systems were entirely separate and operated independently of each other'. The first of these illusions was sustained by the expansion and openness of Great Britain, whose swift emergence as the world's largest economic power from the 1830s onwards provided a 'a single, wide-open and apparently insatiable market for all consumable commodities' and whose currency and banking system became the 'seat of government' for the world economy.[29] The truth was that *Britain* was international and other countries enjoyed a cosmopolitan illusion

26. Carr, *Nationalism and After*, p. 4.   29. Carr, *Nationalism and After*,
27. Carr, *Nationalism and After*, p. 6   pp. 14–15.
28. Carr, *Nationalism and After*, p. 6

under her benevolent prosperity. This fact permitted the continu-
ance of the polite fiction that politics and economics were separate
from each other. Real power was wielded by the financiers of the
City and their counterparts in other European capitals, but since this
power was both hidden from public view and taken for granted, 'it
was not recognized, either by those who exercised control, or by
those who submitted to it, how far the political independence of nations was conditioned by the pseudo-international world economic order based on British supremacy'.[30] Britain infringed the national sovereignty of other nations every time the Bank of England
raised bank rate, but until the late nineteenth century such infringe-
ments were complacently regarded as the working of impartial economic laws; as natural phenomena, not man-made disasters.

The mines that exploded under the foundations of this system
and brought it tumbling down were, of course, nationalism and the
rise of the masses to political power. The dual illusions of the second period allowed European nations to drink these 'heady wines'
without immediate catastrophe, but in retrospect – and here Carr
neatly and I think consciously turns Benedetto Croce on his head
– the nineteenth century was less the story of the triumph of the
'religion of liberty' and the spread of parliamentary institutions and
liberal doctrines than an 'idyllic interlude' from permanent war:
a kind of historical half-time break, or parenthesis, from a very
violent game indeed.[31] The third period of modern European political history, therefore, which began in the late nineteenth century
and which reached its apogee in Nazism, was that of the 'socialized
nation', where the masses' clamour for jobs, economic security and
a higher standard of living are the raison d'etre of politics and where
the rulers' first duty is to satisfy their demands – 'the first obligation
of the modern national government, which no other obligation will
be allowed to override, is to its own people'.[32] Drawing on the work

30. Carr, *Nationalism and After*, p. 16.
31. Carr, *Nationalism and After*, p. 9;
see also E.H. Carr, *The Soviet Impact
on the Western World*, London 1946,
p. 93.

32. Carr, *Nationalism and After*, p. 31.
33. Carr, *Nationalism and After*, p. 19;
F. Borkenau, *Socialism: National
or International*, London 1942.

of Franz Borkenau, Carr added that the 'natural corollary' of the socialized nation had been the 'nationalization of socialism'.[33] The 'counterpart' to a national policy founded 'on the support of the masses,' was the 'loyalty of the masses to a nation which had become the instrument of their collective interests and ambitions'.[34]

The identification of the masses with the nation state was one reason for the intensification of nationalism into the hyper nationalism of fascism. But two other reasons loomed. First, nationalism 'invaded and conquered the economic domain from which the nineteenth century had so cunningly excluded it'.[35] The 'single world economy was replaced by a multiplicity of national economies, each concerned with the well-being of its own members'.[36] Second, in defiance of the trend to greater economic concentration, the number of nation states in Europe grew to over twenty, each of which claimed traditional sovereign rights in the name of 'self-determination' and succumbed to economic nationalism in the name of the same doctrine. As he had written in *The Conditions of Peace*, the Paris treaties of 1919–1920 had 'fostered the disintegration of existing political units and favoured the creation of a multiplicity of smaller units, at a moment when strategic and economic factors were demanding increased integration and the grouping of the world into fewer and larger units of power'.[37] For Carr, the socialization of the nation, the nationalization of economic policy and the multiplication of sovereign states 'have combined to produce the characteristic totalitarian symptoms' of the time.[38]

In effect, Carr was arguing that the doctrine regulating international politics had not kept up with social and economic change. The age of the masses and of mass production had arrived, but the dominant ideological precepts governing international politics were the doctrine of national sovereignty and the belief that nations, as distinct from the human beings that composed them, possessed

34. Carr, *Nationalism and After*, p. 20.
35. Carr, *Nationalism and After*, p. 22.
36. Carr, *Nationalism and After*, p. 22.
37. Carr, *The Conditions of Peace*, pp. 51–52.
38. Carr, *The Conditions of Peace*, p. 26.
39. Carr, *The Conditions of Peace*, p. 31.

rights. Carr was clear that 'the international law of the age of sovereigns is incompatible with the socialized nation'.[39] He was equally clear that the demand of Europe's peoples for welfare, plenty and economic certainty, was the crucial question posed by post-war reconstruction. The dual task facing post-war statesmanship was how to plan, produce and distribute social goods as widely and as fairly as possible and how to evolve new 'forms of organization' that would facilitate the fulfilment of this duty. This concrete objective was obviously widely acknowledged in government circles at the time. It underlay such wartime initiatives as the Beveridge report and the Butler education act, and the post-war Labour government's determination to clear slums and build a national health service 'free at the point of use'.

Carr became convinced that the USSR was the laboratory society for this fourth phase in the development of the European state system. The 'Soviet Impact on the Western World',[40] to quote the title of a book of lectures that he delivered at Oxford in February-March 1946, lay precisely in the fact that the USSR represented the harbinger of the planned, multi-national society that was civilization's most promising future. The Russian regime's ruthlessness took second place in his thought to a fixed conviction that Stalinism had been broadly historically beneficial. Why? Because the Soviet Union created since 1917 was (a) a successful example of the power of planning; (b) a multi-national 'Grossraum' that could act in a coherently in international affairs – one which, specifically, had 'consistently supported the view that there can be no political equality between great and small Powers, and that a system based on the pretence of an equality which does not necessarily exist is a sham'.[41]

Carr agreed that it was impossible to have democracy between nations of unequal size and power and have peace. Nations were not equal in size, in fertility, in economic power, in social system or in the will to power and it was irrational to act as if they were. One

40. E.H. Carr, *The Soviet Impact on the Western World*, London 1946.

41. Carr, *The Soviet Impact on the Western World*, p. 83.

only had to look at the wartime fate of the Baltic republics, or the Netherlands, Belgium, Denmark, Norway or Poland to grasp that such countries were, literally, indefensible.[42] But the rationale for Carr's critique of the 'small states' was not, on close examination, solely a question of might makes right. It was also rooted in a palpable sense of frustration that, for him, the false doctrine of the equality of states was contributing to diminish the human rights of their citizens. His wartime thought amounts to 'a protest against an international order which accepts as its basis the submersion of the rights of the individual in the rights of the nation'.[43]

Carr considered that if the peoples of Europe had had to endure foreign conquest and oppression because their political units were inadequate to defend them, and if their welfare had been impoverished because their national resources and industries were too small to achieve economies of scale, then the time had come to abandon the 'unattainable' search for parity between nations and concentrate upon achieving 'a freedom and equality which will express themselves in the daily lives of men and women'.[44] His support for an EPA and for post-war economic cooperation was an attempt to persude statesmen to listen to history's libretto – though he was always conscious that political leaders and whole peoples might be deaf to history's call. In fact, it should be added that by 1945, when he published *Nationalism and After*, he was a good deal less confident of Europe's chances than he had been in the darkest moment of the war. In the absence of British leadership, Carr thought that Western Europe was destined to a 'tragic' future. Her 'outlook' remained 'dark and uncertain'. Western Europe was the 'home of the national epoch from which the world was now emerging'. Western Europe, moreover, lacked 'the leadership and the central focus of power which would be necessary to place her among the great multi-national civilizations of the 'hemisphere' or Grossraum epoch'.[45]

---

42. Carr, *Nationalism and After*, p. 54.
43. Carr, *Nationalism and After*, p. 43.
44. Carr, *Nationalism and After*, p. 43.
45. Carr, *Nationalism and After*, pp. 75–76.

Changing the Intellectual Milieu

It is interesting to compare Carr to other contemporary writers and intellectuals. We normally think of the quality of a thinker as being closely related to his or her originality and sophistication. This essay has shown that Carr was undoubtedly a sophisticated interpreter of his times. Yet it is also true that an undeniable part of the importance of Carr's ideas lies in the fact that others were thinking along the same lines: his work was part of a broader climate of opinion constructed by thinkers and scholars who were trying to get to grips with the causes of the upheaval and destruction of their times.

I have argued elsewhere that Carr's ideas on European reconstruction were essentially similar to those of the important 'progressive' intellectuals gathered around the leading weekly of socialist opinion in Britain, the *New Statesman and Nation*.[46] The pre-war and wartime writings of the progressives were not purely antifascist (as some of them subsequently claimed in their memoirs), nor crudely pro-Soviet (as has sometimes been alleged), but centred upon the need to renew liberal civilization in the face of the totalitarian challenge. These writers were convinced that the Soviet Union represented a realler historical dynamic than liberal capitalism and – if you caught them in a reflective mood – were even willing to acknowledge the same of Fascism. Like Carr, they believed liberal capitalist society was moribund and totalitarianism was one of the symptoms of its disease.[47]

It is true that some of the other writers and intellectuals with whom I am linking Carr here had mostly been enthusiastic 'utopians' – to adopt the terminology of the *Twenty Years' Crisis* – in the 1920s and 1930s. Writers such as Harold J. Laski, who as chairman of the Labour Party during the war was not without political visi-

46. M. Gilbert, "Il futuro socialista dell'Europa. Gli intellettuali progressisti britannici e il federalismo europeo, 1935–1945," *Contemporanea* vol. XI 2008, no. 1, pp. 23–45; M. Gilbert, "The Sovereign Remedy of European Unity: The Progressive Left and Supranational Government 1935–1945", *International Politics*, vol. 47, no. 1, 2009, pp. 27–46.

47. See also: E.H. Carr (Michael Cox (ed.)), *The Twenty Years' Crisis*, London 2001, p. 208.

bility, and the editor of the *New Statesman*, Kingsley Martin, had been passionate partisans of the League of Nations and of liberal internationalist ideas until well into the 1930s. Carr, by contrast, was regarded then and by many still is regarded as the quintessential theorist of power politics. Nevertheless, during the war their ideas converged. Unsurprisingly, because they all shared the view that the 'lesson' of recent history was the dangerous anachronism of the survival of national sovereignty, especially for the 'small states'. As Laski commented: 'To speak of Denmark or Portugal as sovereign states is to dwell in a purely formal realm'.[48] G.D.H. Cole, an Oxford don who was a regular contributor on international affairs to the *New Statesman*, and who on this subject was even more outspoken than Carr, said in a deliberately provocative, indeed in places outrageous, book (*Europe, Russia and the Future*) that the consequences of Europe's pre-war 'economic atomism' had been so 'dire' that:

> From the purely economic point of view, it is quite arguable that it would be better to let Hitler conquer all of Europe short of the Soviet Union, and thereafter exploit it ruthlessly in the Nazi interest, than go back to the pre-war order of independent Nation States with frontiers drawn so as to cut across natural units of production and exchange.[49]

Elsewhere in the same work he affirmed that it was 'much better' to be ruled by Stalin than by a 'pack of half-witted Social Democrats' who 'believe in the "independence" of separate, obsolete, nation states'.[50]

The same broad themes that Carr had raised dominate Laski's wartime book *Reflections on the Revolution in Our Time*. In this work, Laski argued for 'freedom in a planned democracy'; suggested

48. H.J. Laski, *Reflections on the Revolution in Our Time*, London 1943, p. 213.

49. Cole, *Europe, Russia and the Future*, p. 122.

50. Cole, *Europe, Russia and the Future*, p. 9.

that war, by giving individual Britons a sense of duty and purpose, had brought about a 'genuine liberation'[51]; proposed a 'Society of Nations', dominated by the big three military powers, which would coordinate the activities of functional bodies working on the reconstruction of Europe; echoed Carr's arguments about how military might and the need to plan the economy had rendered the sovereignty of the 'small state' obsolete. Laski was not plagiarizing Carr; rather both were shaping the prevailing analytical mood among a particular intellectual community.

The progressives could be ruthless with those states, or individuals, that did not share their views about the undesirability of the small states. Cole's *Europe, Russia and the Future* was condemned by the emigré community in Britain as an apologia for Stalinism. Cole replied by fulminating that 'doctrinaire democrats' who defended national self-determination were the worst enemies that the socialist movement faced.[52] More generally, the *New Statesman* somewhat besmirched its reputation by running a prolonged campaign of denigration from 1942 onwards in its columns against the Polish government-in-exile in London, which was obsessively caricatured as reactionary, anti-Soviet, and anti-Semitic. Shamefully, the London Poles, whose resistance to Nazism can only be described as heroic, were even compared by the *New Statesman* to the Vichy regime in France.[53] Superficially, this campaign might seem a case of straightforward fellow-travelling with Moscow. In fact, a close reading of the paper throughout the last two years of the war shows clearly that what the progressives objected to was the Poles' *national assertiveness*: their determination to re-establish a Polish state that was fully sovereign and, if possible, bigger and stronger than the one that had existed between 1919 and 1939. The Poles' crime was not anti-communism, but refusing to acknowledge the lessons of recent history.

51. Laski, *Reflections on the Revolution in Our Time*, p. 339.
52. Gilbert. "The Sovereign Remedy of European Unity", p. 39.

53. M. Gilbert, "Foreign Policy and Propaganda in the Progressive Press 1936–1945", PhD dissertation, University of Wales, 1990, pp. 222–223.

The comparison of Carr with British progressives is an obvious one. What is equally instructive is to compare Carr's ideas with the *Manifesto di Ventotene*, a document that is canonical for the European Movement and which was written almost contemporaneously with *The Conditions of Peace*. The differences between Carr's ascetic, controlled prose and the more rhetorical style of the *Manifesto* are obvious; moreover, his opinions on the Soviet Union and communism more generally are light years away from Altiero Spinelli, Ernesto Rossi, Eugenio Colorni and Ursula Hirschmann's hostility to the 'bureaucratic despotism' of the Soviet Union, and from their belief that '[a] situation in which the Communists became a dominant political force would represent less a revolutionary turn than an early failure of European renewal'. Most important of all, the *Manifesto* is an explicit call for the 'definitive abolition of the division of Europe into sovereign nation states' and the creation of a 'European Federation'. Carr, as we have seen, was dismissive of British proponents of such ideas.

The similarities between Carr's thought and the ideas of the *Manifesto*'s authors, however, are far greater than a superficial reading might suggest. *The Manifesto*, especially by people who haven't read it, is often depicted outside of Italy as an emblematic document of a popular mood of revulsion against war and nationalism. In fact, it is an analysis of the 'crisis of modern civilization' by a small group of intellectuals who were acutely aware, like Carr, both that powerful reactionary forces would strive to reinstate national sovereignty after the war and that the masses, unsure of what they wanted and misled by their instinctive patriotism, might fall into the trap. Just as Carr could conceive with equanimity an Anglo-Soviet military imposition of European-wide planning on recalcitrant small states, so the authors of the *Manifesto* argued, with Rousseauean panache, that it would be necessary for the revolutionary parties of Europe, 'deeply conscious of representing the most profound needs of modern society', to take the lead in forming the 'new order', by dictatorial means if necessary. There was no need for the uninformed masses to vote. More important was to ensure that the levers of power did not fall into the hands of reactionary classes (or indeed, the Communists) and to guarantee that the powers of the state were used in the new Europe to alleviate the masses from want and misery. Such a federal state would be the 'finest and most innovative creation to emerge for centuries in Europe'.[54]

It will be seen that what Carr, the British progressives and the authors of the *Manifesto* shared was the notion that building a post-national Europe was a primary value over and above even the democratic choices of Europe's peoples, or their right to self-determination. This was a very powerful (and ambiguous) concept that arguably still exercises a real influence on politics in Europe. The undeniable moral force possessed by the institutions of European integration in my view does ultimately derive from the persuasive (or, at any rate, pervasive) historical narrative that depicts the subdivision of Europe into sovereign nation states as the principal cause of political catastrophe and economic under-development in the first half of the twentieth century, but it is also not fanciful to suggest that the EU's 'democratic deficit' has its roots in the same tale. The weapon of last resort for the EU against member states that cling to the trappings of national sovereignty is the warning that a disunited Europe will lapse back, if not into war, then certainly into economic nationalism and political chaos. The 'construction of Europe' is ethically prior to the decisions of the electors in the EU's member states who must 'vote again' if they don't vote the right way the first time. Carr was one of the many wartime thinkers who helped to drape this cloak of historical progress over European integration, but I would argue that he did so less by his somewhat sketchy advocacy of pan-European institutions than by the plausibility and sophistication of the reading he gave to his time. Intellectuals invent their own times: their power lies in their interpretative gift, not in their ability to condition policy. Carr's interpretative gifts were simply enormous.

54. A. Spinelli et al.. *Il Manifesto di Ventotene*, 1941. Available at: http://www.altierospinelli.org/manifesto/manifesto_it.html

Conclusions

Like Marx, or indeed Francis Fukuyama, who greatly resembles Carr in method, if not in political sympathy, Carr's political thought was founded on a cast-iron belief that he had figured out History and others had not. Carr's grand narrative can, in fact, be critiqued, like any other depiction, and not just because subsequent events, such as the stagnation, decline and implosion of communism, and the proliferation of nation states in Europe and elsewhere, disproved his predictions. His analysis of the causes of fascist totalitarianism – socialized nations + nationalization of economic policy + too many small states – in hindsight seems oddly formulaic and psychologically extremely thin. Nationalism was a necessary but not sufficient condition for the rise of fascism, which, if poetic license may be permitted, was propelled by the darker side of the European soul just as much as by economic and social forces. Carr never gives the impression of understanding why Germans and Italians enjoyed marching in unison in torchlight parades, or why categories of human being should have been subordinated to slave or inhuman status.

It should be said, however, that Carr got a lot right. Jonathan Haslam has written that ' [u]nlike many of his riskier predictions, Carr's anticipation of the process of western European unification has proved astonishingly accurate'.[55] Insofar as Carr hypothesized a Europe managed by technocrats, whose nations cooperated in loose supranational institutions to maximize welfare for their citizens, this comment is not hyperbolic. He certainly grasped earlier than most the difficulties that would be faced by any form of European federalism.

But one can perhaps expand upon Haslam's praise. Carr's vision of the direction that post-war Europe would take was superseded almost as he published it by the Cold War – indeed, though there is no space to discuss the issue here, it is remarkable how little attention he paid to the likely role the United States would play in post-

55. Haslam, *The Vices of Integrity*, p. 117.

war Europe, particularly since he had been an attentive reader of Borkenau, whose *Socialism: National or International* predicted with remarkable accuracy that post-war hopes for democratic socialism in Europe would depend upon the construction of a security organization under 'Anglo-American joint international leadership'.[56] But Carr's picture of a world based upon multi-national conglomerations of states, now the Cold War has defrosted, is looking genuinely perceptive. As we head towards a world where the US, via NAFTA and various free trade agreements, dominates the Americas; where China's expanding economy is absorbing the resources of central Asia, Australia and Africa; where Russia remains a huge territory with pretensions to reasserting its control over some of the nationalities it lost after the collapse of the USSR; where the European Union has encompassed 27 states and is pushing to arrive at well over 30, spanning, potentially, a territory stretching from Iceland to Iraq; where oil producers in the Middle East and elsewhere form a de facto transnational organization capable of exercising enormous power; where South Africa will either create a regional community or be submerged in the problems created by the economic and political anarchy raging to its north, Carr looks like a serious thinker again.

This is because world politics today increasingly is about managing the tensions and interests of multi-national blocs that are in competition for scarce resources and are facing powerful internal demands for the immediate satisfaction of social goods. It is a world where the same driving historical forces that Carr identified in the 1940s – the desire of the masses for ever higher levels of welfare and the greater democratization of domestic political power – are now working their impersonal, but unstoppable effects on the gigantic societies of Asia, Africa and Latin America. If so, a shift in the structure of the global system of power relations, and its mode of governance, will be an inevitable concomitant. Carr's historicism led him down some grim blind alleys. But unlike the many present-day

56. Borkenau, *Socialism: National or International*, p. 170.

IR theorists who are stuck in the static world of their models, Carr teaches that international relations are a function of broader social-political change and that our primary duty as analysts is to identify historical trends. His influence was less on day-to-day decisions than on the interpretative climate of his time, to the construction of whose meaning he made a lasting contribution.

Bibliography

Adler, E. and Barnett, M. (eds.), *Security Communities*, Cambridge 1998.

Adonnino, P., "A People's Europe: Reports from the Ad Hoc Committee", *Bulletin of the European Communities*, Supplement 7/85, 1985.

Albrecht, S., *Hermann Hellers Staats und Demokratieauffassung*, Frankfurt am Main 1983.

Albrecht, S., "Rechtsstaat, autoritäre Demokratie und der europäische Faschismus. Hermann Hellers Grundlegungen einer starken Demokratie", in M. Schmeitzner (ed.): *Totalitarismuskritik von links. Deutsche Diskurse im 20. Jahrhundert*.

Ambjörnsson, R., Ringby, P. and Åkermann (eds.), S., *Att skriva Människan. Essäer om biografin som livshistoria och vetenskaplig genre*, Stockholm 1997.

American Historical Review (vol. 114, 2009).

An International Bill of Human Rights, London (HMSO) 1947.

Andresen, K., *Schleswig-Holsteins Identitäten. Die Geschichtspolitik des Schleswig-Holsteinischen Heimatbundes*, Neumünster 2010.

Assmann, A. und Frevert, U., *Geschichtsvergessenheit – Geschichtsvergessenheit. Vom Umgang mit deutschen Vergangenheit nach 1945*, Stuttgart 1999.

Auster, P., *The Book of Illusions*, London/New York 2002.

Banner, L.W., "Biography as History", *American Historical Review*, vol. 3, 2009, pp. 579–586.

Barnouw, D., "The New Nazi Order and Europe", in: M. Wintle (ed.), *Imagining Europe. Europe and European Civilisation as seen from its Margins and by the Rest of the World in the Nineteenth and Twentieth Centuries*.

Baumann, Z., *Europe – An Unfinished Adventure*, Cambridge 2004.

Bayly, C.A., Beckert, S., Connelly, M., Hofmeyr, I., Kozol, W. and Seed, P., "AHR Conversation: On Transnational History", *American Historical Review*, vol. 111, 2006, pp. 1440–64.

Beck, U. and Grande, E. *Cosmopolitan Europe*, Cambridge 2007.

Becker, W. et al. (eds.), *Lexikon der Christlichen Demokratie in Deutschland*, Paderborn 2002.

Begtrup, B., *Kvinde i et verdenssamfund*, Viby J. 1986.

Benvenuto, B. and Kennedy, R., *The Works of Jacques Lacan*, London 1986.

Berghahn, V. and Lässing, S. (ed.), *Biography between Structure and Agency. Central European Lives in International Historiography*, New York 2008.

Bessel, R. and Schumann, D. (eds.) *Life after Death. Approaches to a Cultural and Social History of Europe during the 1940s and 1950s*, Cambridge 2003.

Blau, J., *Sozialdemokratische Staat-slehre in der Weimarer Republik. Dar-stellung und Untersuchung der staats-theoretischen Konzeptionen von Hermann Heller, Ernst Fraenkel und Otto Kirchheimer*, Marburg 1980.

Bödecker, H.E., (ed.), *Biographie schreiben*, Göttinger Gespräche zur Geschichtswissenschaft, vol. 18, Göttingen 2003.

Borkenau, F., *Socialism: National or International*, London 1942.

Bösch, F., "Politische Skandale in Deutschland und Großbritannien", *Aus Politik und Zeitgeschichte*, Vol. 53, No. 7, 2006, pp. 25–32.

Bösch, F., *Das konservative Milieu. Vereinskultur und lokale Sammlungs-spolitik*, Göttingen 2002.

Bourdieu, P., *Sketch for a Self-Analysis*, Chicago 2008.

Bourdieu, P., "The biographical illu-sion", *Working Papers and Proceed-ings of the Centre for Psychosocial Studies*, University of Chicago, vol. 14, Chicago 1987.

Bourdieu, P., "L'Illusion biografique", in *Actes de la recherche en sciences sociales*, no. 62/63, June 1986, Editions de Minuit, Paris 1986. Danish translation by Eva Bertram in *Kontext 2*, pp. 39–45, Politisk Revy, Copenhagen 1988.

Braunschweiger Zeitung (various).

Bredsdorff, N., *Fremtidens Danmark, socialdemokraterne og keynesianis-men. En doktrinhistorisk under-søgelse*, Roskilde 2000.

Brown, J.M., "'Life Histories' and the History of Modern South Asia", *American Historical Review*, vol. 114, 2009, pp. 587–595.

Bulletin of the European Communities (various).

Bullock, A., *Ernest Bevin: Foreign Secretary, 1945–1951*, London 1983.

Byman, D. L. and Pollack, K. M., "Let Us Now Praise the Great Men. Bringing the Statesman Back In", *International Security*, vol. 25, No. 4, 2001, pp. 107–146.

Carr, E. H., *What is History?*, London 2003.

Carr. E.H., *The Twenty Years' Crisis*, London 2001.

Carr, E.H., *The Soviet Impact on the Western World*, London 1946.

Carr, E.H., *Nationalism and After*, London 1945.

Carr, E.H., *The Conditions of Peace*, New York 1943.

Chiesa, L., *Subjectivity and Otherness – A philosophical Reading of Lacan*, Cambrdige, MA 2007.

Christensen, C.B., Lund, J., Olesen, N. W., and Sørensen, J., *Danmark besat. Krig og hverdag 1940–1945*, Copen-hagen 2005.

Christiansen, N.F., *Den politiske ordfører. Hartvig Frisch 1935–1940*, Copenhagen 1999, pp. 57–61.

Christiansen, N.F., *Hartvig Frisch – mennesket og politikeren. En biografi*, Copenhagen 1993.

Churchill, W., Speech: Congress of Europe, The Hague, Plenary Session, Verbatim Report, 7 May 1948, Coun-cil of Europe Publishing 1999.

Cini, M. and Bourne, A. K., (eds.), *Palgrave Advances in European Union Studies*, London 2005.

Clavin, P. "Defining Transnational-ism", *Contemporary European History*, vol. 14, no. 4, 2005, pp. 421–439.

Cole, G.D.H., *Europe, Russia and the Future*, New York 1942.

Collini, S., *Common Reading: Critics, Historians, Publics*, Oxford 2008.

Coltheart, L. "Citizens of the World. Jessie Street and International Feminism", Hecate, vol. 31, no. 1, 2005.

Con Davis, R. (ed.), *The Fictional Father – Lacanian Readings of the Text*, Amherst 1981.

Constantin, C., "'Le future passé' de l'intégration européenne. Discours et pratiques mémoriels des élites européennes (1950–2007). *Congrès AFSP* 2009.

Damm, H. *På trods. 100 års kvindehistorie. Danske Kvinders Nationalråd 1899–1999*, Copenhagen 1999.

Davídsdottir, S., *Håndskriftsagaens Saga – i politisk belysning*, Odense 1999.

De Europæiske fællesskabers tidende (various).

Deacon, D., Russell, P. and Woollacott, A. (eds.), "Introduction", in: Deacon, Russell and Woollacott, *Transnational Lives. Biographies of Global Modernity, 1700 – Present*, Basingstoke 2010.

Deighton, A., "Entente Neo-Coloniale? Ernest Bevin & the Proposals for an Anglo-French Third World Power, 1945–1949", *Diplomacy and Statecraft*, vol. 17, no. 4, 2006.

Delors, J. (with J.-L. Arnaud), *Mémoires*, Paris 2004.

Der Spiegel (various).

Die Welt (various).

Die Zeit (various).

Draht, M. et al (eds.), *Hermann Heller, Gesammelte Schriften*, vol. I-III, Leiden 1971.

Duchêne, F., *Jean Monnet. The First Statesman of Interdependence*, New York 1994.

Dybdal, V. (ed.), *Dansk Biografisk Leksikon*, Copenhagen 1978–83.

Dyrberg, T.B., Hansen, A. D. and Torfing, J. (eds.), *Diskursteorien på arbejde*, Roskilde 2000.

Dyzenhaus, D. *Legality and Legitimacy. Carl Schmitt, Hans Kelsen and Hermann Heller in Weimar*, Oxford 1997.

Edel, L., *Literary Biography*, London 1957.

Edel, L., *Writing Lives. Principia Biographia*, New York 1984.

Edelman, M., "The Council of Europe 1950", *International Affairs*, XXVII,/1, 1951, 29.

Ekman, S. and Edling, N. (eds.), *War Experience, Self-Image and National Identity. The Second World War as Myth and History*, Stockholm 1997.

Elias, N., *Mozart: Portrait of a Genius*, Berkeley 1993.

Engberg, J. *I minefeltet, Træk af Arbejderbevægelsens Erhvervsråd historie siden 1936*, Copenhagen 1986.

Eriksen, S., "Niels Thomsens relevans", *Historisk Tidsskrift* (Copenhagen) 1997, no. 2, pp. 432–438

Esser, F. and Hartung, U., "Nazis, Pollution, and No Sex: Political Scandals as a Reflection of Political Culture in Germany", *The American Behavioral Scientist*, vol. 47, no. 8, 2004, pp. 1040–1071.

Europa Parlamentets forhandlinger (various).

European Commission, Completing the Internal Market – White Paper from the Commission to the European Council, COM(85)310 final, 14 June 1985.

European Commission, First Communication of the Commission about the Community's Policy on the Environment. SEC(71)2616 final, 22 July 1971.

European Commission, From the Single Act to Maastricht and Beyond : The Means to Match our Ambitions, COM(92)2000 final, 11 February 1992.

European Parliament Session Documents (various).

Federspiel, P., "Aktiv neutralitetspolitik", *Fremtiden*, Vol. 1, No. 7, 1946, pp. 7–9.

Ferenczi, S., *First Contributions to Psychoanalysis*, London 1952.

Fink, B. *The Lacanian subject*, Princeton 1995.

Finnemann, N.O., *I Broderskabets Aand. Den socialdemokratiske arbejderbevægelses idehistorie 1871–1977*, Copenhagen 1985.

Finnemore, M., *National Interests in International Society*, Ithaca 1996.

Finney, P. (ed.), *Palgrave Advances in International History*, London 2005.

Fonnesbech-Wulff, B. and Roslyng-Jensen, P. (eds.), *Historiens Lange Linjer*, Copenhagen 2006.

Fonsmark, H., *Historien om den danske utopi. Et idepolitisk essay om danskernes velfærdsdemokrati*, Copenhagen 1990.

Fontaine, P., *Jean Monnet – A Grand Design for Europe*, Luxembourg 1988.

France, P. and St. Clair, W. (eds.), *Mapping Lives. The Uses of Biography*, Oxford 2002

Frankfurter Allgemeine Zeitung, 25 June 1979, 16 June 1979.

Frankfurter Rundschau, 23 May 1979.

Fransen, F.J., *The Supranational Politics of Jean Monnet*. Westport, 2001.

Freitas, G. And H. de, *The Sligther Side of a Long Public Life*, [publishing place unknown] 1985.

Freud, S., *Group Psychology and the Analysis of the Ego*, New York 1922 (rev. ed. 1959).

Freud, S., *The Ego and the Id*, London 1927.

Frevert, U. *Eurovisionen: Ansichten guter Europäer im 19. und 20. Jahrhundert*, Frankfurt 2003.

Frisch, H., *Pest over Europa*, (2nd ed.), Copenhagen 1950.

Frisch, H., *Pest over Europa*, Copenhagen 1933.

Frisch, H., *Europas Kulturhistorie*, Copenhagen 1928.

Frisch, H., "Hvad er aktiv neutralitetspolitik?", *Fremtiden*, vol. 1, no. 8, 1946, pp. 11–12.

Frisch, H.,"Denmark and the League of Nations", *The International Observer: A Popular Quarterly*, 1937, pp 92–107.

Frisch, H. and Husfeldt, E., *Rapporter fra De Delegerede ved De Forenede Nationers Konference i San Francisco*, Copenhagen 1945.

Garff, J., *Søren Kierkegaard. A Biography*, translated from Danish by B. H. Kirmmse, New Jersey 2005.

Geschichte im Wissenschaft und Unterricht (10/09).

Gienow-Hecht, J. and Schumacher, F. (eds.), *Culture and International History*, Oxford/New York 2003, pp. 3–26.

Gilbert, M., "Foreign Policy and Propaganda in the Progressive Press 1936–1945", PhD dissertation, University of Wales 1990.

Gilbert, M., "The Sovereign Remedy of European Unity: The Progressive Left and Supranational Government 1935–1945", *International Politics*, vol. 47, no. 1, 2009, pp. 27–46.

Gilbert, M., "Il futuro socialista dell'Europa. Gli intellettuali progressisti britannici e il federalismo europeo, 1935–1945," *Contemporanea* vol. XI 2008, no. 1, pp. 23–45.

Gilbert, M., *Winston Churchill. A Life,* London 1992.

Goldstein, J. and Keohane, R. O. (eds.), *Ideas & Foreign Policy. Beliefs, Institutions and Political Change,* London 1993.

Gosewinkel, D., *Adolf Arndt. Die Wiederbegründung des Rechtsstaats aus dem Geist der Sozialdemokratie (1945–1961),* Bonn 1991.

Götz, N., *Deliberative Diplomacy. The Nordic Approach to Global Governance and Societal Representation at the United Nations,* Dordrecht 2011.

Gowan, P. and Anderson, P. (eds.), *The Question of Europe,* London 1997.

Gram-Skjoldager, K., *Fred og folkeret. Dansk internationalistisk udenrigspolitik 1899–1939,* Copenhagen 2012.

Gründler, G. and Manikowsky, A. von, *Das Gericht der Sieger. Der Prozeß gegen Göring, Heß, Ribbentrop, Keitel, Kaltenbrunner u.a.,* Oldenburg 1967.

Gründler, G., *Erinnerung an Arnim von Manikowsky* [obituary], 2010, available from: http://www.gerdgruendler.de/Manikowsky, Arnim%v..html.

Grünthal, W., *Festschrift für Dr. Hans Edgar Jahn zur Vollendung des 80. Lebensjahres: Dr. Hans Edgar Jahn – ein Mann der erste Stunde,* Bonn 1994.

Hamburger Morgenpost (various).

Handelsblatt (various).

Handlin, O., *Truth in History,* Cambridge, Mass. 1979.

"Hans-Edgar Jahn", *Internationales Biographisches* Archiv, Vol. 45, 2000.

Hansard (various).

Hansen, H.C. and Bomholt, J. (eds.), *Idé og arbejde. En bog til hans Hedtoft på 50–årsdagen,* Copenhagen 1953.

Hansen, K and Torpe, L., *Socialdemokratiet og krisen i 30'rne,* Aarhus 1977.

Hansen, O., "Til min ven den unge nationaløkonom", *Verdens Gang* 1952.

Hansen, S. (ed.), *Krag – som vi kendte ham,* Copenhagen 1978.

Harryvan, A.G. and Harst, J. van der, *Max Kohnstamm. Leven en werk van een Europeaan,* Utrecht 2008.

Harryvan, A. G. and Harst, Jan van der, *Max Kohnstamm: A European's Life and Work,* Baden-Baden, 2011.

Harryvan, A.G., Harst, Jan van der, and Voorst, S. van (eds.), *Voor Nederland en Europa. Politici en ambtenaren over het Nederlandse Europabeleid en de Europese integratie, 1945–1975,* Amsterdam 2001.

Harzburger Zeitung (various).

Haslam, J., *The Vices of Integrity: E.H. Carr 1892–1982,* London 1999.

Hathaway, R. M., *Ambiguous Partnership: Britain and America, 1944–1947,* New York 1981.

Heller, H., *Staatslehre*, Leiden 1934.

Heller, H., "Die Gefahr des Faschismus", *Vorwärts*, 17 November 1930.

Heller, H. *Europa und der Fascismus*. Berlin/Leipzig 1929.

Heller, H. *Hegel und der nationale Machtstaatsgedanke in Deutschland*, Leipzig/Berlin 1921.

Hermann, L., *Jean Monnet*, Freudenstadt 1968.

Hirdman, Y., *Det tänkende Hjärtat. Bokan om Alva Myrdal*, Stockholm 2006.

Hobsbawm, E., *Nations and Nationalism since 1780 – Programme, Myth, Reality*, Cambridge 1991.

Hobsbawm, E. and Ranger, T., *The Invention of Tradition*, Cambridge 1983.

Hoffmann, Aa., "'Fremtidens Danmark'. En analyse af Socialdemokratiets efterkrigsprogram, dets tilblivelse, indhold og formål", Årbog for arbejderbevægelsens historie 1993.

Hoffmann, S., "Reflections on the Nation State in Western Europe Today", *Journal of Common Market Studies*, vol. 21, no. 1, 1982, pp. 21–37.

Hoffmann, S., "Obstinate or obsolete? The Fate of the Nation State and the Case of Western Europe", *Daedalus* vol. 95, 1966, pp. 862–915.

Høibraaten, H. and Hille, J. (eds.), *Northern Europe and the Future of European Union*, Berlin 2010.

Homer, S., *Jacques Lacan*, London/New York 2005.

Ignatieff, M., *Isaiah Berlin: A Life*, London 1998.

Iriye, A. and Saunier, P.-Y. (eds.), *Palgrave Dictionary of Transnational History: From the Mid-19th Century to the Present Day*, London 2008.

Iriye, A., *Global Community. The Role of International Organizations in the Making of the Contemporary World*, Berkeley 2004.

Jahn, H. E. and Roth, A., *Spionage in Deutschland*, Preetz/Holstein 1962.

Jahn, H.E., *10 Jahre Arbeitsgemeinschaft Demokratischer Kreise. Eine Bilanz staatsbürgerlicher Bildungsarbeit*, Bad Godesberg 1961.

Jahn, H.E., *An Adenauers Seite. Sein Berater erinnert sich*, Munich 1987.

Jahn, H.E., *Gesellschaft und Demokratie in der Zeitwende*, Cologne 1955.

Jahn, H.E., *Pommersche Passion*, Preetz/Holstein 1964.

Jahn, H.E., *Rede, Diskussion, Gespräch*, Frankfurt 1954.

Jahn, H.E., *Vertrauen, Verantwortung, Mitarbeit. Eine Studie über public relations Arbeit in Deutschland*, Oberlahnstein/Rhein 1953.

Jahn, H.E., *Vom kap nach Kairo. Afrikas Weg in die Weltpolitik*, Munich 1963.

Jahn, H.E., *Von Feuerland nach Mexiko. Lateinamerika am Scheideweg*, Munich 1962.

Jahn, H., *Der Steppensturm. Der jüdisch-bolschewistische Imperialismus*, Dresden 1943.

Jean Monnet – et Budskab til Europa (Kontoret for de Europæiske Fællesskabers Officielle Publikationer), Luxembourg 1988.

Jenkins, R., *Churchill. A Biography*, London 2001.

"Jens Otto Krag", in V. Dybdal (ed.), *Dansk Biografisk Leksikon*.

Jensen, J. I., *Carl Nielsen – danskeren: musikbiografi*, Copenhagen 1991.

Jones, C., *E.H. Carr and International Relations: A Duty to Lie*, Cambridge 1998.

Jørgensen, J., "Velfærdsstatens arkitekt", in: S. Hansen (ed.), *Krag – som vi kendte ham.*

Kaarsted, T., *De danske Ministerier 1953–1972*, Copenhagen 1992.

Kaiser, W., *Christian Democracy and the Origins of European Union*, Cambridge, 2007.

Kaiser, W., Leucht, B. and Gehler, M. (eds.), *Transnational Networks in Regional Integration. Governing Europe 1945–83*, London 2010.

Kaltenmark, M., *Biographies des femmes illustrés,* Peking 1953.

Kammen, M. (ed.), *The Past Before Us: Contemporary Historical Writing in the United States*, Ithaca 1980.

Kampmann, V. and Bomholt, J. (eds.), *Bogen om H.C. Hansen*, Copenhagen 1961.

Kertzer, D. I., *Ritual, Politics and Power*, New Haven 1988.

Kirchhoff, H. "Foreign Policy and Rationality – the Danish Capitulation of 9 April 1940. An Outline of a Pattern of Action", *Scandinavian Journal of History*, vol. 16, 1991, pp. 237–268.

Klein, A. et al., *Bürgerschaft, Öffentlichkeit und Demokratie in Europa*, Opladen, 2003.

Knudsen, A.-C.L. and Gram-Skjoldager, K., "Hvor gik statens repræsentanter hen, da de gik ud? Nye rolleforståelser hos diplomater og parlamentarkere efter 1945", *Temp – Tidsskrift for Historie*, vol. 1, no. 1, 2010, pp. 82–113.

Knudsen, A.-C.L., *Farmers on Welfare. The Making of Europe's Common Agricultural Policy*, Ithaca 2009.

Kofod, J. and Staunæs, D. (eds.), *Magtballader. 14 fortællinger om magt, modstand og menneskers tilblivelse,* Copenhagen 2007.

Kohnstamm, M., *"Nog is er geen oorlog." Briefwisseling tussen Max en Philip Kohnstamm*, Amsterdam 2001.

Kohnstamm, M., *Brieven uit "Hitler's Herrengefängnis" 1942–1944*, Amsterdam 2005.

Kohnstamm, P., *Hoe mijn "Bijbels personalisme" ontstond*, Haarlem 1952.

Kølvraa, C., *Imagining Europe as a Global Player. The Ideological Construction of a New European Identity within the EU*, Bruxelles 2012.

Koselleck, R. (ed.), *Vergangene Zukunft: Zur Semantik geschichtlicher Zeiten*, Frankfurt 1995 [1979].

Krag, J.O., *Travl tid, god tid*, Copenhagen 1974.

Krag, J.O., *Dagbog 1971–1972*, Copenhagen 1973.

Krag, J.O. and Andersen, K. B., *Kamp og fornyelse*, Copenhagen 1971.

Krag, J.O., *Ung mand fra trediverne*, Copenhagen 1969.

Krag, J.O., "Manddomsgerning", in: H.C. Hansen and J. Bomholt (eds.), *Idé og arbejde. En bog til hans Hedtoft på 50–årsdagen*

Krag, J.O., "H.C. Hansens politiske indsats indtil hans gerning som statsminister", in: V. Kampmann and J. Bomholt (eds.), *Bogen om H.C. Hansen.*

Kunczik, M., "Die Arbeitsgemeinschaft Demokratischer Kreise (ADK)", *PR-Magazin*, vol. 29, 1998, pp. 53–77.

Kunz, A. *Wehrmacht und Niederlage.*
Die bewaffnete Macht in der End-
phase der nationalsozialistischen
Herrschaft 1944–1945, Munich 2005.

Lacan, J., Écrits, London 1977.

Lammers, K.C., "Fascismens og
diktaturets tidsalder", in: B. Fonnesbech-Wulff and P. Roslyng-Jensen
(eds.), *Historiens Lange Linjer.*

Lammers, K.C., "Antifascismen
i SPD. Fascismeopfattelse og imødegåelse af den tyske fascisme op til
1933", in: H. Löe and J. L. Kristensen
(eds.), *Kritisk fascismeforskning*
i Norden.

Laqua, D. (ed.), *Internationalism*
Reconfigured: Transnational Ideas
and Movements between the World
Wars, London 2011.

Larsson, L., *Sanning och konsekvens:*
Marika Stiernstedt, Ludvig Nord-
ström och de biografiska berättelser-
na, Stockholm 2001.

Larsson, L. "Biografins återkomster",
in: Rosengren and Östling (eds.),
Med livet som insats.

Laski, H.J., *Reflections on the Revo-*
lution in Our Time, London 1943.

Lässig, S. "Die historische Biographie
auf neuen Wegen", *Geschichte*
in Wissenschaft und Unterricht,
vol. 60, no. 10, 2009, pp. 540–553.

Latour, B., *The Pasteurization of*
France, Cambridge MA 1993.

Laursen, J. "Denmark, Scandinavia
and the Second Attempt to Enlarge
the EEC, 1966–67", in W. Loth (ed.),
Crises and Compromises: The
European Project 1963–1969.

Laursen, J., "De nye mandariner
i dansk markedsdiplomati. Jens
Otto Krag og embedsmændene,
1953–1962", *Vandkunsten,*
vol. 9/10, 1994, pp. 132–144.

Lefort, C., *The Political Forms of*
Modern Society, Cambridge 1986.

Lidegaard, B. *Jens Otto Krag,* vol. 1–2,
Copenhagen 2001–2003.

Lidegaard, B., "Overleveren", *Dansk*
Udenrigspolitiks Historie 1914–1945.
Danmarks Nationalleksikon, Vol. 4,
Copenhagen 2003.

Lidegaard, B., *Defiant Diplomacy.*
Henrik Kauffmann,Denmark and
the United States in World War II
and the Cold War, 1939–1958,
New York 2003.

Lidegaard, B., *Jens Otto Krag*
1962–1978, Copenhagen 2002.

Lidegaard, B., *Jens Otto Krag*
1914–1961, Copenhagen 2001.

Lidegaard, B., *I Kongens navn.*
Henrik Kauffmann i dansk diplomati
1918–1958, Copenhagen 1996.

Linder, D.H., "Equality For Women.
The Contribution of Scandinavian
Women at the United Nations,
1946–66", *Scandinavian Studies,*
vol. 73, no. 2, 2001, pp. 165–208.

Löe, H. and Kristensen, J.L., (eds.),
Kritisk fascismeforskning i Norden,
Aalborg 1982.

Long, D. and Wilson, P. (eds.),
Thinkers of the Twenty Years' Crisis.
Inter-War Idealism Reassessed,
Oxford 1995.

Longerich, P., *Deutschland 1918–1933.*
Die Weimarer Republik, Hannover
1995.

Lönne, K.-E., *Faschismus als Heraus-*
forderung. Die Auseinandersetzung
der "Roten Fahne" und des "Vor-
wärts" mit dem italienischen
Faschismus, Cologne 1981.

Los Angeles Times (various).

Loth W. and Osterhammel, J. (eds.), *Internationale Geschichte*: *Themen, Ergebnisse, Aussichten*, Oldenbourg, 2000.

Loth, W. (ed.), *Crises and Compromises: The European Project 1963–1969*, Baden-Baden, 2001, pp. 407–436.

Macey, D., *The Lives of Michel Foucault*, London 1993.

Mackay, R.W.G., *Heads in the Sand: A criticism of the official Labour Party attitude to European Unity*, Oxford 1950.'

Mak, Geert, *In Europe: Travels Through the Twentieth Century*, New York 2007.

Malmborg, M. a fand Stråth, B. (eds.), *The Meaning of Europe. Variety and Contestation within and among Nations*, Oxford 2002.

Manikowsky, A. von, "Christdemokraten: Ein Mann für Europa? Über die NS-Vergangenheit eines CDU Spitzenkandidaten für die Europa-Wahl", *Stern*, no. 21, 23 May 1979.

Manniche, J.C., "Om biografi", in: *Jens Christian Manniche 1942–2003. Biograf, historiograf, kolonihistoriker*, Den jyske Historiker, Aarhus 2003.

Margadent, J.B. (ed.), *The New Biography. Performing Femininity in 19th Century France*, Berkeley 2000.

Marklund, A., *Stenbock. Ära och ensamhet i Karl XII's tid*, Lund 2008.

Maurizio Bach (ed.), *Die Europäisierung nationaler Gesellschaften* (Kölner Zeitschrift für Soziologie und Sozialpsychologie, special issue), Opladen 2000.

Mayhew, C., *A War of Words: Cold War Witness*, London 1998.

Mazower, M. "The Strange Triumph of Human Rights, 1933–1950", *Historical Journal*, Vol. 47, No. 2, 2004.

Mazower, M., *Dark Continent. Europe's Twentieth Century*, London 1998.

Mentz, S. (ed.), *Rejse gennem Islands historie den danske forbindelse*, Copenhagen 2008.

Meyer, C.O., *Die Wächterfunktion von europäischer Öffentlichkeig. Das Brüsseler Pressecorps und der Rücktritt der EU-Kommission*, in A. Klein, et al., *Bürgerschaft, Öffentlichkeit und Demokratie in Europa*.

Meyer, J.-H., "Green Activism. The European Parliament's Environmental Committee Promoting a European Environmental Policy in the 1970s", *Journal of European Integration History*, vol. 17, no. 1, 2011, pp. 73–65.

Meyer, J.-H., *The European Public Sphere. Media and Transnational Communication in European Integration 1969–1991*, Stuttgart 2010.

Meyer, J.-H., "Saving Migrants. A Transnational Network Supporting Supranational Bird Protection Policy in the 1970s", in: W. Kaiser, B. Leucht and M. Gehler (eds.), *Transnational Networks in Regional Integration. Governing Europe 1945–83*.

Michalka, W., *Das Dritte Reich. Dokumente zur Innen- und Aussenpolitik*, vol. 1 (Munich 1985).

Midtgaard, K., "Bodil Begtrup and the Universal Declaration of Human Rights: Individual Agency, Transnationalism and Intergovernmentalism in the Early UN Human Rights Field", *Scandinavian Journal of History*, vol. 36, no. 4, 2011, pp. 479–499.

Milward, A.S. et al., *The Frontier of National Sovereignty. History and Theory, 1945–1992*, London 1994.

Milward, A.S., *The European Rescue of the Nation-State*, London 1992.

Milward, A.S., *The Reconstruction of Western Europe 1945–1951*, Berkely 1984.

Mitteilungsblatt des Instituts für soziale Bewegungen (45, 2011).

Moi, T., *Simone de Beauvoir: The Making of an Intellectual Woman*, Oxford 1994.

Mommsen, H., "Die verspielte Freiheit. Der Weg der Republik von Weimar in den Untergang 1918 bis 1933", *Propyläen Geschichte Deutschlands*, vol. 8, Berlin 1989.

Monnet, J., *Memoirs*, New York 1978.

Montaigne, M. de, *Essays*, vol. 3 [1580], translated by C. Cotton, revised by W.C. Hazlett and E.C. Hill, New York 1910.

Moor, L. and Simpson, B., "Ghosts of Colonialism in the European Convention on Human Rights", *The British Year Book of International Law*, 2005, Oxford 2006.

Morsink, J., "Women's Rights in the Universal Declaration", *Human Rights Quarterly*, vol. 13, 2, 1991, pp. 229–256.

Morsink, J., *The Universal Declaration of Human Rights: Origins, Drafting and Intent*, Philadelphia 1999.

Müller, C. and Staff, I. (eds.), *Staatslehre in der Weimarer Republik. Hermann Heller zu Ehren*, Baden-Baden 1984.

Müller, M.G. and Torp, C., "Conceptualising transnational spaces in history", *European Review of History – Revue européenne d'histoire*, Vol. 16, No. 5, 2009, pp. 609–617.

Müller-Bauseneik, J., "Die US-Fernsehserie 'Holocaust' im Spiegel der deutschen Presse", *Historical Social Research*, vol. 30, no. 4, 2005, pp. 128–140.

Munk Rösing, L., *Autoritetens genkomst*, Copenhagen 2007.

Nasaw, D., "AHR Roundtable. Historians and Biography. Introduction", *American Historical Review*, Vol. 114, 2009, pp. 573–78.

Nasaw, D., "AHR Roundtable: Historians and Biography: Introduction", *American Historical Review*, vol. 114, 2009, no. 3, pp. 573–8.

New York Times (various).

Nicholls, S.C.J., *The Burning of the Synagogue in Neustettin. Ideological Arson in the 1880s*, Centre for German Jewish Studies, University of Sussex, 1999

Nilsson, G.B., "Biografi som spjutspetsforskning", in: R. Ambjörnsson, P. Ringby and S. Åkermann (eds.), *Att skriva Människan. Essäer om biografin som livshistoria och vetenskaplig genre*, Stockholm 1997.

Nora, P., "From lieux de mémoire to Realms of Memory", in: P. Nora and L.D. Kritzman (eds.), *Realms of Memory*.

Nora, P, and Kritzman, L.D. (eds.),
*Realms of Memory: Rethinking
the French Past.* vol. 1: *Conflicts and
divisions,* New York/Chichester
1996.
Nürnberger Nachrichten (various).
Odermatt, P. "The use of Symbols
in the Drive for European Integra-
tion", in *Yearbook of European
Studies,* vol. 4, 1991, pp. 217–238.
*Official Journal of the European
Communities, Annex: Proceedings
of the European Parliament*
(Various).
Olesen, N.W., *Jens Otto Krag.
En socialdemokratisk politiker.
De unge år 1914–1950,* PhD Disser-
tation, University of Southern
Denmark 2002.
Olesen, N.W., "Jens Otto Krag
og Keynes", *Arbejderhistorie,*
nr. 1, 2001.
Olesen, T.B., "A Nordic *Sonderweg*
to Europe. Integration History from
a Northern Perspective", in H.
Høibraaten and J. Hille (eds.), *North-
ern Europe and the Future of Euro-
pean Union.*
Olesen, T.B. and Villaume, P.,
"I blokopdelingens tegn 1945–1972",
Dansk udenrigspolitiks historie,
Vol. 5, Copenhagen 2005.
Pagden, A. (ed.), *The Idea of Europe:
From Antiquity to the European
Union,* Cambridge 2002.
Parsons, C., *A Certain Idea of Europe,*
Ithaca 2003.
Patel, K.K. "Transatlantische Perspek-
tiven transnationaler Geschichte",
Geschichte und Gesellschaft, vol. 29,
2003, pp. 625–647.
Pedersen, S., 'Back to the League
of Nations', *American Historical
Review* vol. 112, 2007, no. 4,
pp. 1091–1117.

Politiken (various).
Poulsen, H., "Denmark at War?
The Occupation as History", in
S. Ekman and N. Edling (eds.), *War
Experience, Self-Image and National
Identity. The Second World War
as Myth and History.*
Possing, B., *Uden omsvøb. Et portræt
af Bodil Koch,* Copenhagen 2007.
Possing, B., *Awakening the Promise
of the Soul,* Copenhagen 2001.
Possing, B., *Viljens Styrke. Natalie
Zahle – en biografi om køn, dannelse
og magtfuldkommenhed,* vol. 1–2,
Copenhagen 1992 and 1997.
Possing, B., "The Historical
Biography", in: N.J. Smelser
and P.B. Baltes, *Encyclopedia of
Social and Behavioral Sciences,*
vol. 2, Amsterdam 2001.
Possing, B., "Biografien – en frisk
eller en skæv bølge", *Historisk
Tidsskrift* (Copenhagen) 1997,
No. 2, pp. 439–450.
Pyta, W. *Gegen Hitler und für
die Republik. Die Auseinanderset-
zung der deutschen Sozialdemokratie
mit der NSDAP in der Weimarer
Republik,* Düsseldorf 1989.
Rabaté, J.-M., "A Clown's Inquiry
into Paternity: Fathers, Dead or
Alive, in Ulysses and Finnegans
Wake", in: R. Con Davis (ed.),
*The Fictional Father – Lacanian
Readings of the Text.*
Rasmussen, E., "H.C. Hansen, J.O.
Krag og udenrigsministeriet. Kom-
mentarer omkring efterkrigstidens
socialdemokratiske lederskikkelser",
Historie, N.R., No. 3, 1982.
Rasmussen, H. and Koch, H. et al.
(eds.), *Europe: The New Legalism:
Essays in Honor of Hjalte Rasmussen,*
Copenhagen, 2010.

Rigsdagstidende (various).

Robertson, A.H., *The Council of Europe*, London 1961.

Rosengren, H. and Östling, J. (eds.) , *Med livet som insats. Biogrqfin som humanistisk genre*, Lund 2007.

Samnøy, A., *Human Rights as International Consensus: The Making of the Declaration of Human Rights, 1945–1948*, Bergen 1993.

Sassoon, D. *One Hundred Years of Socialism: The West European Left in the Twentieth Century*, London 1996.

Saunier, P.-Y., "Circulations, connexions et espaces transnationaux", *Genèses*, vol. 57, 2004, pp. 110–126

Schluchter, W., *Entscheidung für den sozialen Rechtsstaat. Hermann Heller und die staatstheoretische Diskussion in der Weimarer Republik*, Cologne 1968.

Schmeitzner, M., (ed.): *Totalitarismuskritik von links. Deutsche Diskurse im 20. Jahrhundert*, Göttingen 2007.

Segers, M.L.L., *Europese dagboeken van Max Kohnstamm. Augustus 1953–September 1957*, Amsterdam 2008.

Seidel, K., *The Process of Politics in Europe. The Rise of European Elites and Supranational Institutions*, London/New York 2010.

Sevaldsen, J., *Statsmand og myte*, Copenhagen 2004.

Shore, C. *Building Europe – The Cultural Politics of European Integration*, Houndsmill 2000.

Simpson, A.W.B., *Human Rights and the end of Empire*, Oxford, 2001.

Smelser, N.J., and Baltes, P.B., *Encyclopedia of Social and Behavioral Sciences*, vol. 2, Amsterdam 2001.

Smith, A.D., "National Identity and European Unity", in: P. Gowan and P. Anderson (eds.), *The Question of Europe*.

Smith, M.L. and Stirk, P.M.R. (eds.), *Making the New Europe – European Unity and the Second World War*, London 1990.

Smith, M.L., "The Anti-Bolshevik Crusade and Europe", in M. L. Smith and P.M.R. Stirk (eds.), *Making the New Europe – European Unity and the Second World War*.

Sontheimer, K., *Antidemokratisches Denken in der Weimarer Republik. Die politischen Ideen des deutschen Nationalismus zwischen 1918 und 1933* (Munich 1962).

Spaak, P.-H., *Strasbourg: The Second Year*, Oxford 1952.

Spinelli, A. et al.. *Il Manifesto di Ventotene*, 1941. Available at: http://www.altierospinelli.org/manifesto/manifesto_it.html

Staff, I., "Staatslehre in der Weimarer Republik", in: C. Müller and I. Staff (eds.), *Staatslehre in der Weimarer Republik. Hermann Heller zu Ehren*.

Stern (various).

Stosch, S., *Die Adenauer-Legion. Geheimauftrag Wiederbewaffung*, Konstanz 1994.

Strachey, L., *Eminent Victorians*, London 1918.

Strauss, E., *Common Sense about the Common Market*, Crows Nest, NSW 1958

Süddeutsche Zeitung, 23 May 1979.

Suganami, H., *The Domestic Analogy and World Order Proposals*, Cambridge 1989.

Tamm, D., *Federspiel. En dansk europæer*, Copenhagen 2005.

Tamm, D., *Per Federspeil. A Fighter for Danish and European Freedom*, Copenhagen 2005.

The Times (various).

Thing, M., *Portrætter af ti kommunister,* Copenhagen 1996.

Thomsen, N., "Biografiens nye bølge – en skæv sø?", *Historisk Tidsskrift* (Copenhagen) 1997, no. 2, pp. 414–429.

Time magazine (various).

Tindemans, L., "European Union", in: *Bulletin of the European Communities*, Supplement 1/76, 1976.

Torfing, J., "Velfærdsstatens ideologisering", in: T. B. Dyrberg, A.D. Hansen and J. Torfing, (eds.), *Diskursteorien på arbejde.*

Trachtenberg, M., *The Craft of International History. A Guide to Method*, Princeton 2006.

Treaty of Economic, Social and Cultural Collaboration and Collective Self-Defence, (The Brussels Treaty), Cmnd.7599, HMSO 1948.

Trenz, H.-J., "Korruption und politischer Skandal in der EU. Auf dem Weg zu einer Europäischen Öffentlichkeit?", in: Maurizio Bach (ed.), *Die Europäisierung nationaler Gesellschaften.*

Tumber, H. and Waisbord, S.R., "Introduction: Political Scandals and Media Across Democracies Volume 1", *The American Behavioral Scientist*, vol. 47, no. 8, 2004, pp. 1031–1040.

Verhaeghe, P., "The collapse of the function of the father and its effect on gender roles", in *Journal for the Psychoanalysis of Culture and Society*, vol. 4, no. 1, 1999, pp. 18–30.

Walton, S. J., *Ivar Aasens kropp,* Oslo 1996.

Walton, S.J., *Skaff deg eit liv! Om biografi*, Oslo 1998.

Warner, G. (ed.), *In the Midst of Events: the Foreign Office papers and diaries of Kenneth Younger,* London 2005.

Weisbrod, B., "Generation und Generationalität in der Neueren Geschichte", *Aus Politik und Zeitgeschichte*, vol. 52, no. 8, 2005, pp. 3–9.

Wengraf, T., Chamberlayne, P. and Bornat, J., "A Biographical Turn in the Social Sciences? A British-European View", *Cultural Studies – Critical Methodologies*, 2002, no. 2, pp. 245–269.

Wette, W. (ed.), *Filbinger – eine deutsche Karriere*, Springe 2006.

Wilson, K. and Dussen, J. van der, *The History of the Idea of Europe*, Houndsmill 1993.

Winkler, H.A., *Der Schein der Normalität. Arbeiter und Arbeiterbewegung in der Weimarer Republik 1924 bis 1930*, Berlin/Bonn 1985.

Winkler, H.A., *Deutsche Geschichte vom 'Dritten Reich' bis zur Wiedervereinigung*, vol. 2, Munich 2000.

Winkler, H.E., "Der lange Weg nach Westen", *Deutsche Geschichte vom Ende des Alten Reiches bis zum Untergang der Weimarer Republik*, vol. 1, Munich 2000.

Wintle, M. (ed.), *Imagining Europe. Europe and European Civilisation as seen from its Margins and by the Rest of the World in the Nineteenth and Twentieth Centuries*, Brussels 2008.

Wæver, O. "Insecurity, Security and Asecurity in the West European Non-War Community", in: E. Adler and M. Barnett (eds.), *Security Communities.*